T0296769

Multi-Criteria Decision-Making Sorting Methods

Multi-Criteria Decision-Making Sorting Methods

Applications to Real-World Problems

Luis Martínez López
Department of Computer Science
University of Jaén
Jaén, Spain

Alessio Ishizaka
NEOMA Business School
Mont-Saint-Aignan, France

Jindong Qin
School of Management
Wuhan University of Technology
Wuhan, Hubei, China

Pavel Anselmo Álvarez Carrillo
Department of Management and Economic Sciences
Universidad Autónoma de Occidente
Culiacan, Mexico

ACADEMIC PRESS

An imprint of Elsevier

Academic Press is an imprint of Elsevier
125 London Wall, London EC2Y 5AS, United Kingdom
525 B Street, Suite 1650, San Diego, CA 92101, United States
50 Hampshire Street, 5th Floor, Cambridge, MA 02139, United States
The Boulevard, Langford Lane, Kidlington, Oxford OX5 1GB, United Kingdom

Notices

Knowledge and best practice in this field are constantly changing. As new research and
experience broaden our understanding, changes in research methods, professional practices, or
medical treatment may become necessary.

Practitioners and researchers must always rely on their own experience and knowledge in
evaluating and using any information, methods, compounds, or experiments described herein. In
using such information or methods they should be mindful of their own safety and the safety of
others, including parties for whom they have a professional responsibility.

To the fullest extent of the law, neither the Publisher nor the authors, contributors, or editors,
assume any liability for any injury and/or damage to persons or property as a matter of products
liability, negligence or otherwise, or from any use or operation of any methods, products,
instructions, or ideas contained in the material herein.

ISBN: 978-0-323-85231-9

For information on all Academic Press publications
visit our website at https://www.elsevier.com/books-and-journals

Publisher: Mara Conner
Editorial Project Manager: Tom Mearns
Production Project Manager: Punithavathy
Govindaradjane
Cover Designer: Mark Rogers

Typeset by VTeX

Working together
to grow libraries in
developing countries

www.elsevier.com • www.bookaid.org

Contents

Foreword

The current problems of our world require us to make increasingly complex and articulated decisions. With this in mind, there is a growing need for methodologies that, on the basis of the ever-increasing wealth of data available, are able to take into account all the relevant points of view, technically called criteria, and all the actors involved. For example, economic criteria (e.g., income produced), environmental criteria (e.g., emission of pollutants), social criteria (e.g., working conditions), and cultural criteria (e.g., preservation of cultural heritage) must be taken into account in decision-making issues related to sustainable growth. It is also necessary to actively involve businesses, central and local authorities, trade unions, environmental protection associations, and so on in the decision-making process. Over the last 50 years, an area of research has developed that elaborates methodologies to deal with this type of problem, under the name of multicriteria decision analysis. In this area, observations that at first sight might seem only doctrinal have turned out to be fraught with consequences and results. In particular, it was pointed out [1] that choice and decision are not synonymous, and that there are in fact different types of decision problems, of which choice is a special case. In particular, taking into consideration the most important decision-making problems, we must distinguish between:

- choice problems, in which the objective is to select one or a small set of alternatives that is considered better;
- ranking problems, in which the objective is to order the alternatives from best to worst; and
- sorting problems, where the objective is to assign the alternatives to some predefined classes and sort them according to preferences.

The latter type of problem, although it has been neglected by traditional decision analysis that is focused more on choice and ranking problems, has significant practical relevance and is becoming increasingly important as new and more advanced methodologies are proposed to deal with it. To show how sorting problems differ from choice and ranking problems, consider the case of a bank that wants to distinguish between applicants who are worth financing and others for whom it would be too risky to grant credit. Suppose the bank in question ranks the applicants from best to worst. This would be sufficient to support the choice or ranking. However, the problem in this case is different. In fact, all applicants could be bad creditors and thus financing only the "best" one is too risky—just as all applicants could be good creditors, meaning that not financing even the "worst" applicant could result in the loss of a profit opportunity for the bank. Of course, similar reasoning could be made for intermediate cases and, in any case, the conclusion to be drawn is that even the most accurate order of preference of applicants does not provide the decision support that is sought.

From this perspective, this book makes a very important contribution to the theory and practice of multicriteria decision analysis, because it takes stock systematically of sorting methodologies, reconstructs their theoretical foundations, and envisages their future development, but without ever losing sight of the practical interest in the numerous real problems that find formulation in terms of sorting. The reader will be able to appreciate the comprehensive coverage of the broad spectrum of methodologies that have been proposed to tackle sorting problems, ranging from the outclassing approach to the full aggregation approach, via models with goals and reference levels, to nonclassical approaches. Another interesting peculiarity of the work is the large space devoted to applications, which allows the reader to become aware of the relevance of the subject and to understand the reasons for the rich and sophisticated range of models proposed in the literature precisely because of the specific requirements dictated by operational practice. From this perspective, the discussion on the fuzzy extension of multicriteria decision analysis appears particularly relevant. Indeed, fuzzy sets make it possible to manage the uncertainty and indeterminacy inherent in decision problems due to imprecisions in the data, lack of information, understanding of the parameters of the models adopted, and the expression of knowledge and preferences in verbal and qualitative terms, which are very important issues in real-world decision problems.

In the light of these observations and reflections, it seems inarguable that anyone wishing to deal seriously and systematically with multicriterial ordering problems in the future will not be able to ignore this work. It will therefore prompt many interesting new theoretical developments and many new real-life applications of methodologies in this field, which is of such great interest. Therefore, I can only congratulate Luis Martínez, Alessio Ishizaka, Jindong Qin, and Pavel A. Alvarez for offering such a rich and convincing monograph on the theory and practice of multicriterial analysis.

References

[1] B. Roy, Méthodologie Multicritère d'aide à la Dècision, Economica, Paris, 1985.

Salvatore Greco
Catania, March 2023

Chapter 1

Multi-Criteria Decision-Making

1.1 Introduction

Decision making is a common task in human beings' daily lives. They often face situations in which they need to analyze alternatives, which may be mutually exclusive, and it is necessary to choose one of them. To make the right decision about what alternative(s) could be the best or the most suitable for the situation, empirical and scientific methods are used. These decision situations may affect a wide range of problems, from very simple ones such as choosing which shirt to wear to highly complex ones such as selecting the right type of maintenance for a key tool in a complex engineering system, and so on.

Decision making has been a subject of active research in many different fields and studied from several perspectives [1]. Decision making includes multiple processes and activities such as information gathering, preference modeling, and data analysis, among others. It also implies the need for computing with objective values as well as subjective judgments that can appear in different ways when dealing with particular situations in different environments. It is therefore not surprising that several disciplines, such as philosophy, logic, computer sciences, mathematics, and operational research, are concerned with decision making. Due to the fact that these disciplines are often completely separate from each other, work in an independent way, and do not involve cross-disciplinary communication, the term *decision* is often interpreted and defined in different ways in each discipline. This may lead to misunderstandings among scientists from these disciplines when researching and discussing decision making.

Since ancient times, philosophers such as Aristotle, Plato, and Thomas Aquinas have discussed the capacity of human beings to make decisions, and some have claimed that this capacity makes a clear distinction between humans and animals [2,3], showing the importance of decision making for the development of social and civil societies.

Decisions can be made under different conditions depending on distinct aspects such as number of experts, number of criteria, or definition environment [2]. Therefore, depending on the characterization of the decision and situation, different types of problems have been defined and structured by decision theory to solve them. In this book, we focus on Multi-Criteria Decision-Making (MCDM).

Multi-Criteria Decision-Making Sorting Methods. https://doi.org/10.1016/B978-0-32-385231-9.00006-7

The discipline of Multi-Criteria Decision-Making (MCDM) is a recent branch of decision theory and a subfield of operational research. It deals with finding optimal results in complex scenarios in which scientific methods are used by decision-makers to make decisions where more than one criterion/attribute for evaluating each alternative is considered. It has been used as a generic term for all techniques that assist humans making decisions according to their preferences, in situations where there are multiple conflicting criteria. MCDM is applied to most of the everyday decisions in organizations and companies [4]. The approach of MCDM involves decision making concerning quantitative and qualitative factors [2,5–7]. Since its initial foundations in the 1950s and 1960s, MCDM has experienced exponential growth in terms of research publications, citations, and applications [2], and it has been influenced by many rational foundations of different disciplines [8]. During its evolution, MCDM has provided: (i) new decision models [4] able to aggregate different types of information (qualitative, quantitative, fuzzy, etc.); (ii) new multiobjective optimization tools for decision support [9]; and (iii) intelligent decision support systems for better data management/visualization [10].

The relevance and success of MCDM are due to the fact that it has successfully dealt with different types of decision problems [11], from *choice, sorting, ranking*, and *description* problems to *elimination* [12] and *design* [13] ones. Most of the problems studied in the literature are choice and ranking problems, thus many approaches have been developed and applied accordingly in real-world problems. However, this book focuses on MCDM sorting approaches not only because the scientific literature shows a great diversity of interesting techniques, but also and mainly because the applications that have been and can be solved by these sorting techniques are increasingly important in real-world decision-making problems nowadays, such as financial and investment decisions, environmental decisions, or medical decisions. For instance, an MCDM problem regarding the location of a new photovoltaic solar plant can be initially studied as a choice problem, because the goal is to select the most suitable location according to different related criteria. On the other hand, an evaluation of the efficiencies of different engines for a car can be studied as a ranking problem, since the objective is to estimate the relative performance of each engine compared to the others. Finally, failure mode and effect analysis can be studied as an MCDM sorting problem [14]: device analysis can indicate low, medium, or high risk of failure for further maintenance, according to its risk level.

Therefore, MCDM sorting methods aim at classifying the alternatives in homogeneous classes defined a priori [15], with interest shown in the development of quantitative models that may achieve higher classification accuracy and predicting ability. The practice of MCDM sorting justifies the need for a proper research document (book) of sorting methods, such as this one, to consolidate recent research conducted on this area of study.

Although the focus of this book is MCDM sorting, the remainder of this chapter will be devoted to providing a clear categorization of MCDM problems.

A further description of the types of problems in MCDM will be supplied for better comprehension, along with a short review of the different methods that have been developed for MCDM and subsequently extended for MCDM sorting.

1.2   MCDM: elements and classification

It is not common even for decision problems with just one decision-maker that she/he is clear about the evaluation of alternatives and has only one single criterion. Most decision real-world problems are usually evaluated by means of multiple and conflicting criteria. Consequently, MCDM and the diversity of problems to which they are successfully applied [9] may imply some heterogeneity in the definitions of such problems. However, all MCDM problems share several common characteristics pointed out by Hwang and Yoon [5] as follows:

- Multiple criteria: each problem has multiple criteria, and depending on the solution space of the MCDM problem, such criteria can be objectives or attributes.
- Conflicting criteria: it is common that in the set of criteria, some of them conflict with each other.
- Incommensurable units: often the criteria may involve different units of measurement.
- Design/selection: the solutions of MCDM problems are either to design the best alternative(s) or to select the best one among a predefined, finite set of alternatives.

It has been pointed out that criteria can be divided into two types, *objectives* and *attributes*, which leads to the classification of MCDM problems into two broad categories [5]:

1. Multi-objective decision-making (MODM) problems: these problems are focused on continuous solution spaces and are solved by means of mathematical programming models (linear programming, goal programming, etc.) or metaheuristics.
2. Multi-attribute decision-making (MADM) problems: these are defined on discrete solution spaces.

For a better understanding and further discussion of these types of MCDM problems, the basic concepts provided by [5,9] are enumerated and briefly described as follows:

- *Criteria* are the standard of judgment or rules to test acceptability. In MCDM-specific literature, they may indicate objectives and/or attributes. Therefore, an MCDM problem may mean either MODM or MADM; however, MCDM usually means MADM.[1]
- *Objectives* are the reflection of the decision-maker's preference and indicate the direction which she/he wishes to follow. MODM problems, as a result,

---

[1] In this book, we will use MCDM to refer to MADM problems. Therefore, the MCDM sorting problems studied across the book will be MADM sorting problems.

involve the design of alternatives that optimize or best satisfy the decision-maker's objectives.

- *Goals* are elements desired by a decision-maker and are expressed in terms of a specific state in space and time. Unlike objectives, which give the desired direction, goals provide a desired target level to achieve.
- *Attributes* are the characteristics, qualities, or performance parameters that define the alternatives of the MADM problem. The selection of the best alternative implies the evaluation of the selected alternatives according to the attributes.
- *MODM* problems are a continuous type of MCDM in which decision-makers aim to achieve multiple objectives that are incommensurable and conflicting with each other. An MODM model includes a vector of decision variables, objective function(s) that describe the objectives, and constraints. Decision makers attempt to optimize (maximize or minimize) the objective functions. Therefore, an MODM problem can be formulated mathemetically as shown in Eq. (1.1):

$$(MODM) \begin{cases} \max f(x) \\ \text{s.t. } x \in X = \{x \in R^n | g(x) \leq b, x \geq 0\} \end{cases} \quad (1.1)$$

Here, $f(x)$ are the k objective functions to be optimized, which can be in conflict, $g(x) \leq b$ are the m constraints that must fulfill the solution, and x is a vector of n decision variables.

- *MADM* problems involve aiming to make a preference decision (that is, comparison, choice, prioritization, sorting, and/or ordering) over the set of alternatives characterized by multiple, usually conflicting, attributes. MADM usually deals with a limited number of predetermined alternatives, which are associated with a level of achieving the attributes used for the final decision.
- *Alternatives* are key elements in MCDM, and it is important to note that in MODM problems, they are generally developed automatically by the math models in the continuous solution space. However, in MADM problems the solution space is discrete and the alternatives must be generated manually, which usually implies greater complexity. From a formal mathematical point of view, an MADM (referred to as MCDM in this book) can be formulated as in Eq. (1.2):

$$(MADM) \begin{cases} Choose \ O_1, O_2, ..., O_n \\ \text{s.t. : } C_1, C_2, ..., C_m \end{cases} \quad (1.2)$$

Here, O_i are the n alternatives of the decision problem and C_j are the m attributes (usually called *criteria*) that describe and characterize the alternatives for the decision situation. The *choose* function here means the optimization (either maximizing or minimizing) of a multicriteria-based value (which usually represents the utility of the alternative) defined by either decision-makers or stakeholders of the decision-making problem.

1.3 Types of MCDM problems

In section 1.1 it was pointed out that MCDM methods can deal with different types of problems to support decision-makers (DMs) [15–18] such as ranking, choice, sorting, description, elimination, and design. This section provides further details about these types of problems in order to clarify the basics to differentiate and understand the importance of different MCDM problems; ranking, choice, and sorting types are the most common MCDM problems in the real world, and this section highlights the importance of sorting problems to which this book is devoted.

1. The *choice* problem [19,20]: Dealing with this involves selecting the best alternative or reducing the set of alternatives that will contain incomparable *satisfactory* ones, by identifying as *satisfactory* those alternatives that perform better than all the others that are comparable. Examples of choice problems are an IT manager choosing the right enterprise resource planning (ERP) system for her/his company or a manager selecting the best location for a new branch of the company.

2. The *ranking* problem [18,21]: To solve this, one orders the alternatives from best to worst by using utility scores or pairwise comparisons, etc. The order obtained by this method can be partial if there are incomparable alternatives, or complete if there are no incomparable alternatives. An example of ranking problems is the ranking of employees to increase their salary according to different criteria, such as sales or quality feedback from customers.

3. The *sorting* problem [20,22]: In this type of problem the alternatives are sorted into ordered classes, or categories, from most to least or the other way around. Such categories are defined a priori in the problem by stakeholders or are inherent to the problem (the method is not intended to discover pre-existing categories). Solving these problems involves grouping the alternatives with similar performance regarding multiple attributes for descriptive, organizational, or predictive reasons. For instance, university lecturers can be assessed for classification into different categories such as *outstanding lecturer, average lecturer*, and *poor lecturer*. From these classifications, different measures can be taken to improve poor and average sorted lecturers. It is remarkable that sorting methods are useful in decision-making situations in which repetition or automation of the methods is required. Additionally, sorting methods can be used for screening processes in MCDM to reduce the number of alternatives to be considered in a subsequent decision step. A graphical explanation of the different types of solutions provided by these three types of problems is shown in Fig. 1.1.

4. The *description* problem [15,23]: The goal for this problem is not to rank or classify the alternatives, but to describe the alternatives and their consequences if they are taken as solutions for the MCDM problem. This type of MCDM process is usually applied at the beginning of the MCDM problem to gain a better understanding of its characteristics.

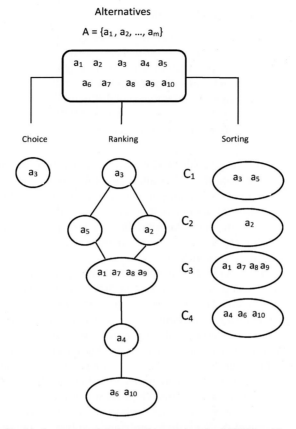

FIGURE 1.1 Graphical summary of choice, ranking, and sorting MCDM problems.

5. The *elimination* problem [12,20]: This type of problem has been regarded as a branch of sorting MCDM problems in which the alternatives are classified into two different classes: *accepted* and *eliminated*.
6. The *design* problem [13,18]: Solving this MCDM problem involves identifying or creating a new course of action that will meet the decision-maker's requirements and goals.

1.4 Categorization of MCDM methods

MCDM has been researched and applied to real-world problems since the 18th century (although not using that name) [24]. Interest in MCDM has led to the development of methods able to solve problems with different characteristics and complexity. Due to the increasing number of MCDM methods existing in the literature [2,4], it is necessary and convenient to clarify the common elements of

TABLE 1.1 Categorization of MCDM methods.

Categorization in this book	D. Bouyssou et al. [25]	Ishizaka and Nemery [20]	Greco et al. [2]
Full aggregation	Additive value model	Full aggregation	Multi-attribute utility and value theories
Outranking	Outranking methods	Outranking	Outranking
Goal, aspiration, or reference-level		Goal, aspiration, or reference-level	
Nonclassical MCDM approaches	Decision rules		Nonclassical MCDM approaches
			Multi-objective mathematical programming

different methods by grouping them into different categories according to their characterization. Consequently, different attempts to categorize MCDM methods have been made [2,20,25]. Bouyssou et al. [25] first attempted to categorize the MCDM methods into an additive value model, with outranking methods and decision rules. Subsequently, Ishizaka and Nemery [20] developed a novel and relevant description of MCDM methods according to their characteristics, dividing them into full aggregation, outranking approach, and reference-level categories. Recently, Greco et al. [2] analyzed the MCDM approaches and concluded by discussing the importance of the outranking methods, multiattribute utility and value theories, nonclassical MCDM approaches, and multiobjective mathematical programming. Nonclassical MCDM approaches describe how to deal with uncertainty, decision rules, fuzzy measures, and verbal decision analysis. Multi-objective mathematical programming includes interactive methods and multi-objective programming.

In order to clarify the categories that will be used in this book and according to [22], Table 1.1 summarizes the different categories into which such methods have been placed and the categorizations that will be considered in this book.

It is important to note that the management of uncertainty in MCDM has attracted a huge amount of research attention, and multiple methodologies have been used to deal with the uncertainty in MCDM. Fuzzy sets theory [26] has been widely and successfully applied to different complex MCDM problems and many MCDM methods have been extended to include fuzzy MCDM methods [7], to deal with uncertainty modeled by fuzzy information that accord better with real-world situations on many occasions. Consequently, and due to the importance and application of fuzzy sets to MCDM, this book will review in Chapter 4 the basics of fuzzy sets in order to understand the multiple fuzzy

TABLE 1.2 MCDM methods.

Full aggregation	Outranking	Goal, aspiration, or reference-level	Nonclassical MCDM approaches
AHP [27,28]	ELECTRE I, II, III [29,30]	DEA [31,32]	Decision rules [33,34]
ANP [35,36]	PROMETHEE I, II, III [37,38]	VIKOR [39,40]	Rough sets [41,42]
MACBETH [43,44]	PAMSSEM I, II [45]	TOPSIS [5,46]	
MOORA [47,48]	ORESTE [53,54]	CODAS [49,50]	
UTADIS [51,52]	QUALIFLEX [55,56]		
WASPAS [57,58]			

extended classical MCDM sorting methods that have been introduced in the literature.

1.5 MCDM methods

The huge amount of decision making required for real-world problems that demand MCDM methods for their resolution has led to the development of many ad hoc methods [2,4]. This section presents the most widespread MCDM methods according to their categories which have mostly been extended to *sorting* approaches, and the most important ones will be revised and described in further detail across the different chapters of this book (these are italicized in Table 1.2).

1.6 Structure of the book

After this introduction, in which basic concepts of MCDM are revised and explained, six chapters revise, describe, and introduce the major concepts, methods, and applications of MCDM sorting. Each chapter provides knowledge that supports the contents of the other chapters in order to understand more thoroughly the proposals of MCDM sorting and its application to different real-world problems.

- Chapter 2 provides a historical perspective of sorting problems and its application of real-world problems. It also provides an overview of the development of MCDM methods for sorting issues.
- Chapter 3 revises 10 classical MCDM methods and details their extensions to MCDM sorting methods, providing mathematical formulations for these methods and showing different examples of their application.
- Chapter 4 reviews the fuzzy sets concepts and their application in MCDM sorting problems.
- Chapter 5 analyzes MCDM sorting methods to characterize them and evaluate their necessity and suitability.

- Chapter 6 shows the application of MCDM sorting methods to different types of real-world problems.
- Chapter 7 concludes the book and provides insightful conclusions along with a view about the future challenges of MCDM sorting.

References

[1] D. Kahneman, A. Tversky, Choices, Values, and Frames, Cambridge University Press, 2000.
[2] J. Figueira, S. Greco, M. Ehrgott, Multiple Criteria Decision Analysis: State of the Art Surveys, 2nd edition, Springer, New York, 2016.
[3] D. Bouyssou, D. Dubois, H. Prade, M. Pirlot, Decision Making Process: Concepts and Methods, Wiley-ISTE, 2009.
[4] A. Alinezhad, J. Khalili, New Methods and Applications in Multiple Attribute Decision Making (MADM), International Series in Operations Research & Management Science, vol. 32, Springer, Cham, 2019.
[5] C-L. Hwang, K. Yoon, Multiple Attribute Decision Making: Methods and Applications, Springer, New York, 1981.
[6] R. Keeney, H. Raiffa, Decision with Multiple Objectives: Preferences and Value Tradeoffs, Wiley, New York, 1976.
[7] W. Pedrycz, P. Ekel, R. Parreiras, Fuzzy Multicriteria Decision-Making: Models, Methods and Applications, Wiley, 2011.
[8] Edmundas Kazimieras Zavadskas, Zenonas Turskis, Simona Kildiene, State of art surveys of overviews on MCDM/MADM methods, Technological and Economic Development of Economy 20 (1) (Mar. 2014) 165–179.
[9] J. Lu, G. Zhang, D. Ruan, F. Wu, Multi-Objective Group Decision Making, Imperial College Press, 2007.
[10] J. Castro, J. Lu, G.Q. Zhang, Y.C. Dong, L. Martinez, Opinion dynamics-based group recommender systems, IEEE Transactions on Systems, Man and Cybernetics 48 (12) (December 2018) 2394–2406.
[11] B. Roy, The optimisation problem formulation: criticism and overstepping, Journal of the Operational Research Society 32 (6) (1981) 427–436.
[12] C. Bana e Costa, A multicriteria decision aid methodology to deal with conflicting situations on the weights, European Journal of Operational Research 26 (1) (1996) 22–34.
[13] R. Keeney, Value-Focused Thinking: A Path to Creative Decision Making, Harward University Press, Cambridge, 1992.
[14] P. Nemery, C. Lamboray, FlowSort: a flow-based sorting method with limiting or central profiles, Top 16 (1) (2008) 90–113.
[15] M. Doumpos, C. Zopounidis, Multicriteria Decision-Aid Classification Methods. Applied Optimisation, Kluwer Academic Publishers, New York, 2002.
[16] B. Roy, The optimisation problem formulation: criticism and overstepping, Journal of the Operational Research Society 32 (6) (1981) 427–436.
[17] B. Roy, Methodologie multicriteres d'aide a la decision (Paris: Economica), 1985.
[18] Roy Bernard, Multicriteria Methodology for Decision Aiding, vol. 12, Springer, 1996.
[19] Fernando Sitorus, Jan J. Cilliers, Pablo R. Brito-Parada, Multi-criteria decision making for the choice problem in mining and mineral processing: applications and trends, Expert Systems with Applications 121 (2019) 393–417.
[20] A. Ishizaka, P. Nemery, Multi-Criteria Decision Analysis, John Wiley & Sons Inc, Chichester, 2013.
[21] Aleksandras Krylovas, Edmundas Kazimieras Zavadskas, Natalja Kosareva, Stanislav Dadelo, New KEMIRA method for determining criteria priority and weights in solving MCDM problem, International Journal of Information Technology & Decision Making 13 (06) (2014) 1119–1133.

[22] Pavel Anselmo Alvarez, Alessio Ishizaka, Luis Martínez, Multiple-criteria decision-making sorting methods: a survey. Expert systems with applications, Expert Systems with Applications 183 (2021) 115368.

[23] Masurah Mohamad, Ali Selamat, Ondrej Krejcar, Kamil Kuca, A recent study on the rough set theory in multi-criteria decision analysis problems, in: Manuel Núñez, Ngoc Thanh Nguyen, David Camacho, Bogdan Trawiński (Eds.), Computational Collective Intelligence, Springer, Cham, 2015, pp. 265–274.

[24] Murat Köksalan, Jyrki Wallenius, Stanley Zionts, Multiple Criteria Decision Making, World Scientific, 2011.

[25] D. Bouyssou, Thierry Marchant, P. Perry, M. Pirlot, A. Tsoukias, P. Vincke, Evaluation and Decision Models: a Critical Perspective, International Series in Operations Research & Management Science, vol. 32, Kluwer, 2000.

[26] L.A. Zadeh, Fuzzy sets, Information and Control 8 (1965) 338–353.

[27] T. Saaty, The Analytic Hierarchy Process, McGraw-Hill, New York, 1980.

[28] A. Ishizaka, D. Balkenborg, T. Kaplan, Does AHP help us make a choice? An experimental evaluation, Journal of the Operational Research Society 62 (10) (2011) 1801–1812.

[29] José Figueira, Vincent Mousseau, Bernard Roy, Electre Methods, Springer New York, New York, NY, 2005, pp. 133–153.

[30] Xiaohan Yu, Suojuan Zhang, Xianglin Liao, Xiuli Qi, Electre methods in prioritized MCDM environment, Information Sciences 424 (2018) 301–316.

[31] R.D. Banker, A. Charnes, W.W. Cooper, Some models for estimating technical and scale inefficiencies in data envelopment analysis, Management Science 30 (9) (1984) 1078–1092.

[32] K. Tone, A slacks-based measure of efficiency in data envelopment analysis, European Journal of Operational Research 130 (3) (2001) 498–509.

[33] P. Fortemps, S. Greco, R. Slowinski, Multicriteria choice and ranking using decision rules induced from rough approximation of graded preference relations, in: S. Tsumoto, R. Slowinski, J. Komorowski, J.W. GrzymalaBusse (Eds.), Rough Sets and Current Trends in Computing, 4th International Conference on Rough Sets and Current Trends in Computing, Uppsala Univ, Uppsala, Sweden, Jun. 1–5, 2004, in: Lecture Notes in Artificial Intelligence, vol. 3066, 2004, pp. 510–522.

[34] K. Niki Kunene, H. Roland Weistroffer, An approach for predicting and describing patient outcome using multicriteria decision analysis and decision rules, European Journal of Operational Research 185 (3) (2008) 984–997, 23rd EURO Summer Institute on OR in Health Care, Univ Southampton, Southampton, England, Jul. 24, 2005.

[35] T. Saaty, Making and validating complex decisions with the AHP/ANP, Journal of Systems Science and Systems Engineering 14 (1) (2005) 1–36.

[36] T.L. Saaty, L.G. Vargas, Decision Making with the Analytic Network Process: Economic, Political, Social and Technological Applications with Benefits, Opportunities, Costs and Risks, International Series in Operations Research & Management Science, vol. 95, 2006, pp. 1–278.

[37] J. Karkazis, Facilities location in a competitive environment: a promethee based multiple criteria analysis, European Journal of Operational Research 42 (3) (1989) 294–304.

[38] Jean-Pierre Brans, Bertrand Mareschal, Promethee Methods, Springer New York, New York, NY, 2005, pp. 163–186.

[39] S. Opricovic, G-H. Tzeng, Compromise solution by MCDM methods: a comparative analysis of VIKOR and TOPSIS, European Journal of Operational Research 156 (2) (2004) 445–455.

[40] Serafim Opricovic, Gwo-Hshiung Tzeng, Extended VIKOR method in comparison with outranking methods, European Journal of Operational Research 178 (2) (2007) 514–529.

[41] Liping An, Zengqiang Chen, Lingyun Tong, Generation and application of decision rules within dominance-based rough set approach to multicriteria sorting, International Journal of Innovative Computing, Information & Control 7 (3) (Mar. 2011) 1145–1155.

[42] S. Greco, B. Matarazzo, R. Slowinski, Rough sets theory for multicriteria decision analysis, European Journal of Operational Research 129 (1) (2001) 1–47.

[43] C.A. Bana, E. Costa, M.P. Chagas, A career choice problem: an example of how to use macbeth to build a quantitative value model based on qualitative value judgments, European Journal of Operational Research 153 (2) (2004) 323–331, 12th Mini Euro Conference, Brussels, Belgium, Apr. 02–05, 2002.

[44] Carlos A. Bana, E. Costa, Jean-Marie De Corte, Jean-Claude Vansnick, On the mathematical foundations of MACBETH, in: J. Figueira, S. Greco, M. Ehrgott (Eds.), Multiple Criteria Decision Analysis: State of the Art Surveys, in: International Series in Operations Research & Management Science, vol. 78, 2005, pp. 409–442.

[45] Micheline Belanger, Jean-Marc Martel, Explanations for a decision support system based on MCDA, Computing and Informatics 25 (2-3) (2006) 195–221, Symposium on Explanation Aware Computing, Washington, DC, Nov. 03–06, 2005.

[46] Mahmood M. Salih, B.B. Zaidan, A.A. Zaidan, Mohamed A. Ahmed, Survey on fuzzy TOPSIS state-of-the-art between 2007 and 2017, Computers & Operations Research 104 (Apr. 2019) 207–227.

[47] Willem K. Brauers, Edmundas K. Zavadskas, Robustness of the multi-objective MOORA method with a test for the facilities sector, Technological and Economic Development of Economy 15 (2) (2009) 352–375.

[48] Willem Karel M. Brauers, Multi-objective seaport planning by MOORA decision making, Annals of Operations Research 206 (1) (2013) 39–58.

[49] A.I. Maghsoodi, H. Rasoulipanah, L.M. Lopez, H.C. Liao, E.K. Zavadskas, Integrating interval-valued multi-granular 2-tuple linguistic BWM-CODAS approach with target-based attributes: site selection for a construction project, Computers & Industrial Engineering 139 (January 2020).

[50] Mehdi Keshavarz Ghorabaee, Edmundas Kazimieras Zavadskas, Zenonas Turskis, Jurgita Antucheviciene, A new combinative distance-based assessment (CODAS) method for multi-criteria decision-making, Economic Computation and Economic Cybernetics Studies and Research 50 (3) (2016) 25–44.

[51] J. Devaud, G. Groussaud, E. Jacquet-Lagrèze, UTADIS: Une méthode de construction de fonctions d'utilité additives rendant compte de jugements globaux, in: European Working Group on Multicriteria Decision Aid, Bochum, 1980.

[52] C. Zopounidis, M. Doumpos, Business failure prediction using the UTADIS multicriteria analysis method, Journal of the Operational Research Society 50 (11) (1999) 1138–1148, 39th Annual Conference of the Operational-Research-Society, Bath Univ., Bath, England, Sep. 1997.

[53] P. Mercier, J. Teghem, H. Pastijn, Assignment of available products to orders with the MCDM software ORESTE, Applied Mathematics and Computation 54 (2–3) (1993) 183–196.

[54] H. Pastijn, J. Leysen, Constructing an outranking relation with ORESTE, Mathematical and Computer Modelling 12 (10–11) (1989) 1255–1268.

[55] J.H.P. Paelinck Qualiflex, A flexible multiple-criteria method, Economics Letters 1 (3) (1978) 193–197.

[56] D. Banerjee, B. Dutta, D. Guha, L. Martinez, SMAA-QUALIFLEX methodology to handle multicriteria decision-making problems based on q-rung fuzzy set with hierarchical structure of criteria using bipolar Choquet integral, International Journal of Intelligent Systems 35 (3) (March 2020) 401–431.

[57] Adil Baykasoglu, Ilker Golcuk, Revisiting ranking accuracy within WASPAS method, Kybernetes 49 (3) (2020) 885–895.

[58] E.K. Zavadskas, D. Kalibatas, D. Kalibatiene, A multi-attribute assessment using WASPAS for choosing an optimal indoor environment, Archives of Civil and Mechanical Engineering 16 (1) (Jan. 2016) 76–85.

Chapter 2

Multiple-Criteria Decision-Making sorting method

2.1 Introduction

It has been pointed out in Chapter 1 that Multi-Criteria Decision-Making (MCDM) can deal with different types of problems to support decision makers (DMs) [60,161,162,164] such as choice, sorting, description, design, and ranking.

In the sorting problem, a set of classes must be defined a priori, and actions are assigned to them regardless of other actions [73]. In this problem, the DM attempts to partition the set of alternatives into several categories [20].

Sorting MCDM methods helps decision makers to assign each action to a category. The categories are either previously characterized by the DMs or inherent to the problem. In this sense, the multi-criteria sorting methods do not intend to discover categories [71]. When categories are discovered, it is a clustering problem.

The sorting problems are highly relevant to MCDM for solving complex problems. Sorting approaches have undoubtedly received a great deal of attention from practitioners and research studies. The scientific literature has presented a great diversity of interesting sorting techniques and many applications to real-world decision-making problems. Different applications have been solved using multi-criteria decision-sorting methods, such as maintenance management [146], education [139], and policy analysis (smart grids) [51]. This chapter is an adaptation of [3]. It shows the different classification and sorting methods developed and applied in the context of real problems.

Following the characterization of Chapter 1, this chapter will categorize the sorting method into four approaches based on the classifications found in the literature [19,20,80,95]. The classification comprises four categories in which MCDM methods are assigned: *full aggregation approach*; *goal, aspiration, or reference-level*; *nonclassical MCDM approach*; and *outranking approach*. The objective behind grouping methods by approach is to understand how the MCDM sorting methods have been developed from the initial study of this problem until now.

This chapter presents how the development of multi-criteria sorting methods and problems has increased, mainly in the last two decades. In addition, it shows how each approach has developed and evolved. It also lists the application areas.

We will also point out the deficiencies that must be addressed. The chapter shows where there is a lack of solved real problems, software development, support for selecting the utility function, and support to define the information required by methods. We will see that more fuzzy research needs to be developed, such as multi-granulation and attribute reduction.

2.2 Background

This section briefly describes and revises different concepts concerning MCDM sorting, and provides a categorization of such problems that will be used in subsequent sections.

2.2.1 Basic concepts concerning MCDM sorting

MCDM sorting refers to instances where alternatives are assigned to classes ordered from the most preferred to the least preferred. The MCDM community regards the sorting problem as the assignment of alternatives into categories on the basis of their evaluation on a set of criteria [75].

The sorting problem involves a set of alternatives $A = \{a_1, a_2, \ldots, a_m\}$. Each alternative is evaluated on n criteria $G = \{g_1, g_2, \ldots, g_n\}$. Then, each alternative is assigned to one class (category) or a range of classes. The classes are denoted by $C_1, C_2, \ldots, C_k$. The classes correspond to a complete or partial preorder. The expression $h > j$ denotes that class C_h is preferred to class C_j $(C_h \succ C_j)$. Fig. 2.1 illustrates an instance of a sorting outcome, where C_1 is preferred over the rest of the classes and C_4 is the least preferred class.

Each class is defined by a reference profile, which can be either the central profile(s) or the limiting profile(s). When classes are defined by limiting profiles, the profile lp is the vector of attributes values $(lp_1, \ldots, lp_j, \ldots, lp_{k-1})$. The class C_j is delimited by its lower limit profile lp_j and its upper limit profile lp_{j+1}, which is also the lower limit profile of class $C_j + 1$. When classes are defined by central profiles (or centroids), the profile cp is denoted by $(cp_1, \ldots, cp_j, \ldots, cp_k)$, where cp_j is the centroid of class C_j. Sorting the alternatives requires them to be compared to the reference profiles that distinguish the classes.

2.2.1.1 Computational complexity

As stated in the previous section, the sorting problem consists of assigning alternatives to ordered classes. Most of the multi-criteria decision sorting methods require an interaction with the decision maker (DM). In this sense, some methods implement the extraction of preference from the information expressed in a reference set of assigned alternatives from the DM. Two steps can be iden-

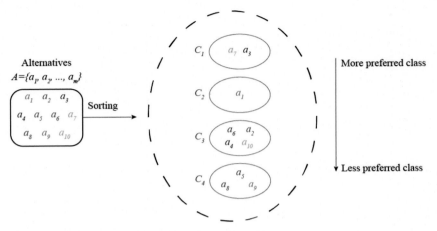

Alternatives
$A=\{a_1, a_2, ..., a_m\}$

a_1 a_2 a_3
a_4 a_5 a_6 a_7
a_8 a_9 a_{10}

Sorting

C_1 a_7 a_3

C_2 a_1

C_3 a_6 a_2 a_4 a_{10}

C_4 a_5 a_8 a_9

More preferred class

Less preferred class

FIGURE 2.1 Schematic representation of the sorting problem.

tified. The first is the preference disaggregation analysis (PDA) of the holistic decisions given by the DM. In the second step, an MCDM sorting method compares alternatives against limiting profiles (or centroids) and assigns alternatives in classes.

The models based on assignment examples such as preference information should generate more computational cost, and this will depend on the kind of model or approach applied. Kadzinski, Greco, and Slowinski [108] reported a rule-based preference model with an adaptation from robust ordinal regression. The model presents exponential complexity, and it is reported to be an NP-hard problem (non-deterministic polynomial-time hardness). However, even with this complexity in the model, it does not seem very complicated. The number of assignment examples commonly used in MCDM sorting would usually be below 100 [108].

Liu, Liao, Huang, and Yang [126] proposed an algorithm to balance active reference alternatives across categories from an imbalanced set of assignment examples. The algorithm is reported to have a complexity $O(n^2)$, where n is the number of categories. One of the few studies explicitly reports the computational complexity in one function (algorithm).

In the second step, as mentioned above, the sorting problem from the MCDM discipline seems easy to solve. Typically, the sorting applications include relatively small sizes; there are around 100 alternatives, there are fewer than 100 decision criteria, and there are fewer than 50 total classes. The dimensions of MCDM sorting problems are relatively small [106].

Algorithm 1 illustrates very general instructions for the MCDM sorting in the second step. In line 3, the aggregation of alternatives is performed. The complexity of the current line is $n \cdot m = O(n)$. In line 7, the assignment in the worst case is $n \cdot k = O(n)$. This computational complexity description is an overall

Algorithm 1. General instructions of a MCDM sorting algorithm.

Data:
n: is the number of alternatives
k: is the number of categories
m: is the number of criteria

```
1  for i ← 1 to n do
2  |   for j ← 1 to m do
3  |   |   a_i = Σ_{j=1}^{m} w_j g_j
4  |   end
5  |   for r ← 1 to k do
6  |   |   if a_i belong to C_r then
7  |   |   |   Assign( a_i to C_r)
8  |   |   end
9  |   end
10 end
```

and simple description, and it does not intend to explain the complexity of all methods. It can be assumed that most of the methods will present a quadratic function or other higher function while still belonging to the class of polynomial problems.

The computational complexity of each method needs to be analyzed. The analysis needs to focus on the aggregation function and other complex procedures that support the decision maker. In the same manner, the runtime needs to be tested to better understand the methods' complexity.

2.2.2 The categorization of MCDM sorting methods

The papers published during the development of MCDM show an increase in the number of methods developed for each approach. The approach corresponds to the way in which the multi-criteria problem is addressed. Thus, we assign the developed sorting methods to the proper approach in order to analyze them correctly.

For the sake of clarity when reviewing different MCDM sorting methods, it is convenient to establish the different categories into which the MCDM methods will be classified. The methods are categorized in four categories, as shown in Table 1.1.

To analyze the sorting studies properly, we include categorizations by both Ishizaka and Nemery [95] and Greco et al. [80]. The current categorization is justified due to the full diversity of methods and approaches that deal with specific hypothetical and real-life problems taken from the sorting problems in MCDM.

Initial MCDM sorting methods were based on the following paradigms: multi-attribute value theory (MAVT) [116], the outranking approach [163], and decision rules using "if-then" statements, which can, for example, be inferred using a dominance-based rough set approach [83]. However, with the improvement of some methods and the development of new ones, the classification of MCDM sorting approaches has improved.

In the literature, we found a wide variety of methods addressing the sorting problem formulation. This categorization is based on approaches that have been evolving over the years in the development of MCDM. These approaches are described here with the most commonly cited paper in each approach.

Full aggregation approach

Ishizaka and Nemery [95] defined full aggregation approaches, where a score is evaluated for each criterion and then synthesized into a global score. In this approach, a bad score on one criterion can be compensated by a good score on another criterion. The well-known UTADIS is the first sorting method developed in this approach.

UTADIS is a method where the decision maker (DM) must define a set of imprecise assignment examples from actions to one or several contiguous classes. The assignments are considered reference actions that represent the DM's preference, which is used to build the preference model of the DM represented by a set of general additive value functions that are compatible with the assignment examples. The additive value function U that represents the DM's preference is $U(a) = \sum_{j=1}^{n} u_i(g_j(a))$, where u_j is the marginal value function of the evaluation of criterion g_j from the alternative a. The additive value function satisfies some linear constraints, solving an ordinal regression problem.

UTADIS GMS is a new ordinal regression method developed by Greco, Mousseau, and Slowinski [88]. The method considers all compatible additive value functions, while the classical UTADIS deals with a subset of the entire set of compatible additive value functions.

Based on the set of all compatible value functions, two binary relations can be defined in the set of all actions A:

- A necessary weak preference relation $\succsim^N$, in cases where $U(a) \geq U(b)$ for **all** compatible value functions.
- A possible weak preference relation $\succsim^P$, in cases where $U(a) \geq U(b)$ for **at least one** compatible value function.

The binary relations redefine the indices of minimum possible and necessary classes and the maximum of possible and necessary classes. Those indices are defined to be used directly to calculate the possible and necessary assignments of any action based on the necessary weak preference relation $\succsim^N$ and possible weak preference relation $\succsim^P$ representing the preferences of the DM.

Outranking approach

A complete category is dedicated to the outranking approach due to the number of publications and methods developed. This is considered a noncompensatory approach. The order of the actions may be partial because the relation of incomparability is allowed. In this approach, two actions can have similar score values, but their behaviors may be different and therefore they are incomparable [95]. The most representative models are those based on ELECTRE or PROMETHEE. However, the outranking approach shows new and interesting method proposals that should be considered.

In the outranking approach, the most cited paper describes a PROMETHEE-based sorting method named PROMSORT [5]. The assignment of an alternative to a certain category is performed by using both profiles and reference alternatives in different steps. PROMSORT constructs an outranking relation using PROMETHEE I to assign alternatives to categories except for the incomparability and indifference situations. The final assignment of the remaining alternatives is based on pairwise comparison with the reference alternatives.

The construction of the outranking relation is performed with PROMETHEE I, defining preference $a\mathrm{P}b_h$, indifference $a\mathrm{I}b_h$, and incomparable $a\mathrm{R}b_h$ formulations for comparison of an alternative a with the limit profiles b_h [5]. An alternative is assigned in one of the $h + 1$ ordered categories $C_{h+1}, C_h, \ldots, C_1$ when the alternative a is compared with the profile b_i and the preferences relation $a\mathrm{P}b_h$ is defined. When the outranking relation indicates that a is indifferent or incomparable to a limit profile, it is not assigned to a category directly. The assigned alternatives are reference actions of the categories and are used to assign the alternatives that have not yet been assigned.

For nonassigned alternatives a, the distance to the cutoff point b is determinating. b would reflect the DM's point of view, which is referred to as either pessimistic or optimistic. If the distance is further than the cutoff point, then assign alternative a to the category C_{t+1}; otherwise, assign it to C_t.

Goal, aspiration, or reference-level approach

This is the approach required to define a reference level (goal) on each criterion and then to identify the closest option to this ideal reference level [95]. The alternatives are evaluated on each criterion that allows one to define how far the alternatives fall from the final objective. In this chapter, TOPSIS and DEA are the considered methods. We have also included the distance function implementation with Euclidean distance. This distance is expected to be useful to help understand the relation among alternatives [32].

This approach could be represented by the data envelopment analysis (DEA) method. DEA was developed by Charnes, Cooper, and Rhodes [29] to evaluate public programs. However, it is suitable for private organizations and even for entities such as regions or countries [91]. It is a measure that estimates the performance of decision-making units (DMUs) that are evaluated by common inputs and outputs. It is estimated that an efficiency frontier has a score of 1 (or 100%). In that sense, DMUs operating beneath the frontier have an efficiency score of less than 1 and thus have the capacity to improve future performance [91].

For the sorting problem, the research presented by Karasakal and Aker [114] has received the most attention in this approach. In their study, the DEA-based sorting method is used for sorting research and development (R&D) projects instead of ranking. DEA was previously used to rank projects, but Karasakal and Aker's proposal was developed for sorting R&D.

In the R&D problem, the analytic hierarchy process (AHP) is first applied to provide upper and lower bounds on the criteria weights [114]. These are the interval importance values, which have been incorporated into the DEA-based sorting method as assurance regions from preferential information of the DM. The authors proposed some models for classifying the alternatives by comparing their performances with the reference set alternatives, using preference disaggregation analysis (PDA).

Nonclassical MCDM approaches

The methods based on decision rules are included in this approach. The rough set is the representative method. The methods based on decision rules incorporate logic statements of the type "if ..., then ...." The set of decision rules represents a preference model of the decision-maker who made the classification decisions described by a data set.

The most cited paper dealing with sorting approaches belongs to the nonclassical approach [87]. It is the dominance rough set method. The preference model is inferred from preferential information of the DM, and provides a set of "if ..., then ..." decision rules. The rules are derived from rough approximations of decision classes made up of reference actions.

The subset Y can be characterized by two ordinary sets called lower and upper approximations, which define the rough set. The zone between the upper and the lower approximation constitutes the boundary region, including objects that cannot be properly classified as belonging or not to Y, using the available knowledge [175].

The reference actions are represented in the form of an information table. The rows are reference actions, whereas columns are attributes, and entries of the table are attribute values, called descriptors. The descriptors are attribute values of reference actions represented in an information table. As presented by Pawlak [149], the information table is the 4-tuple $S = \langle U, Q, V, f \rangle$, where U is a finite set of reference actions, Q is a finite set of attributes, $V = \cup_{q \in Q} V_q$ and V_q is a domain of the attribute q, and $f : U \times Q \longrightarrow V$ is a total function such that $f(x, q) \in V_q$ for every $q \in Q$, $x \in U$, called an information function.

Let S be the information table and let $P \subseteq Q$ and $x, y \in U$. It is said that x and y are indiscernible by the set of attributes P in S iff $f(x, q) = f(y, q)$ for every $q \in P$. Thus, every $P \subseteq Q$ generates a binary relation on U, the **indiscernibility relation** I_P [149].

It is defined as a quality of **approximation** of classification by the set of attributes P. It expresses the ratio of all P-correctly classified objects to all objects in the system [87]. Discovering **dependencies** between attributes is of primary importance in the rough set approach to information table analysis. An information table can be seen as a decision table. From the decision table S, a set of **decision rules** can be derived. A decision rule can be expressed as a logical statement.

The extension of the dominance rough set for sorting problems proposed by Greco et al. [87] consists of building rough approximations of decision classes using a "granule of knowledge." It is defined by three relations considered jointly: indiscernibility, defined on qualitative attributes; similarity, defined on quantitative attributes; and dominance, defined on criteria. The novelty is a joint consideration of criteria and regular attributes in one sorting problem. The original rough set method is not able to discover inconsistencies related to consideration of criteria (attributes with preference-ordered domains, scales).

The notion of an attribute differs from that of a criterion because the domain (scale) of a criterion has to be ordered according to a decreasing or increasing preference, while the domain of the attribute does not have to be ordered. Part of the innovation in this extension concerns the substitution of the indiscernibility relation by a dominance relation in the rough approximation of decision classes developed in [84].

2.3 Publications on sorting methods

Publication in the Web of Science databases of articles concerning the MCDM sorting problem began in 1997, as shown in Fig. 2.2. There seems to be an increase of publications in 2002, with 10 publications in that year. A consistent increase in the number of publications per year is then evident until 2007. From 1997 to 2021, the average number of publications concerning the MCDM sorting problem is 6.5 articles per year. Regarding citations, the first one appeared in 2002 and is shown in Fig. 2.3. Since then, the number of cited articles per year has increased at almost a linear scale until 2018, surpassing 300 citations. The sum of citations in the Web of Science in MCDM sorting is 2299, with an average citation of 114 per year. Table 2.1 shows the detailed number of publications and citations from 1997 to 2020.

Table 2.2 shows the top 10 cited papers of MCDM sorting. We can identify the review made by [187] and the sorting model rough set by [87] as the most cited articles. The first presents 350 citations and the second 283 citations. In the top 10 cited papers, the outranking methods are the most cited with six methods, reaching 616 citations in total.

Fig. 2.4 shows the papers categorized in 16 main fields of study. Popular fields in MCDM for applying sorting methods are risk assessment and education problems. Risk assessment presents 17 articles, and education presents 15 articles.

The development of MCDM methods for the sorting problem and their applications shows a tendency for more scientific studies in the full aggregation

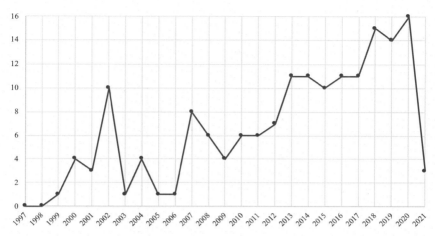

FIGURE 2.2   Total number of articles published by year.

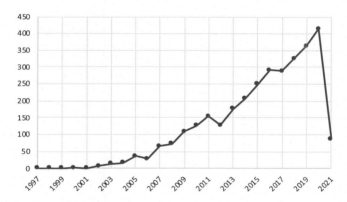

FIGURE 2.3   Sum of cited articles per year.

and outranking approaches. Fig. 2.5 shows this tendency with an emphasis observed from 2007 until now. The development of sorting methods in MCDM is growing. This study is focused on 17 areas of research, where risk assessment and education are the most addressed. It seems that other areas such as policy analysis, inventory management, facility location, and democracy lack development.

Recent publications from 2019 to 2021 show the following number of articles in each approach. The full aggregation and outranking approaches present 14 and 15 articles, respectively. The goal, aspiration, or reference-level approach and the nonclassical approach each show two publications in the same period.

TABLE 2.1 Number of publications and times cited per year.

Year	Publication	Citation
2021	16	87
2020	14	414
2019	14	363
2018	15	326
2017	11	289
2016	11	291
2015	10	250
2014	11	208
2013	11	177
2012	7	128
2011	6	154
2010	6	126
2009	4	109
2008	6	72
2007	8	66
2006	1	28
2005	1	37
2004	4	16
2003	1	13
2002	10	7
2001	3	0
2000	4	1
1999	1	0
1998	0	0
1997	0	0

2.3.1 Contributions and applications of the MCDM sorting methods

This section aims to show the contribution, development, strengths, and weaknesses of sorting MCDM methods.

The methods can be divided into five types of contributions (Fig. 2.6):

- novel, the development of a new method for solving MCDM problems;
- extension, a paper that extends an existing method by presenting an improvement;
- hybrid, a scientific contribution that merges two or more methods;
- application, solves a particular problem with one or more existing methods; and

TABLE 2.2 Top ten cited articles in multi-criteria sorting.

Position	Article	Method	Times cited
1	C. D. Zopounidis, M. [187]	Review	350
2	Greco et al. [87]	Dominance rough-set	283
3	Araz and Ozkarahan [5]	PROMSORT	171
5	Almeida-Dias, Figueira, and Roy [1]	ELECTRE TRI-C	102
4	Brito, de Almeida, and Mota [22]	ELECTRE TRI integrating utility theory	101
6	Tervonen et al. [178]	ELECTRE TRI and SMAA	94
9	Ishizaka, Pearman, and Nemery [97]	AHPsort	83
7	Greco et al. [88]	UTADIS	81
8	S. Damart, Dias, and Mousseau [38]	GDM ELECTRE TRI	75
10	Almeida-Dias, Figueira, and Roy [2]	ELECTRE TRI-NC	73

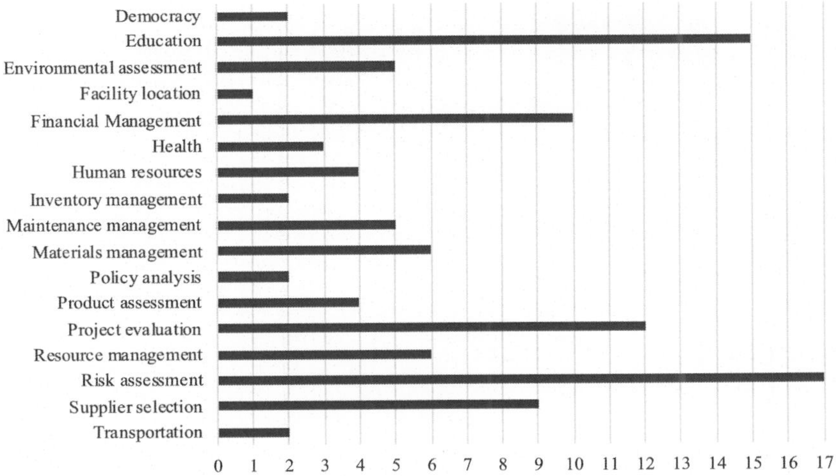

FIGURE 2.4 Sorting problem applications.

- review, summarizes the current state of the art on a topic.

Fig. 2.6 shows the percentages of papers distributed in each type of contribution. The sorting methodological development is still in a growing phase because most contributions are focused on the novel category. Almost the same trend is shown by application and extension contributions. Few hybrid contributions are shown. Only one paper review has been developed. In the following

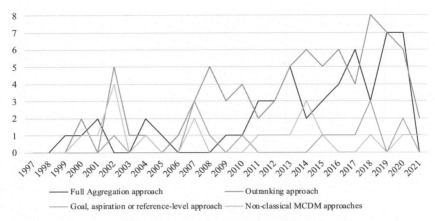

- Full Aggregation approach
- Goal, aspiration or reference-level approach
- Outranking approach
- Non-classical MCDM approaches

FIGURE 2.5 Development of each approach by the number of publications per year.

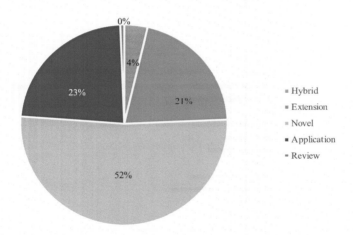

- Hybrid
- Extension
- Novel
- Application
- Review

FIGURE 2.6 Types of articles in MCDM sorting.

subsections, for each approach, we show the method, its contribution, and also the main topic in which the sorting method was applied.

2.3.1.1 Full aggregation approach

This approach presents methods with preference functions in additive and multiplicative forms that synthesize evaluations into a global score. The sorting methods presented in the current approach are AHPSort, ANPSort, CORT, DIS-CARD, MACBETHSort, MHDIS, Multimoora Sort, TchSort, and some extensions of UTADIS. Table 2.3 shows each multiple-criteria sorting method, identifying the type of contribution and the application area.

TABLE 2.3 MCDM sorting methods by the full aggregation approach.

Article	Method	Contribution	Application
[147]	Additive-veto sorting	Novel	Supplier selection
[97]	AHPsort	Novel	Supplier selection
[6]	IAHP	Extension	Risk assessment
[135]	AHPSort II and GIS	Novel	Risk assessment
[129]	GAHPSort	Novel	Supplier selection
[99]	AHP-fuzzy sorting	Extension	Risk assessment
[94]	Cost-benefit AHPSort	Extension	Supplier selection
[184]	IT2FS AHPSort II	Extension	Supplier selection
[98]	ANPSort	Novel	Education
[107]	Contingent sort (CORT)	Novel	Education
[110]	DIS-CARD	Novel	Human resources
[92]	MACBETHSort	Novel	Materials management
[57]	MHDIS	Novel	Risk assessment
[119]	Multimoora Sort	Novel	Environmental assessment
[177]	TchSort	Novel	Numerical example
[146]	Category size restrictions for MR-Sort and UTADIS	Extension	Maintenance management
[34]	Hierarchical-UTADIS	Novel	Financial management
[24]	PUTADIS	Novel	Education
[63]	PUTADIS with PSO-GA	Hybrid	Health
[105]	ROR-UTADIS	Novel	Product assessment
[148]	ROR-UTADIS	Application	Supplier selection
[113]	Flexible and interactive tradeoff elicitation sorting	Novel	Project evaluation
[186]	UTADIS	Application	Financial management
[58]	UTADIS	Application	Numerical example
[118]	Interactive-UTADIS	Novel	Education
[181]	UTADIS	Extension	Risk assessment
[158]	UTADIS	Application	Human resources
[121]	UTADIS	Extension	Numerical example
[124]	Preference learning for sorting	Novel	Education
[186]	UTADIS (UTADIS I, UTADIS II, UTADIS III)	Application	Risk assessment
[117]	UTADIS-CS	Novel	Education
[82]	UTADIS^{GM}	Novel	Education

continued on next page

TABLE 2.3 (*continued*)

Article	Method	Contribution	Application
[88]	UTADIS^{GMS}	Novel	Maintenance management
[81]	UTADIS$^{GMS-GROUP}$	Novel	Maintenance management
[56]	NAROR-HC for sorting	Novel	Financial management
[58]	MHDIS	Extension	Risk assessment
+ [62]	Inverse sorting with goal programing	Novel	Resource management

Table 2.4 shows some MCDM methods adapted to solve the sorting problem. In this approach, the most used method is the UTADIS method with various extensions. The AHP-based methods have been gaining attention, and five methods have been shown to solve the sorting problem. The most recent methods are AHP-fuzzy sorting [99], contingent sort (CORT) [107], preference learning for sorting [124], NAROR-HC for sorting [6], sorting with partial monotonicity constraints [109], flexible and interactive tradeoff elicitation sorting [113], and Inverse sorting with goal programing [62].

Some recent adapted MCDM methods for sorting are nonmonotonic sort [90] and with monotonicity constraints [109]. Education is the most addressed application area, followed by supplier selection and risk assignment. Fig. 2.7 presents a summary of the application fields where each contribution has been developed.

As identified, the most used method is UTADIS and its extensions. There are some new approaches that could be suggest as emerging lines of research: the nonmonotonic problem [90,125], partial monotonicity [109], interactivity with the DM with a specific case [23,25,180], and an inverse problem performing actions that have an impact on object evaluations [139].

An important strength that can be used in this approach is the support to the DM in its problem definition. Preference disaggregation analysis (PDA) is a common technique used to support the DM in the decision process to find parameters that fill its preferences.

2.3.1.1.1 Lack of development in the full aggregation approach

The full aggregation approach presents a greater number of theoretical contributions regarding novel, hybrid, or extension methods. However, its lack of ability to solve real problems is remarkable; only six articles (11.5%) have been developed to solve real problems. In other words, the full aggregation approach shows a real development in method and models, but practitioners would be also interested in solving real problems. On the other hand, only four computational programs were explicitly described in the articles in the analysis performed in full-text reading: Freeware TOMASO [132], UTADIS^{GMS} [88], PREFDIS [186], and CRIO [125]. The need to develop more available

TABLE 2.4 Adapted MCDM methods for sorting problems using the full aggregation approach.

Article	Method	Contribution	Application
[90]	Nonmonotonic sort	Novel	Financial management
[125]	Nonmonotonic sort with regularization framework	Novel	Numerical example
[109]	PDA sorting with partial monotonicity constraints	Novel	Materials management
[115]	Inequity-averse sorting	Novel	Financial management
[132]	TOMASO	Application	Education
[126]	CRIO for imbalanced set	Novel	Numerical example
[25]	Interactive GDM sort with RINCON algorithm	Novel	Education
[11]	ISMAUT-based choice-ranking-sorting	Extension	Numerical example
[111]	Possible and necessary sorting procedure with SMAA, ROR	Novel	Democracy
[104]	Post factum analysis for ranking and sorting	Novel	Environmental assessment
[106]	Preferential reducts and constructs sort	Novel	Democracy
[23]	Interactive probabilistic sorting algorithm	Novel	Education
[127]	GDM sort with evidential reasoning	Novel	Product assessment
[139]	Inverse-SORT	Novel	Education
[180]	Interactive Quasiconcave sort	Novel	Education

software for academics and practitioners is evident. A complicated situation for the practitioners could be selecting the utility function, as the evaluation outcomes depend on both choices of the utility function and its parameters [155].

2.3.1.2 Outranking approach

The outranking approach has the highest number of publications. The ELECTRE family presents new and extended models such as ELECTRE Tri, ELECTRE Tri-B, ELECTRE Tri-C, Electre Tri-nC, and ELECTRE-TRI-B-H. Other ELECTRE-based methods are ELECTRE-SORT and MR-Sort. There have also been some PROMETHEE-based methods such as FlowSort, PROMSORT, and β-PROMETHEE. FlowSort is gaining the most attention, with six different

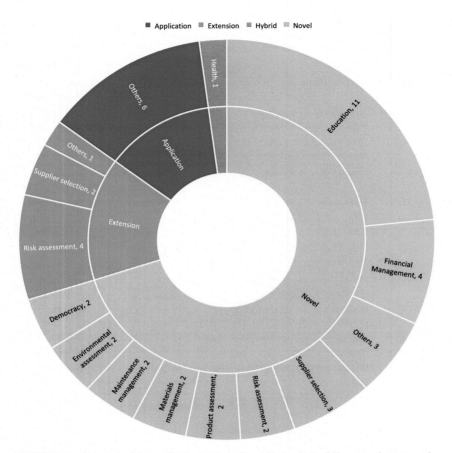

FIGURE 2.7   Summary of the application by type of contribution in the full aggregation approach.

novel and extension papers. There are currently five THESEUS-based papers (see Table 2.5).

Table 2.6 shows some MCDM methods adapted with the outranking approach for sorting problems. Fig. 2.8 shows a summary of the application fields by contribution. Risk assessment is the most common way to apply the proposals in this approach. It is followed by project evaluation. Other areas with fewer applications are resource management, supplier selection, financial management, and health and human resources.

The outranking approach is of interest for the scientific community, and it is also the most widely published, with a total of 52 articles. The ELECTRE-based method and its extension are the most developed. The important improvement shown by the outranking approach is the support to find profiles or other parameters (thresholds and cutting levels).

TABLE 2.5 MCDM sorting methods using the outranking approach.

Article	Method	Contribution	Application
[21]	GDM ELECTRE sort	Novel	Numerical example
[160]	PASA	Hybrid	Human resources
[178]	SMAA-TRI	Novel	Risk assessment
[136]	SMAA-TRI	Applied	Resource management
[102]	SMAA-TRI	Applied	Materials management
[96]	ELECTRE-SORT	Novel	Maintenance management
[7]	ELECTRE TRI	Applied	Resource management
[38]	ELECTRE TRI	Novel	Risk assessment
[143]	ELECTRE-TRI	Applied	Policy analysis
[138]	ELECTRE TRI	Extension	Numerical example
[140]	ELECTRE-TRI	Applied	Maintenance management
[156]	ELECTRE-TRI	Applied	Resource management
[53]	ELECTRE-TRI	Extension	Risk assessment
[50]	ELECTRE-TRI	Extension	Risk assessment
[36]	ELECTRE-TRI	Applied	Facility location
[39]	ELECTRE-TRI	Applied	Transportation
[44]	ELECTRE-TRI	Applied	Education
[52]	ELECTRE-TRI	Novel	Transportation
[22]	ELECTRE TRI	Applied	Risk assessment
[172]	ELECTRE TRI	Applied	Project evaluation
[174]	ELECTRE TRI	Applied	Human resources
[14]	ELECTRE TRI	Applied	Environmental assessment
[171]	ELECTRE TRI	Applied	Supplier selection
[185]	Optimistic ELECTRE TRI	Novel	Numerical example
[157]	Posteriori ELECTRE TRI	Extension	Risk assessment
[123]	ELECTRE TRI-B	Applied	Materials management
[137]	ELECTRE TRI-C	Applied	Project evaluation
[55]	ELECTRE Tri-nC	Applied	Risk assessment
[18]	ELECTRE TRI-B and ELECTRE TRI-C	Extension	Numerical example
[130]	ELECTRE TRI-nC	Novel	Environmental assessment
[47]	ELECTRE-TRI-B-H	Novel	Product assessment
[1]	ELECTRE TRI-C	Novel	Health
[74]	ELECTRE TRI-C	Applied	Health
[2]	ELECTRE Tri-nC	Novel	Numerical example
[112]	ELECTRE Tri-C	Extension	Risk assessment

continued on next page

TABLE 2.5 (*continued*)

Article	Method	Contribution	Application
[71]	ELECTRE TRI-C, ELEC-TRE TRI-nC and THE-SEUS	Applied	Numerical example
[154]	Fuzzy ELECTRE TRI-C	Extension	Facility location
[142]	FlowSort	Novel	Numerical example
[141]	FlowSort	Extension	Financial management
[167]	FlowSort	Applied	Supplier selection
[168]	FlowSort	Applied	Supplier selection
[169]	FlowSort	Applied	Supplier selection
[101]	Interval-FlowSort	Novel	Supplier selection
[26]	F-FlowSort	Extension	Project evaluation
[128]	FlowSort-GDSS	Novel	Risk assessment
[151]	SMAA-FFS (FlowSort)	Extension	Project evaluation
[150]	SMAA–FFS–H (FlowSort)	Extension	Project evaluation
[176]	MR-Sort	Novel	Numerical example
[145]	MR-Sort	Extension	Maintenance management
[134]	MR-sort with large positive and negative performance	Extension	Resource management
[10]	MR-Sort	Applied	Health
[9]	MR-Sort with MIP	Novel	Product assessment
[133]	Extended MR-sort	Extension	Numerical example
[5]	PROMSORT	Novel	Supplier selection
[166]	PCLUST (PROMETHEE CLUSTER)	Extension	Environmental assessment
[59]	PROMETHEE-based sorting	Extension	Risk assessment
[43]	PROMETHEE-based sorting	Applied	Risk assessment
[45]	PROMSORT	Applied	Supplier selection
[173]	β-PROMETHEE	Novel	Materials management
[65]	THESEUS	Novel	project evaluation
[70]	THESEUS	Applied	Risk assessment
[72]	PDA-THESEUS	Extension	Numerical example
[35]	PDA-THESEUS	Novel	Numerical example
[68]	PDA-THESEUS	Applied	Numerical example
[153]	PLTS sorting	Novel	Risk assessment
[144]	Multiprofile sorting	Applied	Project evaluation
[179]	Bipolar sorting	Extension	Numerical example

TABLE 2.6 Adapted MCDM methods for sorting problems using the outranking approach.

Article	Method	Contribution	Application
[51]	Delphi-ELECTRE TRI	Novel	Policy analysis
[100]	Relation H sort	Novel	Numerical example
[69]	Preference closeness sort	Novel	Project evaluation
[67]	Preference closeness clustering	Novel	Project evaluation
[159]	Progressive assisted sorting algorithm	Novel	Financial management
[103]	Integrated framework for outranking sort	Novel	Education
[170]	Intuitionistic GDM outranking sort	Novel	Risk assessment
[37]	I-MCSGA	Novel	Project evaluation
[64]	Extended NOSGA-II	Applied	Project evaluation
[66]	Dominance sort	Novel	Project evaluation

2.3.1.2.1 Lack of development in the outranking approach

Even DM support has been improved, and only 36 methods (45.5%) apply the PDA strategy. This means that more than half of the proposals are not supporting the definition of the parameters. Alternately, the approaches lack the ability to solve group decision-making problems because just nine papers (11.3%) deal with group decision-making. We highlight the fields that are not addressed by the outranking approach: democracy, environmental assessment, and inventory management. The outranking approach presents more applied work (38%), novel contributions (36.7%), and extension (22.7%). The current approach lacks hybrid work (1.2%), and solving real problems should be studied more. On the other hand, in the current approach, only one computational program was explicitly described in the articles: IRIS [38].

The outranking methods are considered to be flexible as they use criteria evaluation. However, some methods, such as the ELECTRE and PROMETHE families, among others, require threshold parameters. To support decision-makers, some parameters are inferred as the indifference, preference, and veto thresholds (q, p, and v) and the degree of importance (w). This means that the outranking methods still require significant support for analysts and DMs. As stated by de Boer, van der Wegen, and Telgen [40], we should consider that these methods do not guide how to define weight, thresholds, or the information to be gathered.

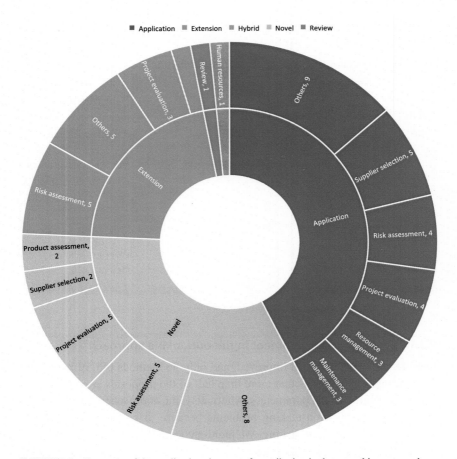

FIGURE 2.8 Summary of the applications by type of contribution in the outranking approach.

2.3.1.3 Goal, aspiration, or reference-level approach

This approach encompasses sorting methods such as DEASort, VIKOR-SORT, AHP–TOPSIS-2N, TOPSIS-SORT, and TOPSIS-Sort-C (see Table 2.7). Other MCDM methods have been adapted to solve sorting problems such as probabilistic-based and distant-based methods (Table 2.8). The most recent methods in this approach are the novel DEASort [95], VIKORSORT [51], and AHP–TOPSIS-2N [46]. The areas of application carried out by the current approaches are environmental assessment, financial management, inventory management, materials management, project evaluation, and resource management. Fig. 2.9 shows a summary of the application fields by contribution in the current approach.

The goal, aspiration, or reference-level approach typically uses some distance functions for criteria aggregation. The current approach is more focused

TABLE 2.7 MCDM sorting methods by the goal, aspiration, or reference-level approach.

Article	Method	Contribution	Application
[93]	DEASort	Novel	Materials management
[114]	DEA-based sorting	Novel	Project evaluation
[31]	Sequential sorting	Novel	Inventory management
[49]	VIKORSORT	Novel	Environmental assessment
[46]	AHP–TOPSIS-2N	Hybrid	Project evaluation
[165]	TOPSIS-SORT	Novel	Environmental assessment
[42]	PDTOPSIS-Sort	Novel	Financial management
[41]	TOPSIS-Sort-C	Novel	Financial management

TABLE 2.8 Adapted MCDM methods for sorting problems by the goal, aspiration, or reference-level approach.

Article	Method	Contribution	Application
[152]	Inverse-DEA	Novel	Financial management
[27]	Probabilistic sorting	Novel	Resource management
[30]	Weighted Euclidean sort	Novel	Resource management
[183]	Case-based distance sort	Applied	Numerical example
[33]	Case-based distance sort	Extension	Inventory management
[13]	Fuzzy-c-means sort	Hybrid	Materials management

on designing and developing novel methods. The goal, aspiration, or reference-level approach has only one applied study. It seems that this would be an excellent opportunity in this approach to exploit applied methods in new problems. Half of the contributions are able to support the decision process with PDA, and only one method deals with the group decision-making context.

2.3.1.3.1 Lack of development in the goal, aspiration, or reference-level approach

An evident disadvantage of working with the current approach is the a priori information that the decision-maker needs to define, which consists of the goal target values [182]. This could be difficult for some problems, e.g. to determine the return in a stock exchange portfolio. On the other hand, some criticisms were stated regarding the application of different distance norms. One distance norm would perform in a different way for each data set. As stated, different distance norms may fit a data set better [27]; in consequence, different distance norms could fit the data set less well, resulting in worse performance. In this sense, it is difficult to choose a norm for the specific data set. One significant issue in the

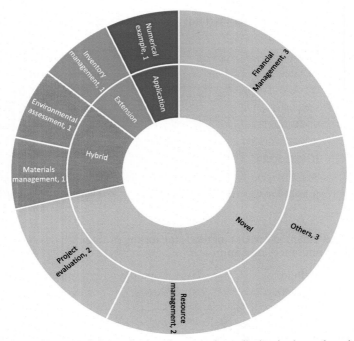

FIGURE 2.9 Summary of the applications by type of contribution in the goal, aspiration or reference-level approach.

current approach is software development. The development of any software in the current approach has not been explicitly stated.

2.3.1.4 Nonclassical MCDM approach

The current approach is gaining relevance, and 19 papers have been published (see Table 2.9). The adapted methods are mostly rule-based, such as rough-set, dominance-based rough set, TRINOMFC, prediction sorting, and the conjoint measurement technique for the nonclassical MCDM approach. We found two hybrid, six extension, and 10 novel contributions, and one application contribution. A seminal contribution was presented by [87], the most cited paper in MCDM sorting literature. Risk assessment (three), theoretical foundations (two), and education (four) are the areas of greater application for the current approach. Other areas of application are financial management (three), Materials management (one), and resource management (two). Fig. 2.10 shows a summary of the application fields by contribution.

The first publications concerning this approach appeared in 2002, consisting of four papers. Since then, six more papers have been produced. The rough-set-based sorting method by [87] has been of great interest for the scientific community, as it is the most cited paper on the sorting problem.

TABLE 2.9 Adapted MCDM methods for sorting problems using the non-classical MCDM approach.

Article	Method	Contribution	Application
[76]	STEPCLASS	Novel	Financial management
[8]	STEPCLASS and UniComBOS	Hybrid	Resource management
[16]	Conjoint measurement techniques	Novel	Theoretical foundations
[17]	Conjoint measurement techniques	Novel	Theoretical foundations
[87]	Rough-set	Extension	Resource management
[48]	Rough-set	Extension	Education
[4]	Rough-set	Novel	Education
[85]	Dominance-based rough set approach	Extension	Financial management
[86]	Dominance-based rough set approach	Extension	Education
[108]	Dominance-based rough set approach	Novel	Risk assessment
[32]	Dominance-based rough set approach, Dempster–Shafer theory of evidence	Novel	Risk assessment
[89]	Dominance-based rough set approach	Applied	Product assessment
[78]	Know-how with dominance-based rough set approach	Novel	Health
[28]	DRSA-condition attributes	Extension	Financial management
[120]	TRINOMFC	Novel	Risk assessment
[79]	TRINOMFC	Extension	Health
[12]	Prediction sorting	Hybrid	Materials management
[61]	Logical multi-criteria sort	Novel	Education
[122]	Fuzzy inference and rule-based classification	Novel	Supplier selection

The decision rules approach shows more development in novel contributions than in applied studies. It seems both are promising areas for development of the current approach. A relevant strength of the nonclassical MCDM is the way it aggregates the DM preferences regarding the adjacent knowledge-constructing decision rules to assign alternatives in the classes. The replication of this knowledge with new alternatives or similar problems seems to be true to the preferences of the DM.

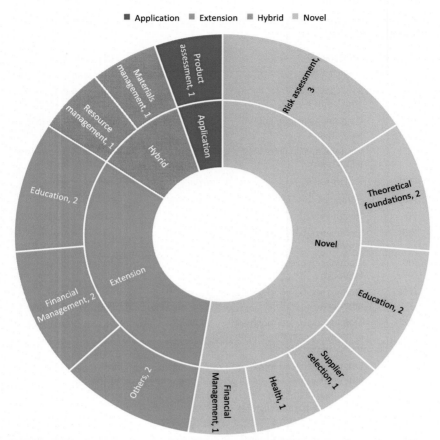

FIGURE 2.10   Summary of the applications by type of contribution in the nonclassical MCDM approach.

It seems that the hybrid methods are a promising path to scale the algorithms to more complex problems with a large volume of data. A trend in this approach seems to be hybrid methods with a machine learning approach to overcome some limitations in MCDM approaches. A total of 57% of the articles help the DM with the parameter definition with the analogous PDA strategy.

2.3.1.4.1   Lack of development in nonclassical MCDM approach

The publications are mostly based on rough-set. Other articles are absent, such as the theory of evidence, and the lack of group decision-making problems is evident in this approach. The study of further research in the nonclassical method is a promising area of study. Notably, more fuzzy studies need to be developed, such as multi-granulation and attribute reduction, as stated in [131]. The development of software is still needed for the current approach. There is no reported software developed in the published studies.

2.4 Trends and future directions for MCDM sorting

In additive utility methods, the input attributes are normally expected to be monotone with respect to the preferences [77]. However, in a decision-aiding context, an important situation can arise, for which the direction of monotonicity cannot be specified a priori. This situation is described by [54], suggesting that each nonmonotonic criterion can be replaced by multiple monotonic criteria. This is an open problem for sorting methods and only three studies [90,109,125] address it.

The representation of knowledge can be useful to estimate the assignment of nonreference alternatives to decision classes by rule inductions. This strategy would be supported by a dominance relation in the rough approximation of decision classes. Some induction strategies offer a minimal set of rules representing the assignment examples in the most concise manner [15]. The development of this approach has not been updated for sorting problems.

The conventional methods deal with few numbers of alternatives and criteria. The MCDM sorting methods presented in the survey lack a methodology to address large numbers of alternatives and criteria. Some studies mentioned that the proposed methods could address a large number of criteria, but no methodological or experimental evidence was shown. The assignment of nonreference alternatives in the presence of a large number of criteria is still an open line of research in MCDM sorting.

Few types of sorting software are available. Regarding the problem features addressed in multi-criteria decision-making (MCDM), most of the methods lack robust solutions. Robust sorting methods still need to be developed to ensure that solutions are not affected significantly by value variations of parameters. A review of the literature shows that few contributions declared the generation of robust solutions.

In MCDM methods, the DM's preference is included as an input parameter. It is well-known that the parameter elicitation process can be a complex task for the DM, requiring great cognitive effort. A technique that uses indirect elicitation that corresponds to the DM's preferences expressed by holistic judgments on representative case sets is preference disaggregation analysis (PDA). We would like to highlight the importance of using PDA in the MCDM context. New methods not supporting the parameter definitions would lack support for the DM. There will be a greater impact when the DM is not experienced in MCDM or in parameter definitions for a particular problem.

Thus, the following key directions should be considered regarding further research in multi-criteria decision sorting problems:

- It is necessary to develop techniques for criteria evaluation using fuzzy logic to capture the true meanings of linguistic assessments in human perceptions.
- The new methods should be capable of representing knowledge. Newly developed methods need to find adjacent knowledge from decision inductions. Some strategies would be based on the dominance relation, machine learning, or other optimization methods for knowledge discovery.
- The MCDM methods need to venture into problems with a large number of criteria. Two possible paths are in the field of MCDM and in nonclassical MCDM. New methods based on PDA in MCDM to deal with preference information with a large number of criteria should be developed. On the other hand, machine learning or unsupervised learning can be implemented to develop new sorting methods that include DMs' preferences.
- More studies are needed to provide DMs with the assignment of alternatives in the appropriate classes that are not affected significantly by value variations of parameters to ensure a robust solution.
- More computational tools are necessary. These will help more practitioners to adopt the current and new multi-criteria sorting models. We found a very small number of computational tools available.

References

[1] J. Almeida-Dias, J.R. Figueira, B. Roy, ELECTRE TRI-C: a multiple criteria sorting method based on characteristic reference actions, European Journal of Operational Research 204 (3) (2010) 565–580, https://doi.org/10.1016/j.ejor.2009.10.018.

[2] J. Almeida-Dias, J.R. Figueira, B. Roy, A multiple criteria sorting method where each category is characterized by several reference actions: the ELECTRE TRI-NC method, European Journal of Operational Research 217 (3) (2012) 567–579, https://doi.org/10.1016/j.ejor.2011.09.047.

[3] Pavel Anselmo Alvarez, Alessio Ishizaka, Luis Martínez, Multiple-criteria decision-making sorting methods: a survey, Expert Systems with Applications 183 (2021) 115368.

[4] L.P. An, Z.Q. Chen, L.Y. Tong, Generation and application of decision rules within dominance-based rough set approach to multicriteria sorting, International Journal of Innovative Computing, Information & Control 7 (3) (2011) 1145–1155.

[5] C. Araz, I. Ozkarahan, Supplier evaluation and management system for strategic sourcing based on a new multicriteria sorting procedure, International Journal of Production Economics 106 (2) (2007) 585–606, https://doi.org/10.1016/j.ijpe.2006.08.008.

[6] S.G. Arcidiacono, S. Corrente, S. Greco, Robust stochastic sorting with interacting criteria hierarchically structured, European Journal of Operational Research (2020), https://doi.org/10.1016/j.ejor.2020.11.024.

[7] C. Arondel, P. Girardin, Sorting cropping systems on the basis of their impact on groundwater quality, European Journal of Operational Research 127 (3) (2000) 467–482, https://doi.org/10.1016/s0377-2217(99)00437-3.

[8] I.V. Ashikhmin, E.M. Furems, Hybrid method for multicriteria items ordering, Scientific and Technical Information Processing 45 (6) (2019) 444–451, https://doi.org/10.3103/s0147688218060023.

[9] K. Belahcene, C. Labreuche, N. Maudet, V. Mousseau, W. Ouerdane, An efficient SAT formulation for learning multiple criteria non-compensatory sorting rules from examples, Computers & Operations Research 97 (2018) 58–71, https://doi.org/10.1016/j.cor.2018.04.019.

[10] S. Ben Souissi, M. Abed, L. El Hiki, P. Fortemps, M. Pirlot, PARS, a system combining semantic technologies with multiple criteria decision aiding for supporting antibiotic prescriptions, Journal of Biomedical Informatics 99 (2019) 103304, https://doi.org/10.1016/j.jbi.2019.103304.

[11] N. Benabbou, P. Perny, P. Viappiani, Incremental elicitation of Choquet capacities for multicriteria choice, ranking and sorting problems, Artificial Intelligence 246 (2017) 152–180, https://doi.org/10.1016/j.artint.2017.02.001.

[12] I. Berget, T. Naes, Sorting of raw materials with focus on multiple end-product properties, Journal of Chemometrics 16 (6) (2002) 263–273, https://doi.org/10.1002/cem.720.

[13] I. Berget, T. Næs, Optimal sorting of raw materials, based on the predicted end-product quality, Quality Engineering 14 (3) (2002) 459–478, https://doi.org/10.1081/qen-120001883.

[14] J. Biluca, C.R. de Aguiar, F. Trojan, Sorting of suitable areas for disposal of construction and demolition waste using GIS and ELECTRE TRI, Waste Management 114 (2020) 307–320, https://doi.org/10.1016/j.wasman.2020.07.007.

[15] J. Błaszczyński, R. Słowiński, M. Szeląg, Sequential covering rule induction algorithm for variable consistency rough set approaches, Information Sciences 181 (5) (2011) 987–1002, https://doi.org/10.1016/j.ins.2010.10.030.

[16] D. Bouyssou, T. Marchant, An axiomatic approach to noncompensatory sorting methods in MCDM, I: the case of two categories, European Journal of Operational Research 178 (1) (2007) 217–245, https://doi.org/10.1016/j.ejor.2006.01.027.

[17] D. Bouyssou, T. Marchant, An axiomatic approach to noncompensatory sorting methods in MCDM, II: more than two categories, European Journal of Operational Research 178 (1) (2007) 246–276.

[18] D. Bouyssou, T. Marchant, On the relations between ELECTRE TRI-B and ELECTRE TRI-C and on a new variant of ELECTRE TRI-B, European Journal of Operational Research 242 (1) (2015) 201–211, https://doi.org/10.1016/j.ejor.2014.09.057.

[19] D. Bouyssou, T. Marchant, M. Pirlot, A. Tsoukias, P. Vincke, Evaluation and Decision Models: A Critical Perspective, vol. 32, Springer, 2000.

[20] D. Bouyssou, T. Marchant, M. Pirlot, A. Tsoukiàs, P. Vincke, Evaluation and Decision Models with Multiple Criteria: Stepping Stones for the Analyst, vol. 86, Springer, 2006.

[21] A. Bregar, J. Gyorkos, M.B. Juric, Interactive aggregation/disaggregation dichotomic sorting procedure for group decision analysis based on the threshold model, Informatica 19 (2) (2008) 161–190.

[22] A.J. Brito, A.T. de Almeida, C.M.M. Mota, A multicriteria model for risk sorting of natural gas pipelines based on ELECTRE TRI integrating utility theory, European Journal of Operational Research 200 (3) (2010) 812–821, https://doi.org/10.1016/j.ejor.2009.01.016.

[23] A.G. Bugdaci, M. Koksalan, S. Ozpeynirci, Y. Serin, An interactive probabilistic approach to multi-criteria sorting, IIE Transactions 45 (10) (2013) 1048–1058, https://doi.org/10.1080/0740817x.2012.721945.

[24] F.L. Cai, X.W. Liao, K.L. Wang, A progressive multiple criteria sorting approach based on additive utility functions considering imprecise information, International Journal of Innovative Computing, Information & Control 7 (5B) (2011) 2727–2738.

[25] F.L. Cai, X.W. Liao, K.L. Wang, An interactive sorting approach based on the assignment examples of multiple decision makers with different priorities, Annals of Operations Research 197 (1) (2012) 87–108, https://doi.org/10.1007/s10479-011-0930-3.

[26] A.C.S.M. Campos, B. Mareschal, A.T. de Almeida, Fuzzy FlowSort: an integration of the FlowSort method and fuzzy set theory for decision making on the basis of inaccurate quantitative data, Information Sciences 293 (2015) 115–124, https://doi.org/10.1016/j.ins.2014.09.024.

[27] B. Celik, E. Karasakal, C. Iyigun, A probabilistic multiple criteria sorting approach based on distance functions, Expert Systems with Applications 42 (7) (2015) 3610–3618, https://doi.org/10.1016/j.eswa.2014.11.049.

[28] S. Chakhar, A. Ishizaka, A. Thorpe, J. Cox, T. Nguyen, L. Ford, Calculating the relative importance of condition attributes based on the characteristics of decision rules and attribute reducts: application to crowdfunding, European Journal of Operational Research 286 (2) (2020) 689–712, https://doi.org/10.1016/j.ejor.2020.03.039.

[29] A. Charnes, W.W. Cooper, E. Rhodes, Measuring the efficiency of decision making units, European Journal of Operational Research 2 (6) (1978) 429–444, https://doi.org/10.1016/0377-2217(78)90138-8.

[30] Y. Chen, K.W. Hipel, D.M. Kilgour, Multiple-criteria sorting using case-based distance models with an application in water resources management, IEEE Transactions on Systems, Man and Cybernetics. Part A. Systems and Humans 37 (5) (2007) 680–691, https://doi.org/10.1109/tsmca.2007.902629.

[31] Y. Chen, K.W. Hipel, D.M. Kilgour, A multiple criteria sequential sorting procedure, Journal of Industrial and Management Optimization 4 (3) (2008) 407–423.

[32] Y. Chen, D.M. Kilgour, K.W. Hipel, A decision rule aggregation approach to multiple criteria-multiple participant sorting, Group Decision and Negotiation 21 (5) (2012) 727–745, https://doi.org/10.1007/s10726-011-9246-6.

[33] Y. Chen, K.W. Li, M.D. Kilgour, K.W. Hipel, A case-based distance model for multiple criteria ABC analysis, Computers & Operations Research 35 (3) (2008) 776–796, https://doi.org/10.1016/j.cor.2006.03.024.

[34] S. Corrente, M. Doumpos, S. Greco, R. Slowinski, C. Zopounidis, Multiple criteria hierarchy process for sorting problems based on ordinal regression with additive value functions, Annals of Operations Research 251 (1–2) (2017) 117–139, https://doi.org/10.1007/s10479-015-1898-1.

[35] E. Covantes, E. Fernandez, J. Navarro, Handling the multiplicity of solutions in a moea based PDA-THESEUS framework for multi-criteria sorting, Foundations of Computing and Decision Sciences 41 (4) (2016) 213–235, https://doi.org/10.1515/fcds-2016-0013.

[36] M.T. Covas, C.A. Silva, L.C. Dias, Multicriteria decision analysis for sustainable data centers location, International Transactions in Operational Research 20 (3) (2013) 269–299, https://doi.org/10.1111/j.1475-3995.2012.00874.x.

[37] L. Cruz-Reyes, E. Fernandez, P. Sanchez, C. Gomez, Incorporation of decision-maker preferences in an interactive evolutionary multi-objective algorithm using a multi-criteria sorting, International Journal of Combinatorial Optimization Problems and Informatics 7 (3) (2016) 28–43.

[38] S. Damart, L.C. Dias, V. Mousseau, Supporting groups in sorting decisions: methodology and use of a multi-criteria aggregation/disaggregation DSS, Decision Support Systems 43 (4) (2007) 1464–1475, https://doi.org/10.1016/j.dss.2006.06.002.

[39] S. Damart, V. Mousseau, I. Sommerlatt, DU Mode D'implication D'acteurs Multiples Dans Le Cadre De L'utilisation D'un MOdèle D'affectation Multicritère: Analyse Au Regard D'une Application à La Tarification Des Transports Publics, INFOR. Information Systems and Operational Research 40 (3) (2016) 199–222, https://doi.org/10.1080/03155986.2002.11732654.

[40] L. de Boer, L. van der Wegen, J. Telgen, Outranking methods in support of supplier selection, European Journal of Purchasing and Supply Management 4 (2–3) (1998) 109–118, https://doi.org/10.1016/s0969-7012(97)00034-8.

[41] D.F. de Lima Silva, A.T. de Almeida Filho, Sorting with TOPSIS through boundary and characteristic profiles, Computers & Industrial Engineering 141 (2020) 106328, https://doi.org/10.1016/j.cie.2020.106328.

[42] D.F. de Lima Silva, L. Ferreira, A.T. de Almeida-Filho, A new preference disaggregation TOPSIS approach applied to sort corporate bonds based on financial statements and expert's assessment, Expert Systems with Applications 152 (2020) 113369, https://doi.org/10.1016/j.eswa.2020.113369.

[43] D.F. de Lima Silva, J.C.S. Silva, L.G.O. Silva, L. Ferreira, A.T. de Almeida-Filho, Sovereign credit risk assessment with multiple criteria using an outranking method, Mathematical Problems in Engineering 2018 (2018) 1–11, https://doi.org/10.1155/2018/8564764.

[44] F. de Morais Bezerra, P. Melo, J.P. Costa, Reaching consensus with VICA-ELECTRE TRI: a case study, Group Decision and Negotiation 26 (6) (2017) 1145–1171, https://doi.org/10.1007/s10726-017-9539-5.

[45] A.L. de Oliveira e Silva, C.A.V. Cavalcante, N.V.C. de Vasconcelos, A multicriteria decision model to support the selection of suppliers of motor repair services, The International Journal of Advanced Manufacturing Technology 84 (1–4) (2015) 523–532, https://doi.org/10.1007/s00170-015-7673-2.

[46] L.P. De Souza, C.F.S. Gomes, A.P. De Barros, Implementation of new hybrid AHP-TOPSIS-2N method in sorting and prioritizing 6 of an it CAPEX project portfolio, International Journal of Information Technology & Decision Making 17 (4) (2018) 977–1005, https://doi.org/10.1142/s0219622018500207.

[47] L. Del Vasto-Terrientes, A. Valls, P. Zielniewicz, J. Borras, A hierarchical multi-criteria sorting approach for recommender systems, Journal of Intelligent Information Systems 46 (2) (2016) 313–346, https://doi.org/10.1007/s10844-015-0362-7.

[48] K. Dembczynski, S. Greco, R. Slowinksi, Methodology of rough-set-based classification and sorting with hierarchical structure of attributes and criteria, Control and Cybernetics 31 (4) (2002) 891–920.

[49] L. Demir, M.E. Akpinar, C. Araz, M.A. Ilgin, A green supplier evaluation system based on a new multi-criteria sorting method: VIKORSORT, Expert Systems with Applications 114 (2018) 479–487, https://doi.org/10.1016/j.eswa.2018.07.071.

[50] L. Dias, J. Clímaco, ELECTRE TRI for groups with imprecise information on parameter values, Group Decision and Negotiation 9 (5) (2000) 355–377, https://doi.org/10.1023/a:1008739614981.

[51] L.C. Dias, C.H. Antunes, G. Dantas, N. de Castro, L. Zamboni, A multi-criteria approach to sort and rank policies based on Delphi qualitative assessments and ELECTRE TRI: the case of smart grids in Brazil, Omega-International Journal of Management Science 76 (2018) 100–111, https://doi.org/10.1016/j.omega.2017.04.004.

[52] L.C. Dias, V. Mousseau, IRIS: a DSS for multiple criteria sorting problems, Journal of Multi-Criteria Decision Analysis 12 (4–5) (2003) 285–298, https://doi.org/10.1002/mcda.364.

[53] L.s. Dias, V. Mousseau, J. Figueira, J. Clímaco, An aggregation/disaggregation approach to obtain robust conclusions with ELECTRE TRI, European Journal of Operational Research 138 (2) (2002) 332–348, https://doi.org/10.1016/s0377-2217(01)00250-8.

[54] M. Doumpos, Learning non-monotonic additive value functions for multicriteria decision making, OR Spektrum 34 (1) (2012) 89–106, https://doi.org/10.1007/s00291-010-0231-2.

[55] M. Doumpos, J.R. Figueira, A multicriteria outranking approach for modeling corporate credit ratings: an application of the Electre Tri-nC method, Omega 82 (2019) 166–180, https://doi.org/10.1016/j.omega.2018.01.003.

[56] M. Doumpos, S.H. Zanakis, C. Zopounidis, Multicriteria preference disaggregation for classification problems with an application to global investing risk, Decision Sciences 32 (2) (2001) 333–386, https://doi.org/10.1111/j.1540-5915.2001.tb00963.x.

[57] M. Doumpos, C. Zopounidis, Assessing financial risks using a multicriteria sorting procedure: the case of country risk assessment, Omega-International Journal of Management Science 29 (1) (2001) 97–109, https://doi.org/10.1016/s0305-0483(00)00028-1.

[58] M. Doumpos, C. Zopounidis, Developing sorting models using preference disaggregation analysis: an experimental investigation, European Journal of Operational Research 154 (3) (2004) 585–598, https://doi.org/10.1016/s0377-2217(02)00815-9.

[59] M. Doumpos, C. Zopounidis, A multicriteria classification approach based on pairwise comparisons, European Journal of Operational Research 158 (2) (2004) 378–389, https://doi.org/10.1016/j.ejor.2003.06.011.

[60] M. Doumpos, C. Zopounidis, Multicriteria Decision Aid Classification Methods, vol. 73, Kluwer Academic Publishers, New York, Boston, Dordrecht, London, Moscow, 2004.

[61] M. Ducassé, P. Cellier, Fair and fast convergence on islands of agreement in multicriteria group decision making by logical navigation, Group Decision and Negotiation 23 (4) (2013) 673–694, https://doi.org/10.1007/s10726-013-9372-4.

[62] B. Ecer, M. Kabak, M. DaĞDevİRen, İki amaçlıters çok kriterli sıralama problemi için hedef programlama modeli, Gazi Üniversitesi Mühendislik-Mimarlık Fakültesi Dergisi, https://doi.org/10.17341/gazimmfd.539218, 2020.

[63] M. Esmaelian, H. Shahmoradi, M. Vali, A novel classification method: a hybrid approach based on extension of the UTADIS with polynomial and PSO-GA algorithm, Applied Soft Computing 49 (2016) 56–70, https://doi.org/10.1016/j.asoc.2016.07.017.

[64] E. Fernandez, E. Lopez, G. Mazcorro, R. Olmedo, C.A.C. Coello, Application of the non-outranked sorting genetic algorithm to public project portfolio selection, Information Sciences 228 (2013) 131–149, https://doi.org/10.1016/j.ins.2012.11.018.

[65] E. Fernandez, J. Navarro, A new approach to multi-criteria sorting based on fuzzy outranking relations: the THESEUS method, European Journal of Operational Research 213 (2) (2011) 405–413, https://doi.org/10.1016/j.ejor.2011.03.036.

[66] E. Fernandez, J. Navarro, S. Bernal, Multicriteria sorting using a valued indifference relation under a preference disaggregation paradigm, European Journal of Operational Research 198 (2) (2009) 602–609, https://doi.org/10.1016/j.ejor.2008.09.020.

[67] E. Fernandez, J. Navarro, S. Bernal, Handling multicriteria preferences in cluster analysis, European Journal of Operational Research 202 (3) (2010) 819–827, https://doi.org/10.1016/j.ejor.2009.05.034.

[68] E. Fernandez, J. Navarro, E. Covantes, J. Rodriguez, Analysis of the effectiveness of the THESEUS multi-criteria sorting method: theoretical remarks and experimental evidence, Top 25 (2) (2017) 314–339, https://doi.org/10.1007/s11750-016-0433-0.

[69] E. Fernandez, J. Navarro, A. Duarte, Multicriteria sorting using a valued preference closeness relation, European Journal of Operational Research 185 (2) (2008) 673–686, https://doi.org/10.1016/j.ejor.2006.12.041.

[70] E. Fernandez, J. Navarro, A. Duarte, G. Ibarra, Core: a decision support system for regional competitiveness analysis based on multi-criteria sorting, Decision Support Systems 54 (3) (2013) 1417–1426, https://doi.org/10.1016/j.dss.2012.12.009.

[71] E. Fernandez, J. Navarro, R. Olmedo, Characterization of the effectiveness of several outranking-based multi-criteria sorting methods, International Journal of Information Technology & Decision Making 17 (4) (2018) 1047–1084, https://doi.org/10.1142/s0219622018500177.

[72] E. Fernandez, J. Navarro, E. Salomon, Automatic enhancement of the reference set for multi-criteria sorting in the frame of THESEUS method, Foundations of Computing and Decision Sciences 39 (2) (2014) 57–77, https://doi.org/10.2478/fcds-2014-0005.

[73] J. Figueira, V. Mousseau, B. Roy, ELECTRE methods, in: J. Figueira, S. Greco, M. Ehrgott (Eds.), Multiple Criteria Decision Analysis: The State of the Art Surveys, Springer, New York, 2005, pp. 133–162.

[74] J.R. Figueira, J. Almeida-Dias, S. Matias, B. Roy, M.J. Carvalho, C.E. Plancha, ELECTRE TRI-C, a multiple criteria decision aiding sorting model applied to assisted reproduction, International Journal of Medical Informatics 80 (4) (2011) 262–273, https://doi.org/10.1016/j.ijmedinf.2010.12.001.

[75] J.R. Figueira, S. Greco, B. Roy, R. Słowiński, An overview of ELECTRE methods and their recent extensions, Journal of Multi-Criteria Decision Analysis 20 (1–2) (2013) 61–85, https://doi.org/10.1002/mcda.1482.

[76] E.M. Furems, Stepclass-based approach to multicriteria sorting, Scientific and Technical Information Processing 42 (6) (2015) 481–489, https://doi.org/10.3103/s0147688215060064.

[77] M. Ghaderi, F. Ruiz, N. Agell, Understanding the impact of brand colour on brand image: a preference disaggregation approach, Pattern Recognition Letters 67 (2015) 11–18, https://doi.org/10.1016/j.patrec.2015.05.011.

[78] S. Ghrab, I. Saad, F. Gargouri, G. Kassel, A decision support system for identifying and representing likely crucial organizational know-how and knowing that, Journal of Decision Systems 23 (3) (2014) 266–284, https://doi.org/10.1080/12460125.2014.886500.

[79]   Y. Goletsis, C. Papaloukas, D.I. Fotiadis, A. Likas, L.K. Michalis, Automated ischemic beat classification using genetic algorithms and multicriteria decision analysis, IEEE Transactions on Biomedical Engineering 51 (10) (2004) 1717–1725, https://doi.org/10.1109/tbme.2004. 828033.

[80]   S. Greco, M. Ehrgott, J.R. Figueira, Multiple Criteria Decision Analysis: State of the Art Surveys, vol. 233, Springer, New York, 2016.

[81]   S. Greco, M. Kadziński, V. Mousseau, R. Słowiński, Robust ordinal regression for multiple criteria group decision: UTAGMS-GROUP and UTADISGMS-GROUP, Decision Support Systems 52 (3) (2012) 549–561, https://doi.org/10.1016/j.dss.2011.10.005.

[82]   S. Greco, M. Kadzinski, R. Slowinski, Selection of a representative value function in robust multiple criteria sorting, Computers & Operations Research 38 (11) (2011) 1620–1637, https://doi.org/10.1016/j.cor.2011.02.003.

[83]   S. Greco, B. Matarazzo, R. Slowinski, A new rough set approach to multicriteria and multi-attribute classification, in: L. Polkowski, A. Skowron (Eds.), Rough Sets and Current Trends in Computing (vol. 1424), Springer, Berlin, Heidelberg, 1998.

[84]   S. Greco, B. Matarazzo, R. Slowinski, Rough approximation of a preference relation by dominance relations, European Journal of Operational Research 117 (1) (1999) 63–83, https://doi.org/10.1016/s0377-2217(98)00127-1.

[85]   S. Greco, B. Matarazzo, R. Slowinski, Extension of the rough set approach to multicriteria decision support, INFOR. Information Systems and Operational Research 38 (3) (2000) 161–195, https://doi.org/10.1080/03155986.2000.11732407.

[86]   S. Greco, B. Matarazzo, R. Slowinski, Rough sets theory for multicriteria decision analysis, European Journal of Operational Research 129 (1) (2001) 1–47, https://doi.org/10.1016/s0377-2217(00)00167-3.

[87]   S. Greco, B. Matarazzo, R. Slowinski, Rough sets methodology for sorting problems in presence of multiple attributes and criteria, European Journal of Operational Research 138 (2) (2002) 247–259, https://doi.org/10.1016/s0377-2217(01)00244-2.

[88]   S. Greco, V. Mousseau, R. Slowinski, Multiple criteria sorting with a set of additive value functions, European Journal of Operational Research 207 (3) (2010) 1455–1470, https://doi.org/10.1016/j.ejor.2010.05.021.

[89]   F. Guo, M. Hu, V.G. Duffy, H. Shao, Z. Ren, Kansei evaluation for group of users: a data-driven approach using dominance-based rough sets, Advanced Engineering Informatics 47 (2021) 101241, https://doi.org/10.1016/j.aei.2020.101241.

[90]   M. Guo, X. Liao, J. Liu, A progressive sorting approach for multiple criteria decision aiding in the presence of non-monotonic preferences, Expert Systems with Applications 123 (2019) 1–17, https://doi.org/10.1016/j.eswa.2019.01.033.

[91]   J.-M. Hugueni, Data envelopment analysis, in: A. Ishizaka, P. Nemery (Eds.), Multi-Criteria Decision Analysis: Methods and Software, Wiley, United Kingdom, 2013.

[92]   A. Ishizaka, M. Gordon, MACBETHSort: a multiple criteria decision aid procedure for sorting strategic products, Journal of the Operational Research Society 68 (1) (2017) 53–61, https://doi.org/10.1057/s41274-016-0002-9.

[93]   A. Ishizaka, F. Lolli, E. Balugani, R. Cavallieri, R. Gamberini, DEASort: assigning items with data envelopment analysis in ABC classes, International Journal of Production Economics 199 (2018) 7–15, https://doi.org/10.1016/j.ijpe.2018.02.007.

[94]   A. Ishizaka, C. López, Cost-benefit AHPSort for performance analysis of offshore providers, International Journal of Production Research 57 (13) (2018) 4261–4277, https://doi.org/10.1080/00207543.2018.1509393.

[95]   A. Ishizaka, P. Nemery, Multi-Criteria Decision Analysis: Methods and Software, Wiley, United Kingdom, 2013.

[96]   A. Ishizaka, P. Nemery, Assigning machines to incomparable maintenance strategies with ELECTRE-SORT, Omega-International Journal of Management Science 47 (2014) 45–59, https://doi.org/10.1016/j.omega.2014.03.006.

[97] A. Ishizaka, C. Pearman, P. Nemery, AHPSort: an AHP-based method for sorting problems, International Journal of Production Research 50 (17) (2012) 4767–4784, https://doi.org/10.1080/00207543.2012.657966.

[98] A. Ishizaka, V. Pereira, Utilisation of ANPSort for sorting alternative with interdependent criteria illustrated through a researcher's classification problem in an academic context, Soft Computing (2019), https://doi.org/10.1007/s00500-019-04405-5.

[99] A. Ishizaka, M. Tasiou, L. Martínez, Analytic hierarchy process-fuzzy sorting: an analytic hierarchy process-based method for fuzzy classification in sorting problems, Journal of the Operational Research Society 71 (6) (2019) 928–947, https://doi.org/10.1080/01605682.2019.1595188.

[100] K. Jabeur, J.M. Martel, An ordinal sorting method for group decision-making, European Journal of Operational Research 180 (3) (2007) 1272–1289, https://doi.org/10.1016/j.ejor.2006.05.032.

[101] P. Janssen, P. Nemery, An extension of the FlowSort sorting method to deal with imprecision, 4OR – A Quarterly Journal of Operations Research 11 (2) (2013) 171–193, https://doi.org/10.1007/s10288-012-0219-7.

[102] D. Jasiński, M. Cinelli, L.C. Dias, J. Meredith, K. Kirwan, Assessing supply risks for non-fossil mineral resources via multi-criteria decision analysis, Resources Policy 58 (2018) 150–158, https://doi.org/10.1016/j.resourpol.2018.04.011.

[103] M. Kadzinski, K. Ciomek, Integrated framework for preference modeling and robustness analysis for outranking-based multiple criteria sorting with ELECTRE and PROMETHEE, Information Sciences 352 (2016) 167–187, https://doi.org/10.1016/j.ins.2016.02.059.

[104] M. Kadzinski, K. Ciomek, P. Rychly, R. Slowinski, Post factum analysis for robust multiple criteria ranking and sorting, Journal of Global Optimization 65 (3) (2016) 531–562, https://doi.org/10.1007/s10898-015-0359-3.

[105] M. Kadzinski, K. Ciomek, R. Slowinski, Modeling assignment-based pairwise comparisons within integrated framework for value-driven multiple criteria sorting, European Journal of Operational Research 241 (3) (2015) 830–841, https://doi.org/10.1016/j.ejor.2014.09.050.

[106] M. Kadzinski, S. Corrente, S. Greco, R. Slowinski, Preferential reducts and constructs in robust multiple criteria ranking and sorting, OR Spektrum 36 (4) (2014) 1021–1053, https://doi.org/10.1007/s00291-014-0361-z.

[107] M. Kadziński, M. Ghaderi, M. Dąbrowski, Contingent preference disaggregation model for multiple criteria sorting problem, European Journal of Operational Research 281 (2) (2020) 369–387, https://doi.org/10.1016/j.ejor.2019.08.043.

[108] M. Kadziński, S. Greco, R. Slowinski, Robust ordinal regression for dominance-based rough set approach to multiple criteria sorting, Information Sciences 283 (2014) 211–228, https://doi.org/10.1016/j.ins.2014.06.038.

[109] M. Kadziński, K. Martyn, M. Cinelli, R. Słowiński, S. Corrente, S. Greco, Preference dis-aggregation for multiple criteria sorting with partial monotonicity constraints: application to exposure management of nanomaterials, International Journal of Approximate Reasoning 117 (2020) 60–80, https://doi.org/10.1016/j.ijar.2019.11.007.

[110] M. Kadzinski, R. Slowinski, DIS-CARD: a new method of multiple criteria sorting to classes with desired cardinality, Journal of Global Optimization 56 (3) (2013) 1143–1166, https://doi.org/10.1007/s10898-012-9945-9.

[111] M. Kadzinski, T. Tervonen, Stochastic ordinal regression for multiple criteria sorting prob-lems, Decision Support Systems 55 (1) (2013) 55–66, https://doi.org/10.1016/j.dss.2012.12.030.

[112] M. Kadzinski, T. Tervonen, J.R. Figueira, Robust multi-criteria sorting with the outranking preference model and characteristic profiles, Omega-International Journal of Management Science 55 (2015) 126–140, https://doi.org/10.1016/j.omega.2014.06.004.

[113] T.H.A. Kang, E.A. Frej, A.T. de Almeida, Flexible and interactive tradeoff elicitation for multicriteria sorting problems, Asia-Pacific Journal of Operational Research 37 (05) (2020) 2050020, https://doi.org/10.1142/s0217595920500207.

[114] E. Karasakal, P. Aker, A multicriteria sorting approach based on data envelopment analysis for R&D project selection problem, Omega-International Journal of Management Science 73 (2017) 79–92, https://doi.org/10.1016/j.omega.2016.12.006.

[115] O. Karsu, Approaches for inequity-averse sorting, Computers & Operations Research 66 (2016) 67–80, https://doi.org/10.1016/j.cor.2015.08.004.

[116] R. Keeney, H. Raiffa, Decisions with Multiple Objectives: Preferences and Value Tradeoffs, John Wiley & Sons, Inc., New York, 1976.

[117] M. Koksalan, V. Mousseau, S. Ozpeynirci, Multi-criteria sorting with category size restrictions, International Journal of Information Technology & Decision Making 16 (1) (2017) 5–23, https://doi.org/10.1142/s0219622016500061.

[118] M. Koksalan, S.B. Ozpeynirci, An interactive sorting method for additive utility functions, Computers & Operations Research 36 (9) (2009) 2565–2572, https://doi.org/10.1016/j.cor.2008.11.006.

[119] F. Küçükbay, E. Sürücü, Corporate sustainability performance measurement based on a new multicriteria sorting method, Corporate Social-Responsibility and Environmental Management 26 (3) (2019) 664–680, https://doi.org/10.1002/csr.1711.

[120] J. Leger, J.M. Martel, A multicriteria assignment procedure for a nominal sorting problematic, European Journal of Operational Research 138 (2) (2002) 349–364, https://doi.org/10.1016/s0377-2217(01)00251-x.

[121] F. Li, K.K. Phoon, X. Du, M. Zhang, Improved AHP method and its application in risk identification, Journal of Construction Engineering and Management 139 (3) (2013) 312–320, https://doi.org/10.1061/(asce)co.1943-7862.0000605.

[122] F.R. Lima, L. Osiro, L.C.R. Carpinetti, A fuzzy inference and categorization approach for supplier selection using compensatory and non-compensatory decision rules, Applied Soft Computing 13 (10) (2013) 4133–4147, https://doi.org/10.1016/j.asoc.2013.06.020.

[123] R.O. Lissouck, R. Pommier, F. Taillandier, J.K. Mvogo, D. Breysse, L.M.A. Ohandja, A decision support tool approach based on the Electre TRI-B method for the valorisation of tropical timbers from the Congo Basin: an application for glulam products, Southern Forests: A Journal of Forest Science 80 (4) (2018) 361–371, https://doi.org/10.2989/20702620.2018.1463153.

[124] J. Liu, M. Kadziński, X. Liao, X. Mao, Y. Wang, A preference learning framework for multiple criteria sorting with diverse additive value models and valued assignment examples, European Journal of Operational Research 286 (3) (2020) 963–985, https://doi.org/10.1016/j.ejor.2020.04.013.

[125] J. Liu, X. Liao, M. Kadziński, R. Słowiński, Preference disaggregation within the regularization framework for sorting problems with multiple potentially non-monotonic criteria, European Journal of Operational Research 276 (3) (2019) 1071–1089, https://doi.org/10.1016/j.ejor.2019.01.058.

[126] J.P. Liu, X.W. Liao, W. Huang, J.B. Yang, A new decision-making approach for multiple criteria sorting with an imbalanced set of assignment examples, European Journal of Operational Research 265 (2) (2018) 598–620, https://doi.org/10.1016/j.ejor.2017.07.043.

[127] J.P. Liu, X.W. Liao, J.B. Yang, A group decision-making approach based on evidential reasoning for multiple criteria sorting problem with uncertainty, European Journal of Operational Research 246 (3) (2015) 858–873, https://doi.org/10.1016/j.ejor.2015.05.027.

[128] F. Lolli, A. Ishizaka, R. Gamberini, B. Rimini, M. Messori, FlowSort-GDSS – a novel group multi-criteria decision support system for sorting problems with application to FMEA, Expert Systems with Applications 42 (17–18) (2015) 6342–6349, https://doi.org/10.1016/j.eswa.2015.04.028.

[129] C. Lopez, GAHPSort: a new group multi-criteria decision method for sorting a large number of the cloud-based ERP solutions (vol 92, pg. 12, 2007), Computers in Industry 92–93 (2017) 219.

[130] P. Madhooshiarzanagh, I. Abi-Zeid, A disaggregation approach for indirect preference elicitation in electre TRI-nC: application and validation, Journal of Multi-Criteria Decision Analysis (2021), https://doi.org/10.1002/mcda.1730.

[131] A. Mardani, M. Nilashi, J. Antucheviciene, M. Tavana, R. Bausys, O. Ibrahim, Recent fuzzy generalisations of rough sets theory: a systematic review and methodological critique of the literature, Complexity 2017 (2017) 1–33, https://doi.org/10.1155/2017/1608147.

[132] J.L. Marichal, P. Meyer, M. Roubens, Sorting multi-attribute alternatives: the TOMASO method, Computers & Operations Research 32 (4) (2005) 861–877, https://doi.org/10.1016/j.cor.2003.09.002.

[133] P. Meyer, A.-L. Olteanu, Handling imprecise and missing evaluations in multi-criteria majority-rule sorting, Computers & Operations Research 110 (2019) 135–147, https://doi.org/10.1016/j.cor.2019.05.027.

[134] P. Meyer, A.L. Olteanu, Integrating large positive and negative performance differences into multicriteria majority-rule sorting models, Computers & Operations Research 81 (2017) 216–230, https://doi.org/10.1016/j.cor.2016.11.007.

[135] F. Miccoli, A. Ishizaka, Sorting municipalities in Umbria according to the risk of wolf attacks with AHPSort II, Ecological Indicators 73 (2017) 741–755, https://doi.org/10.1016/j.ecolind.2016.10.034.

[136] D.C. Morais, A.T. de Almeida, J.R. Figueira, A sorting model for group decision making: a case study of water losses in Brazil, Group Decision and Negotiation 23 (5) (2014) 937–960, https://doi.org/10.1007/s10726-012-9321-7.

[137] C.M.d.M. Mota, A.T. de Almeida, A multicriteria decision model for assigning priority classes to activities in project management, Annals of Operations Research 199 (1) (2011) 361–372, https://doi.org/10.1007/s10479-011-0853-z.

[138] V. Mousseau, L.C. Dias, J. Figueira, Dealing with inconsistent judgments in multiple criteria sorting models, 4OR 4 (2) (2006) 145–158, https://doi.org/10.1007/s10288-005-0076-8.

[139] V. Mousseau, O. Ozpeynirci, S. Ozpeynirci, Inverse multiple criteria sorting problem, Annals of Operations Research 267 (1–2) (2018) 379–412, https://doi.org/10.1007/s10479-017-2420-8.

[140] A. Nafi, C. Werey, Aide à la décision multicritère pour la hiérarchisation de tronçons d'assainissement dans le cadre d'une gestion patrimoniale, Canadian Journal of Civil Engineering 36 (7) (2009) 1207–1220, https://doi.org/10.1139/l09-069.

[141] P. Nemery, A. Ishizaka, M. Camargo, L. Morel, Enriching descriptive information in ranking and sorting problems with visualizations techniques, Journal of Modelling in Management 7 (2) (2012) 130–147, https://doi.org/10.1108/17465661211242778.

[142] P. Nemery, C. Lamboray, FlowSort: a flow-based sorting method with limiting or central profiles, Top 16 (1) (2008) 90–113, https://doi.org/10.1007/s11750-007-0036-x.

[143] L.P. Neves, A.G. Martins, C.H. Antunes, L.C. Dias, A multi-criteria decision approach to sorting actions for promoting energy efficiency, Energy Policy 36 (7) (2008) 2351–2363, https://doi.org/10.1016/j.enpol.2007.11.032.

[144] M.F. Norese, S. Viale, A multi-profile sorting procedure in the public administration, European Journal of Operational Research 138 (2) (2002) 365–379, https://doi.org/10.1016/s0377-2217(01)00252-1.

[145] Ö. Özpeynirci, S. Özpeynirci, V. Mousseau, An interactive approach for inverse multiple criteria sorting problem, Journal of Multi-Criteria Decision Analysis (2020), https://doi.org/10.1002/mcda.1719.

[146] S. Ozpeynirci, O. Ozpeynirci, V. Mousseau, An interactive algorithm for multiple criteria constrained sorting problem, Annals of Operations Research 267 (1–2) (2018) 447–466, https://doi.org/10.1007/s10479-017-2418-2.

[147] R.P. Palha, A.T.D. Almeida, D.C. Morais, K.W. Hipel, Sorting subcontractors' activities in construction projects with a novel additive-veto sorting approach, Journal of Civil Engineering and Management 25 (4) (2019) 306–321, https://doi.org/10.3846/jcem.2019.9644.

[148] R.P. Palha, A.T. de Almeida, L.H. Alencar, A model for sorting activities to be outsourced in civil construction based on ROR-UTADIS, Mathematical Problems in Engineering 2016 (2016) 1–15, https://doi.org/10.1155/2016/9236414.

[149] Z. Pawlak, Rough Sets. Theoretical Aspects of Reasoning About Data, Kluwer Academic Publishers, Dordrecht, 1991.

[150] R. Pelissari, A. José Abackerli, S. Ben Amor, M. Célia Oliveira, K.M. Infante, Multiple criteria hierarchy process for sorting problems under uncertainty applied to the evaluation of the operational maturity of research institutions, Omega 102381 (2020), https://doi.org/10.1016/j.omega.2020.102381.

[151] R. Pelissari, M.C. Oliveira, S. Ben Amor, A.J. Abackerli, A new FlowSort-based method to deal with information imperfections in sorting decision-making problems, European Journal of Operational Research 276 (1) (2019) 235–246, https://doi.org/10.1016/j.ejor.2019.01.006.

[152] P.C. Pendharkar, A potential use of data envelopment analysis for the inverse classification problem, Omega 30 (3) (2002) 243–248, https://doi.org/10.1016/s0305-0483(02)00030-0.

[153] H.-g. Peng, J.-q. Wang, Multi-criteria sorting decision making based on dominance and opposition relations with probabilistic linguistic information, Fuzzy Optimization and Decision Making 19 (4) (2020) 435–470, https://doi.org/10.1007/s10700-020-09330-z.

[154] J. Pereira, E.C.B. de Oliveira, L.F.A.M. Gomes, R.M. Araújo, Sorting retail locations in a large urban city by using ELECTRE TRI-C and trapezoidal fuzzy numbers, Soft Computing 23 (12) (2018) 4193–4206, https://doi.org/10.1007/s00500-018-3068-2.

[155] V. Podvezko, A. Podviezko, Dependence of multi-criteria evaluation result on choice of preference functions and their parameters / Daugiakriteriniu vertinimu rezultatu priklausomybė nuo prioritetu funkciju ir ju parametru pasirinkimo, Economic Development of Economy 16 (1) (2010) 143–158, https://doi.org/10.3846/tede.2010.09.

[156] K.S. Raju, L. Duckstein, C. Arondel, Multicriterion analysis for sustainable water resources planning: a case study in Spain, Water Resources Management 14 (6) (2000) 435–456, https://doi.org/10.1023/a:1011120513259.

[157] R. Ramezanian, Estimation of the profiles in posteriori ELECTRE TRI: a mathematical programming model, Computers & Industrial Engineering 128 (2019) 47–59, https://doi.org/10.1016/j.cie.2018.12.034.

[158] L.A.D. Rangel, L.F.A.M. Gomes, M.E.L. Gonçalves, Classificação multicritério dos fatores de comprometimento organizacional: aplicação do método UTADIS, Sistemas & Gestão 10 (4) (2016) 623–632, https://doi.org/10.20985/1980-5160.2015.v10n4.638.

[159] C. Rocha, L.C. Dias, An algorithm for ordinal sorting based on ELECTRE with categories defined by examples, Journal of Global Optimization 42 (2) (2008) 255–277, https://doi.org/10.1007/s10898-007-9240-3.

[160] C. Rocha, L.C. Dias, I. Dimas, Multicriteria classification with unknown categories: a clustering-sorting approach and an application to conflict management, Journal of Multi-Criteria Decision Analysis 20 (1–2) (2013) 13–27, https://doi.org/10.1002/mcda.1476.

[161] B. Roy, The optimisation problem formulation: criticism and overstepping, Journal of the Operational Research Society 32 (6) (1981) 427–436, https://doi.org/10.1057/jors.1981.93.

[162] B. Roy, Méthodologie multicritère d'aide à la décision, Economica, Paris, France, 1985.

[163] B. Roy, The outranking approach and the foundations of ELECTRE methods, in: C.A. Bana e Costa (Ed.), Reading in Multiple Criteria Decision Aid, Springer, Berlin, 1990, pp. 155–183.

[164] B. Roy, Multicriteria Methodology for Decision Aiding, vol. 12, Springer, Boston, MA, 1996.

[165] H.F. Sabokbar, A. Hosseini, A. Banaitis, N. Banaitiene, A novel sorting method topsis-sort: an application for Tehran environmental quality evaluation, E & M Ekonomie a Management 19 (2) (2016) 87–104, https://doi.org/10.15240/tul/001/2016-2-006.

[166] R. Sarrazin, Y. De Smet, J. Rosenfeld, An extension of PROMETHEE to interval clustering, Omega 80 (2018) 12–21, https://doi.org/10.1016/j.omega.2017.09.001.

[167] M. Segura, C. Maroto, B. Segura, J.C. Casas-Rosal, Improving food supply chain management by a sustainable approach to supplier evaluation, Mathematics 8 (11) (2020) 1952, https://doi.org/10.3390/math8111952.

[168] J. Sepulveda, J. Gonzalez, M. Alfaro, M. Camargo, A metrics-based diagnosis tool for enhancing innovation capabilities in SMEs, International Journal of Computers, Communications & Control 5 (5) (2010) 919, https://doi.org/10.15837/ijccc.2010.5.2255.

[169] J.M. Sepulveda, I.S. Derpich, Multicriteria supplier classification for DSS: comparative analysis of two methods, International Journal of Computers, Communications & Control 10 (2) (2015) 238, https://doi.org/10.15837/ijccc.2015.2.1755.

[170] F. Shen, J.P. Xu, Z.S. Xu, An outranking sorting method for multi-criteria group decision making using intuitionistic fuzzy sets, Information Sciences 334 (2016) 338–353, https://doi.org/10.1016/j.ins.2015.12.003.

[171] A.M.R. Silva, M.F.F. Sobral, Multicriteria model to sort suppliers in a Brazilian dairy industry, International Journal of Decision Support System Technology 9 (3) (2017) 42–53, https://doi.org/10.4018/ijdsst.2017070103.

[172] L.C.E. Silva, A. Costa, IT project investments: an analysis based on a sort and rank problem, International Journal of Information Technology & Decision Making 13 (4) (2014) 699–719, https://doi.org/10.1142/s0219622014500655.

[173] L.G.d.O. Silva, A.T. de Almeida-Filho, A new PROMETHEE-based approach applied within a framework for conflict analysis in evidence theory integrating three conflict measures, Expert Systems with Applications 113 (2018) 223–232, https://doi.org/10.1016/j.eswa.2018.07.002.

[174] M.M. Silva, A. Costa, A.P.H. de Gusmao, Continuous cooperation: a proposal using a fuzzy multicriteria sorting method, International Journal of Production Economics 151 (2014) 67–75, https://doi.org/10.1016/j.ijpe.2014.01.022.

[175] R. Slowínski, C. Zopounidis, A.I. Dimitras, Prediction of company acquisition in Greece by means of the rough set approach, European Journal of Operational Research 100 (1) (1997) 1–15, https://doi.org/10.1016/s0377-2217(96)00110-5.

[176] O. Sobrie, V. Mousseau, M. Pirlot, Learning monotone preferences using a majority rule sorting model, International Transactions in Operational Research 26 (5) (2018) 1786–1809, https://doi.org/10.1111/itor.12512.

[177] B. Soylu, A multi-criteria sorting procedure with Tchebycheff utility function, Computers & Operations Research 38 (8) (2011) 1091–1102, https://doi.org/10.1016/j.cor.2010.09.009.

[178] T. Tervonen, J.R. Figueira, R. Lahdelma, J.A. Dias, P. Salminen, A stochastic method for robustness analysis in sorting problems, European Journal of Operational Research 192 (1) (2009) 236–242, https://doi.org/10.1016/j.ejor.2007.09.008.

[179] T. Trzaskalik, Bipolar sorting and ranking of multistage alternatives, Central European Journal of Operations Research (2021), https://doi.org/10.1007/s10100-020-00733-2.

[180] C. Ulu, M. Koksalan, An interactive approach to multicriteria sorting for quasiconcave value functions, Naval Research Logistics 61 (6) (2014) 447–457, https://doi.org/10.1002/nav.21595.

[181] A. Ulucan, K.B. Atici, A multiple criteria sorting methodology with multiple classification criteria and an application to country risk evaluation, Technological and Economic Development of Economy 19 (1) (2013) 93–124, https://doi.org/10.3846/20294913.2012.763070.

[182] T. Verheyden, L.D. Moor, Multi-criteria decision analysis: methods to define and evaluate socially responsible investments, International Journal of Management and Decision Making 14 (1) (2015) 44, https://doi.org/10.1504/ijmdm.2015.067377.

[183] R. Vetschera, Y. Chen, K.W. Hipel, D.M. Kilgour, Robustness and information levels in case-based multiple criteria sorting, European Journal of Operational Research 202 (3) (2010) 841–852, https://doi.org/10.1016/j.ejor.2009.06.026.

[184] Z. Xu, J. Qin, J. Liu, L. Martínez, Sustainable supplier selection based on AHPSort II in interval type-2 fuzzy environment, Information Sciences 483 (2019) 273–293, https://doi.org/10.1016/j.ins.2019.01.013.

[185] J. Zheng, S.A.M. Takougang, V. Mousseau, M. Pirlot, Learning criteria weights of an optimistic ELECTRE TRI sorting rule, Computers & Operations Research 49 (2014) 28–40, https://doi.org/10.1016/j.cor.2014.03.012.

[186] C. Zopounidis, M. Doumpos, PREFDIS: a multicriteria decision support system for sorting decision problems, Computers & Operations Research 27 (7–8) (2000) 779–797, https://doi.org/10.1016/s0305-0548(99)00118-5.

[187] C. Zopounidis, M. Doumpos, Multicriteria classification and sorting methods: a literature review, European Journal of Operational Research 138 (2) (2002) 229–246, https://doi.org/10.1016/s0377-2217(01)00243-0.

Chapter 3

MCDM sorting methods

3.1 AHPSort: a sorting method based on AHP

When facing a decision problem, the first task of a decision maker is to identify the type of problem. Roy [1] has described four problem formulations including *choice problem*, *sorting problem*, *ranking problem*, and *description problem*. The analytic hierarchy process (AHP) [2] is one of the most popular MCDM methods developed for ranking problems and occasionally for choice problems. However, it is not adapted for sorting problems. Moreover, another practical limitation of AHP is that a high number of alternatives implies a large number of comparisons. AHPSort [3], as a new variant of AHP, is used for sorting alternatives into predefined ordered categories. Furthermore, AHPSort requires far less comparisons than AHP, which facilitates decision making within large-scale problems. This section aims to recall the classical AHP method and, on this basis, introduce its variant AHPSort and other extensions.

3.1.1 Analytic hierarchy process

AHP is a multi-criteria decision-making method combining qualitative and quantitative analysis, which is suitable for solving complex problem with multiple conflicting and subjective criteria. For example, problems in the economic field usually involves various factors, which requires experts to make decisions according their preferences and experience. The steps involved in AHP are as follows:

Step 1: Model the decision-making problem into three levels.

AHP describes the decision-making problem by constructing a hierarchical structure model to reflect the relationship between each item. Generally speaking, the hierarchy can be divided into three types: target level, criteria level, and scheme level.

Target Level: common goal to be achieved.

Criteria Level: factors considered for achieving the common goal.

Scheme Level: alternatives to be evaluated.

Step 2: Pairwise comparison of criteria for achieving the common goal.

Step 3: Pairwise comparison of alternatives concerning each criterion.

Set m alternatives $(x_1, x_2, \ldots, x_m)$ and compare them pairwise according to a certain criterion. The elements in comparison matrix A denote weight of x_i

Multi-Criteria Decision-Making Sorting Methods. https://doi.org/10.1016/B978-0-32-385231-9.00008-0

with respect to x_j. In order to facilitate the comparison process, Saaty proposes a scale of relative importance between items according to the cognitive habits and judgment ability of the ordinary (Table 3.1).

TABLE 3.1 1–9 scale method.

Relative importance	Definition
1	Equal importance
3	Weak importance of one over another
5	Essential or strong importance
7	Demonstrated importance
9	Absolute importance
2,4,6,8	Intermediate values between the two adjacent judgments

The judgment matrix A can be expressed as follows:

$$\mathbf{A} = \begin{pmatrix} a_{11} & a_{12} & \cdots & a_{1m} \\ a_{21} & a_{22} & \cdots & a_{2m} \\ \vdots & \vdots & \ddots & \vdots \\ a_{m1} & a_{m2} & \cdots & a_{mm} \end{pmatrix} = \begin{pmatrix} \frac{w_1}{w_1} & \frac{w_1}{w_2} & \cdots & \frac{w_1}{w_m} \\ \frac{w_2}{w_1} & \frac{w_2}{w_2} & \cdots & \frac{w_2}{w_m} \\ \vdots & \vdots & \ddots & \vdots \\ \frac{w_m}{w_1} & \frac{w_m}{w_2} & \cdots & \frac{w_m}{w_m} \end{pmatrix} \tag{3.1}$$

It has the following properties:

Reciprocity matrix: $a_{ij} = 1/a_{ji}$, $a_{ii} = 1$.

Consistency matrix: $a_{ij} = a_{ik} \times a_{kj}$ ($k = 1, 2, \ldots, m$).

After constructing the judgment matrix, it is necessary to identify priorities for the criteria and goals, respectively. In order to find the priorities of the judgment matrix, we introduce the eigenvector method, geometric mean, and additive method to derive them from the judgment matrix.

(a) Eigenvector method

$$\mathbf{AW} = \begin{pmatrix} \frac{w_1}{w_1} & \frac{w_1}{w_2} & \cdots & \frac{w_1}{w_m} \\ \frac{w_2}{w_1} & \frac{w_2}{w_2} & \cdots & \frac{w_2}{w_m} \\ \vdots & \vdots & \ddots & \vdots \\ \frac{w_m}{w_1} & \frac{w_m}{w_2} & \cdots & \frac{w_m}{w_m} \end{pmatrix} \times \begin{pmatrix} w_1 \\ w_2 \\ w_3 \\ w_4 \end{pmatrix} = \lambda \times \begin{pmatrix} w_1 \\ w_2 \\ w_3 \\ w_4 \end{pmatrix} \tag{3.2}$$

That is $(A - \lambda I)w = 0$, where I is the identity matrix. If the estimated value of A is accurate, the above equation is strictly equal to 0 (m-dimension 0 vector). If the estimate of A is not accurate enough, then:

$$AW = \lambda_{max} W \tag{3.3}$$

where λ_{max} is the maximum eigenvalue of matrix A. The eigenvector can be obtained from the above equation; that is, the weight is $W = (w_1, w_2, \cdots, w_m)^T$.

(b) Basic steps of geometric mean

First, multiply the elements in each row of the judgment matrix A to the power of m.

$$w_i^* = \sqrt[m]{\prod_{j=1}^{m} a_{ij}} \tag{3.4}$$

Then calculate the normalized weight and sum the elements in each column of matrix A.

$$w_i = \frac{w_i^*}{\sum_{i=1}^{m} w_i^*} \tag{3.5}$$

$$s_j = \sum_{i=1}^{m} a_{ij} \tag{3.6}$$

Finally, calculate the value of λ_{max}.

$$\lambda_{max} = \sum_{i=1}^{m} w_i \times s_i \tag{3.7}$$

(c) Basic steps of additive method

First, normalize the elements of the judgment matrix A by column to get the matrix $Q = (q_{ij})_{m \times n}$.

Then add the elements of matrix Q by rows to get a vector $\alpha = (a_1, a_2, ..., a_m)^T$ and normalize the vector α.

$$w_i = \frac{\alpha_i^*}{\sum_{i=1}^{m} \alpha_i} \tag{3.8}$$

Finally, calculate the maximum eigenvalue.

$$\lambda_{max} = \frac{1}{m} \sum_{i=1}^{m} \frac{(AW)_i}{w_i} \tag{3.9}$$

Step 4: Checking the inconsistency ratio of the pairwise comparison.

The judgment matrix generally does not have complete consistency, so it is stipulated that as long as the consistency of the matrix is within a limited range, the judgment matrix is also acceptable. To measure the consistency, we use the consistency index (CI):

$$CI = \frac{\lambda_{max} - m}{m - 1} \tag{3.10}$$

Generally speaking, the greater the CI, the greater the deviation. In addition, the greater the order of the judgment matrix, the greater the deviation caused by

TABLE 3.2 RI index values.

n	2	3	4	5	6	7	8	9	10
RI	0.00	0.58	0.90	1.12	1.24	1.32	1.41	1.45	1.49
λ_{max}		3.12	4.27	5.45	6.62	7.79	8.99	10.16	11.34

the subjective judgment, so the greater the deviation from consistency. At the same time, the random index (RI) is introduced. This is the average consistency index of 500 randomly generated matrices. The RI index changes with the dimension of the judgment matrix. Table 3.2 lists the RI index values of the judgment matrix of 1–10.

The ratio of CI and RI is called the consistency ratio:

$$CR = \frac{CI}{RI} \qquad (3.11)$$

The consistency ratio CR is used to test the consistency of the judgment matrix. The smaller the CR, the better the consistency of the judgment matrix. It is generally believed that when $CR \leq 0.1$, the judgment matrix meets the consistency standard, otherwise the matrix needs to be revised.

Step 5: Sum the local priorities to obtain the final results.

Step 6: Make a final decision based on the results.

Step 7: Sensitivity analysis. Randomly generate 500 or more testing groups with RI index to verify the robustness of this sorting method.

3.1.2 AHPSort

AHPSort [3] is a sorting method based on AHP that retains the advantages of AHP but reduces the problem of the high number of comparisons. The classes are defined in an ordinal way based on decision makers' preferences, which means that classes are ordered from the most to the least preferred. (See Fig. 3.1.)

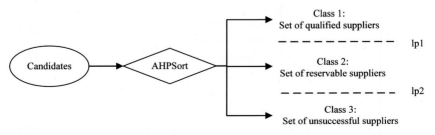

FIGURE 3.1 AHPSort for the sorting process.

AHPSort involves the following three steps.

Step 1: Problem definition

(1) Define the goal, criteria $c_j (j = 1, .., m)$ and alternatives $a_k (k = 1, ..., l)$ of the problem.

(2) Define the classes $C_i (i = 1, ..., n)$, where n is the number of classes. The classes can be ordered and have a label (for example, excellent, good, medium, bad).

(3) Define the profiles of each class. This can be done with local limiting profile lp_i, which indicates the minimum performance needed on each criterion j to belong to the class C_i, or with local central profile cp_i, which is given by a typical example of an element belonging to the class C_i on the criterion j. We need $j \times (n - 1)$ limiting profiles or $j \times n$ central profiles to define each class.

Step 2: Evaluation

(4) Evaluate pairwise the importance of the criteria c_j and derive the weight w_j with the eigenvalue method of the AHP.

$$A \times p = \lambda \times p \qquad (3.12)$$

where:

A is the comparison matrix;

p is the priorities/weight vector; and

λ is the maximal eigenvalue.

(5) Compare in a pairwise comparison matrix a single alternative a_k with each limiting profile lp_i or central profile cp_i for each criterion j.

(6) From the comparison matrices, derive the local priority p_{ik} for the alternative a_k and the local priority p_{ij} of the limiting profiles lp_i or central limiting profiles cp_i with the eigenvalue method in Eq. (3.12).

Step 3: Assignment to classes

(7) Aggregate the weighted local priorities, which provide a global priority p_k for the alternative k, using Eq. (3.13) and a global priority lp_i for the limiting profile or cp_i for the central profiles using Eq. (3.14).

$$p_k = \sum_{j=1}^{m} p_{kj} \times w_j \qquad (3.13)$$

$$lp_i \quad or \quad cp_i = \sum_{j=1}^{m} p_{kj} \times w_j \qquad (3.14)$$

The comparison of p_k with lp_i or cp_i is used to assign the alternative a_k to a class C_i.

(a) Limiting profiles: If limiting profiles have been defined, the alternative a_k is assigned to the class C_i which has the lp_i just below the global priority p_k.

See Fig. 3.2 (left).

$$p_k \geq lp_1 \Rightarrow a_k \subseteq C_1$$
$$lp_2 \leq p_k < lp_1 \Rightarrow a_k \subseteq C_2 \quad\quad\quad\quad (3.15)$$
$$\cdots$$
$$p_k < lp_n - 1 \Rightarrow a_k \subseteq C_n$$

(b) Central profiles: If the decision maker has difficulties defining a limiting profile, they can define a typical example of a class: the central profile cp_i. The limiting profiles are deduced by $(cp_i + cp_{(i+1)})/2$. The alternative a_k is assigned to the class C_i which has the nearest central profile cp_i to p_k (see Fig. 3.2, right). In the case of equal distance between two central profiles, the optimistic assignment vision allocates a_k to the upper class, while the pessimistic assignment vision allocates a_k to the lower class.

$$p_k \geq cp_1 \Rightarrow a_k \subseteq C_1$$
$$cp_2 \leq p_k < cp_1 \quad AND \quad (cp_1 - p_k) < (cp_2 - p_k) \Rightarrow a_k \subseteq C_1$$
$$cp_2 \leq p_k < cp_1 \quad AND \quad (cp_1 - p_k) = (cp_2 - p_k) \Rightarrow a_k \subseteq C_1$$
$$in \quad the \quad optimistic \quad vision$$
$$cp_2 \leq p_k < cp_1 \quad AND \quad (cp_1 - p_k) = (cp_2 - p_k) \Rightarrow a_k \subseteq C_1 \quad (3.16)$$
$$in \quad the \quad pessimistic \quad vision$$
$$cp_2 \leq p_k < cp_1 \quad AND \quad (cp_1 - p_k) > (cp_2 - p_k) \Rightarrow a_k \subseteq C_2$$
$$\cdots$$
$$p_k < cp_n \Rightarrow a_k \subseteq C_n$$

(8) Repeat Steps (5)–(8) for each alternative to be classified.

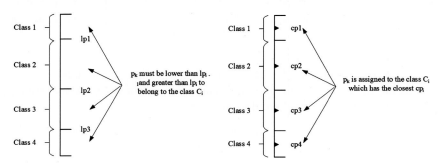

FIGURE 3.2   Sorting with limiting profile or central profile.

The large number of comparisons is a bottleneck problem of AHP. In fact, with l alternatives, $l \times (l-1)/2$ pairwise comparisons are necessary for each criterion considered. The increase in the number of comparisons is quadratic. For m criteria, the total number of pairwise comparisons is:

$$m \times \frac{l \times (l-1)}{2} + \frac{m \times (m-1)}{2} \quad\quad (3.17)$$

In AHPSort, the number of comparisons is reduced. The b limiting or central profiles need first to be compared between themselves: $b \times (b-1)/2$. Then, the l alternatives are compared to the b profiles. Finally, this is repeated for all m criteria:

$$m \times \left(\frac{b \times (b-1)}{2} + (b \times l) \right) \tag{3.18}$$

3.1.3 AHPSort II

3.1.3.1 Methodology

Unfortunately, if the set of alternatives, criteria, and limiting or central profiles analyzed are high, the number of comparisons required is also still high. Therefore, Miccoli and Ishizaka [4] proposed AHPSort II to overcome these problems.

Step 1: Problem definition

(1) Define the goal, criteria $c_j (j = 1, .., m)$ and alternatives $a_k (k = 1, \ldots, l)$ of the problem.

(2) Define the classes $C_i (i = 1, \ldots, n)$ where n is the number of classes. The classes can be ordered and have a label (for example, excellent, good, medium, bad).

(3) Define the profiles of each class. This can be done with local limiting profile lp_i, which indicates the minimum performance needed on each criterion j to belong to the class C_i, or with local central profile cp_i, which is given by a typical example of an element belonging to the class C_i on the criterion j. We need $j \times (n-1)$ limiting profiles or $j \times n$ central profiles to define each class.

Step 2: Evaluation

(4) Evaluate pairwise the importance of the criteria c_j and derive the weight w_j with the eigenvalue method of the AHP.

$$A \times p = \lambda \times p \tag{3.19}$$

where:

A is the comparison matrix;

p is the priorities/weight vector; and

λ is the maximal eigenvalue.

(5) Select for each criterion j a small number of representative points $s_{oj} (o = 1, \ldots, rp_j)$ that are well-distributed on the scale of each criterion.

Compare in a pairwise comparison matrix the representative points and the limiting or central profiles. In this step, it is possible to use clusters to further reduce the number of pairwise comparisons, which involves the following four steps:

(a) For each criterion, the representative points and limiting or central profiles are selected.

(b) Representative points and limiting or central profiles are divided into clusters. Psychologists have observed that it is difficult to evaluate more than seven elements. Therefore, it is recommended to build clusters that do not contain more than seven elements [5]. The last compared element becomes the joining point at the boundary of both clusters.

(c) The elements of the cluster are compared in a matrix and priorities are calculated.

(d) The priorities of the clusters are joined with a common element: "joining point." This is used for the conversion rate between two clusters. (See Fig. 3.3.)

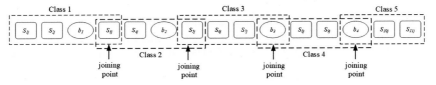

FIGURE 3.3   Clustering with joining point.

From the comparison matrices, derive the local priority p_{oj} for the representative points and the local priority p_{ij} of the limiting profiles or central profiles with the eigenvalue method in Eq. (3.19).

(6) If the alternatives a_k belongs to the interval of two consecutive representative points s_{oj} and s_{o+1j}, we can derive the local priority p_{kj} as follows:

$$p_{kj} = p_{oj} + \frac{p_{o1j} - p_{oj}}{s_{o1j} - s_{oj}} \times \left(g_j\left(a_k \right) - s_{oj} \right) \tag{3.20}$$

where:

s_{oj} and s_{o+1j} are two consecutive representative points on criterion j;

p_{oj} and p_{o+1j} are the local priorities of the two consecutive representative points;

$g_j\left(a_k \right)$ is the score of the alternative a_k on criterion j; and

p_{kj} is the local priority of a_k.

In AHPSort II, the number of pairwise comparisons does not depend on the number of alternatives, but is only based on the number of profiles b and representative points rp_j. The number of required pairwise comparisons is given by:

$$\sum_{j=1}^{m} \frac{\left(b + rp_j \right) \times \left(b + rp_j - 1 \right)}{2} \tag{3.21}$$

where:

rp_j = number of representative points for criterion j;

m = number of criteria; and

b = number of profiles.

An example is given to illustrate the AHPSort II method.

3.1.3.2 Illustrative example

To evaluate the development of employee welfare in the enterprise, some criteria need to be considered comprehensively when making the decision: mobilizing worker labor enthusiasm; raising worker technology culture level; and improving worker material culture life.

(1) Problem structuring and definition of classes

The problem can be structured in a hierarchy with four levels. The top level is the goal of the problem: evaluate the development level of seven enterprises. The second level contains the criteria that are used to quantify their performance:

(a) Expansion of collective welfare facilities (C_1): the number of newly added welfare facilities for employees' leisure and fitness in the company or staff dorm.

(b) Rate of new equipment replacement per year (C_2): replacement rate of office facilities and welfare facilities.

(c) Average of bonus payment (C_3): monthly benefits for each employee.

(d) Average of corporate library (C_4): employee libraries owned by each company (including subsidiaries).

(e) Employees density (C_5): the ratio of the actual number of employees to the capacity of the office.

The third level contains the seven alternatives. The fourth level is dedicated to the classes where the alternatives are sorted. Enterprise will be sorted into four classes, "low performing," "medium-low performing," "medium-high performing," and "high performing," with respect to the development level. The data for all criteria are as follows (Table 3.3). The limiting profiles of each criteria are shown in Table 3.4.

TABLE 3.3 Data on each criterion for all enterprises.

Enterprise	D_1	D_2	D_3	D_4	D_5
E_1	55	1%	1661	0	60.3
E_2	466	10%	3288	39.5	22.1
E_3	1084	42%	1089	0	62.1
E_4	572	38%	5615	0	103.8
E_5	7	2%	781	0	50.3
E_6	147	11%	6034	30	150.5
E_7	54	68%	9956	56.4	17.9

(2) Weighting of criteria

The criteria were compared pairwise in a matrix (Table 3.5).

(3) Selection of the representative points

The representative points were selected by the expert. After an evaluation of the values that the alternatives assume for each criterion, the expert selected an appropriate number of representative points. These must be selected carefully and in the most representative way. The representative points should be

TABLE 3.4 Data on each criterion for limiting profile.

Criteria	lp_1	lp_2	lp_3
D_1	232	464	802
D_2	10	30	40
D_3	2200	4500	6700
D_4	10	30	50
D_5	500	300	200

TABLE 3.5 AHP matrix for weighting criteria.

$C-D$	D_1	D_2	D_3	D_4	D_5	Weight	Inconsistency
D_1	1	1	8	5	7	0.424	
D_2	1	1	7	3	4	0.333	
D_3	$\frac{1}{8}$	$\frac{1}{7}$	1	$\frac{1}{3}$	2	0.056	0.06
D_4	$\frac{1}{5}$	$\frac{1}{3}$	3	1	5	0.140	
D_5	$\frac{1}{7}$	$\frac{1}{4}$	$\frac{1}{2}$	$\frac{1}{5}$	1	0.047	

TABLE 3.6 Representative points and limiting profile for each criteria.

Criteria	D_1	D_2	D_3	D_4	D_5	D_5	D_5	D_5
Rp	0%		20%			50%	60%	70%
Lp		10%		30%	40%			

distributed as homogeneously as possible on the scale of each criterion, in order to highlight marginal changes between them. For example, for the alternatives with respect to the criterion "rate of new equipment replacement per year," assuming values from 0–70%, Table 3.6 shows the five representative points and the three limiting profiles selected by the expert.

(4) Compare the representative points and derive the local priority for the alternatives

In this step, the representative points and the limiting profiles are compared in a matrix in order to obtain the local priorities. The structure of the clusters for the criterion "rate of new equipment replacement per year" is reported in Fig. 3.4.

The local priority p_{kj} of an alternative k that has the presence of 54%, where $s_{o+1j} = 60$, $s_{oj} = 50$, $p_{o+1j} = 0.821$, $p_{oj} = 0.393$, and $g_i(a_k) = 54$, is as follows:

$$p_{kj} = 0.393 + \frac{0.821 - 0.393}{60 - 50} \times (54 - 40) = 0.564 \qquad (3.22)$$

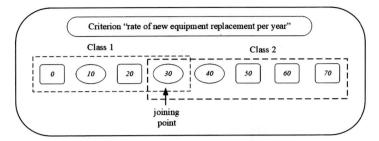

FIGURE 3.4 Cluster for the criteria "rate of new equipment replacement per year".

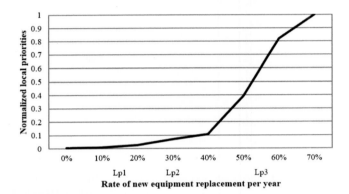

FIGURE 3.5 Graphic of local priorities.

TABLE 3.7 First cluster "rate of new equipment replace-ment per year."

cluster1		0	lp_1	20	lp_2	Local priority
	0	1	$\frac{1}{3}$	$\frac{1}{4}$	$\frac{1}{9}$	0.049
lp_1	10	3	1	$\frac{1}{5}$	$\frac{1}{7}$	0.087
	20	4	5	1	$\frac{1}{4}$	0.242
lp_2	30	9	7	4	1	0.622

The local priorities (Tables 3.7, 3.8) need to be normalized. Fig. 3.5 shows how the rate of equipment replacement per year contributes to the development of enterprises.

(5) Assignment to classes

In this step 5, enterprises are sorted into the respective class. The enterprise with a score below 0.007 have a low performance, between 0.007 and 0.045 a medium-low performance, between 0.045 and 0.122 a medium-high perfor-mance, and 0.122 or above a high performance. (See Table 3.9.)

TABLE 3.8 Second cluster "rate of new equipment replacement per year."

cluster2		lp_2	lp_3	50	60	70	Local priority
lp_2	30	1	$\frac{1}{3}$	$\frac{1}{7}$	$\frac{1}{8}$	$\frac{1}{9}$	0.029
lp_3	40	3	1	$\frac{1}{7}$	$\frac{1}{8}$	$\frac{1}{9}$	0.046
	50	7	7	1	$\frac{1}{3}$	$\frac{1}{5}$	0.164
	60	8	8	3	1	1	0.343
	70	9	9	5	1	1	0.418

TABLE 3.9 Sorting result.

Enterprises	Score	Class
E_1	0.039	Medium-low
E_2	0.056	Medium-high
E_3	0.503	High
E_4	0.051	Medium-high
E_5	0.038	Medium-low
E_6	0.035	Medium-low
E_7	0.430	High

Recently, some studies have extended AHPSort further to group sorting problems with group analytic hierarchy process sorting (GAHPSort) [6], which can sort large number of alternatives into classes according to several decision makers' knowledge. However, the information elicited by the decision makers could lead to significant differences and conflicts in the sorting process. Therefore, situations often emerge in which one or several decision makers do not accept the obtained solution, because they consider that their preferences have not been sufficiently taken into account. To overcome this problem, some studies have applied consensus reaching processes (CRPs) in GAHPSort and proposed a consensual GAHPSort method [7]. This method aims to support decision makers to achieve a satisfactory consensual solution with a minimum cost based on nonlinear programming.

3.2 ANPSort: a sorting method based on ANP

3.2.1 ANP

As a generalization of the AHP, the analytic network process (ANP) is a multi-criteria decision method used to derive relative priority scales of absolute numbers from individual judgments (or from actual measurements normalized to a relative form) that also belong to a fundamental scale of absolute numbers. ANP provides a general framework to deal with decisions without making assumptions about the independence of higher-level elements from lower-level elements and about the independence of the elements within a level as in a hierarchy. In fact, the ANP uses a network without the need to specify levels.

As in the AHP procedure, dominance or the relative importance of influence is a central concept. Priorities are established in the same way they are in the AHP using pairwise comparisons and judgments. The difference between a hierarchy and a network is illustrated in Fig. 3.6. Many decision problems cannot be structured hierarchically because they involve the interaction and dependence of higher-level elements in a hierarchy on lower-level elements. Not only does the importance of the criteria determine the importance of the alternatives as in a hierarchy, but also the importance of the alternatives themselves can determine the importance of the criteria.

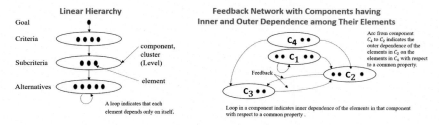

FIGURE 3.6 How a hierarchy compares to a network.

To obtain the overall dependence of elements such as the criteria, one proceeds as follows: construct a zero-one matrix of elements against elements using the number one to signify dependence of one element on another, and zero otherwise. An element does not need to depend on itself as an industry; for example, it may not use its own output. For each column of this matrix, construct a pairwise comparison matrix only for the dependent elements, derive an eigenvector, and augment it with zeros for the elements that are not dependent. If a column is all zeros, then assign a zero vector to represent the priorities. The question in the comparison would be: for a given element, which of two elements depends more on that element with respect to the goal or with respect to a third element?

A hierarchy is comprised of a goal, levels of elements, and connections between the elements. These connections go only to elements in lower levels. A network has clusters of elements, with the elements being connected to elements in another cluster (outer dependence) or the same cluster (inner dependence). A hierarchy is a special case of a network with connections going only in one direction. In a view of a hierarchy, such as that shown in Fig. 3.6, the levels in the hierarchy correspond to clusters in a network. One example of inner dependence in a component consists of a father, a mother, and a baby. The dependence question is on whom does the baby depends more for survival: the mother or himself/herself? The baby depends more on the mother than on himself/herself. Again suppose advertising appears in a newspaper and on television. It is clear that the both influence each other because the newspaper writers watch television and need to make their message unique in some way, and vice versa. From this point of view, all elements can be seen to influence in all of them including itself according to many criteria. The world is far more interdependent than we realize or make use of with our existing ways of thinking and acting. Thus, the ANP appears to be a plausible and logical way to deal with dependence.

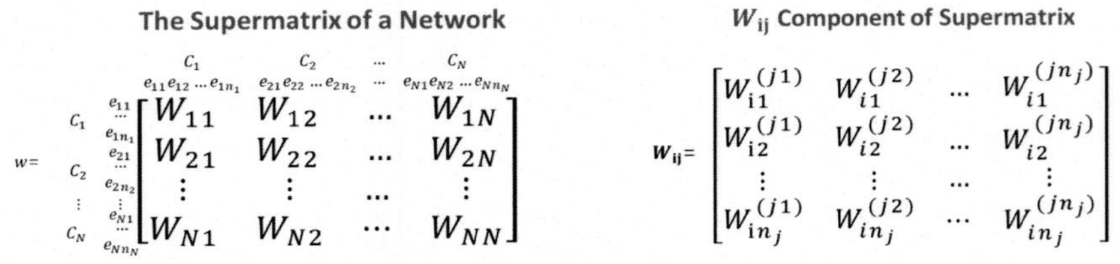

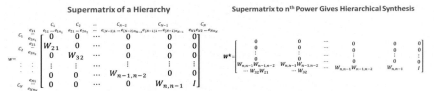

FIGURE 3.7 The supermatrix of a network and detail of a component in it.

Supermatrix of a Hierarchy   **Supermatrix to n^{th} Power Gives Hierarchical Synthesis**

FIGURE 3.8 The supermatrix of a hierarchy with the resulting limit matrix corresponding to hierarchical composition.

The priorities derived from pairwise comparison matrices are entered as parts of the columns of a supermatrix. The supermatrix represents the influence priority of an element on the left of the matrix on an element at the top of the matrix. A supermatrix along with an example of one of its general entry matrices is shown in Fig. 3.7. The component C_i in the supermatrix includes all the priority vectors derived from nodes that are "parent" nodes in the C_i cluster. Fig. 3.8 gives the supermatrix of a hierarchy along with the kth power that yields the principle of hierarchic composition in its $(k, 1)$ position.

In the ANP, we look for steady-state priorities from a limit supermatrix. To obtain the limit, we must raise the matrix to powers. The reason for this is that to capture overall influence (dominance), one must consider all transitivities of different length. These are represented by the corresponding power of the supermatrix. For each matrix, the influence of an element on all others is obtained by taking the sum of its corresponding row. If we do that for all the elements, we obtain a vector of influence from that matrix. The sum of all such vectors gives the overall influence.

For more details of ANP, please refer to [8]; [9] gives an introduction to ANP software.

3.2.2 ANPSort

AHPSort has the advantage of requiring fewer pairwise comparisons as the alternatives are compared only with the profiles representing the classes. It does not require all the alternatives to be compared pairwise. However, it assumes that the criteria are independent, which is often not the case practically speaking. Therefore, a new sorting technique, ANPSort [10], which can deal with interactions and dependencies between the elements in the levels of the hierarchy, has been proposed. Another practical limitation of ANP is that a high number of alternatives imply a large number of comparisons. In comparison, ANPSort requires far fewer comparisons than ANP, which facilitates decision making within large-scale problems. It further allows a structured, transparent, and consistent evaluation integrating qualitative and quantitative criteria.

3.2.2.1 Methodology

ANPSort involves the following seven steps:

- **Problem definition**

    Step 1: Clusters are defined, which include criteria c_j ($j = 1, 2, \ldots, m$), eventually subcriteria and alternatives a_k ($k = 1, 2, \ldots, l$).

    Step 2: The classes C_i ($i = 1, 2, \ldots, n$), where n is the number of classes, are defined. The classes are ordered and have a label (e.g., excellent, good, medium, bad).

    Step 3: The profile of each class is defined.

    This can be done with limiting profiles lp_{ij}, which indicates the minimum performance needed on each criterion j to belong to a class C_i, or with central profiles cp_{ij}, which is given by a typical example of an element belonging to the class C_i. We need $m \times (n - 1)$ limiting profiles or $m \times n$ central profiles to define all n classes. All these profiles and only one alternative to classify will be compared in a matrix.

    Step 4: The influence matrix recording all dependencies is defined.

    The outer dependencies or feedbacks indicate the influence between two clusters. The inner dependencies indicate the influence of elements in the same cluster.

- **Evaluations**

    Step 5: For each dependency, the elements are compared pairwise as regards the parent element. The decision-maker evaluates lp_{ij}, the pairwise comparison between elements i and j, on a discrete 1–9 scale (Table 3.1). All pairwise comparisons are entered in a matrix A. Then, the local priorities are calculated with the eigenvalue method (Eq. (3.3)).

- **Aggregation**

    Step 6: The influence of each element on the other elements, calculated in Eq. (3.3) with the local priorities, is gathered in a supermatrix. If dependencies do not exist between nodes, zero is entered. The columns of the supermatrix must be normalized to 1 in order to have a stochastic matrix that can be used in a Markov chain process. To capture the transmission of the influence along all possible paths of the network, the matrix is raised to powers. The matrix is squared to represent the direct influence of one element on another. The cubic power is taken to express the indirect influence of a second element, and so on. As the matrix is stochastic, it will converge to a limit supermatrix, which contains the global priorities.

- **Assignment to classes**

Step 7: The comparison of p_k, the priority of alternative k, with lp_i, the priority of the limiting profile i, or cp_i, the priority of the central profile i, is used to assign the alternative a_k to a class C_i. p_k and lp_i are the elements of the priority vector. This step is similar to AHPSort.

3.2.2.2 Illustrative example

In this section, we will take the evaluation and classification of world universities in the field of higher education as an example to apply ANPSort with a real dataset, which is collected from the QS World University Ranking.[1] This dataset provides an overall ranking of 500 universities from all over the world. In view of the space available, we only select five universities as alternatives.

- **Problem definition**

Five clusters are defined. The first cluster contains the alternatives, which contains five universities to be classified. Then, six criteria are divided into four clusters:

(a) Research quality

Academic reputation (AR): this collates the expert opinions of more than 100 000 individuals in the higher education space regarding teaching and research quality at the world's universities.

Citations per faculty (CPF): this takes the total number of citations received by all papers produced by an institution across a 5-year period by the number of faculty members at that institution.

(b) Teaching quality

Faculty student ratio (FSR): this is the ratio of teaching staff to students.

(c) Graduate value

Employer reputation (ER): this is based on more than 75 000 responses to the QS Employer Survey, and asks employers to identify those institutions from which they source the most competent, innovative, effective graduates.

(d) Internationalization

International faculty ratio (IFR): this is the ratio of international teachers to the total number of teachers.

International students ratio (ISR): this is the ratio of international students to the total number of students.

---

[1] https://www.qschina.cn/university-rankings/world-university-rankings/2020.

- **Classes definition**

This study is expected to sort five universities into three categories, denoted as C_1, C_2, and C_3.

- **Profile definition**

As there are three classes, we need two limiting profiles to define the classes. The predefined limiting profiles are given in Table 3.10.

TABLE 3.10 Limiting profiles.

	AR	CPF	FSR	ER	IFR	ISR
lp_1	78.66	71.04	69.33	68.50	64.94	58.67
lp_2	49.80	45.89	42.40	44.24	43.32	36.48

- **Influence matrix**

In Table 3.11, "1" means that the criteria on the left side are influencing the criteria on the top of the table, and "0" otherwise. Fig. 3.9 shows the network of the problem, which takes into account the dependencies of Table 3.11. The cluster of the alternatives has: the two limiting profiles and the alternative (university) which will be compared against the two limiting profiles.

TABLE 3.11 Influence matrix.

	AR	CPF	FSR	IFR	ISR	ER
AR	0	1	0	1	1	1
CPF	1	0	0	0	0	0
FSR	1	1	0	1	1	1
IFR	0	0	0	1	1	0
ISR	0	0	0	0	1	0
ER	0	0	0	0	0	0

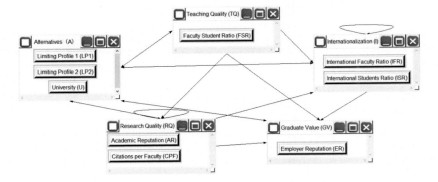

FIGURE 3.9 Network of the problem designed with the software SuperDecisions.

- **Evaluations**

We use the 1–9 Saaty's evaluation scale to provide the pairwise comparisons of the clusters. An extract of the clusters' pairwise comparison matrix is given in Fig. 3.10. The priorities of the clusters are calculated from Fig. 3.10 with Eq. (3.3) and are shown in Table 3.12. A similar matrix is used to compare the criteria (Fig. 3.11).

Similar matrices were employed to evaluate each university, where they were compared with the limiting profile in Table 3.10 as regards the each criterion in Fig. 3.12.

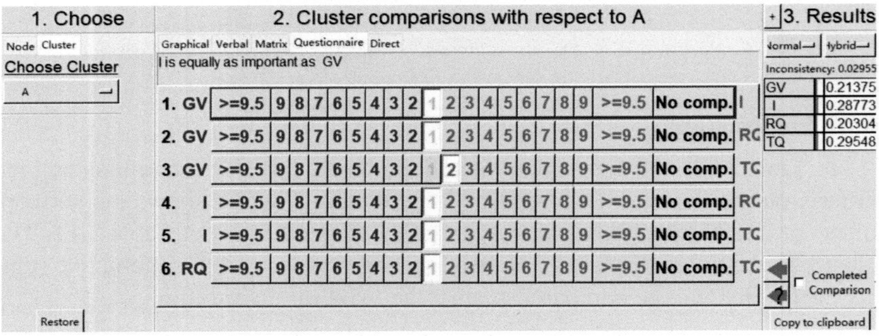

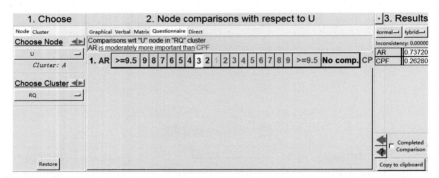

FIGURE 3.10   Extract pairwise comparison matrix from SuperDecisions.

FIGURE 3.11   Pairwise comparison of the criteria of the research quality cluster, done in SuperDecisions.

- **Aggregation**

All the calculated priorities are entered in the supermatrix (Table 3.13). The matrix is then squared until convergence. The priority of the university and limiting profiles are given in Table 3.14. Both can be read from the limit supermatrix of each university (Table 3.15). As the sorting result of the university is relative to the reference profiles and normalized to 1, the priority of the same reference profile changes according to the considered university.

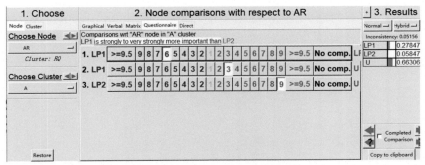

FIGURE 3.12 Evaluation of a university compared to the limiting profiles as regards academic reputation, done in SuperDecisions.

TABLE 3.12 Priorities of the clusters without taking into account the dependencies.

Clusters	Priority
Graduate value	0.21375
Internationalization	0.28773
Research quality	0.20304
Teaching quality	0.29548

- **Assignment to classes**

Universities are classified according to their global priority compared with the priority of the limiting profiles. For example, university A is classified as excellent because its global priority (column 4 in Table 3.14) is greater than the lp_1. In the classification results, two universities are classified into C_1, one into C_2, and two into C_3.

3.3 FlowSort: a sorting method based on PROMETHEE

3.3.1 PROMETHEE

PROMETHEE (the Preference Ranking Organization Method for Enrichment Evaluations) [11] has received a lot of attention from the academia as an outranking method. The ranking result can be received easily by pairwise comparisons between all the alternatives on each criterion. For its simple computation and user friendliness, it has been applied in many fields successfully.

In addition, there are many variants of PROMETHEE, including PROMETHEE I [11] for partial ranking problems, PROMETHEE II [12] for complete ranking problems, PROMETHEE III [13] for problems with interval data, PROMETHEE IV [14] for complete or partial ranking of the alternatives

TABLE 3.13 Supermatrix.

	IFR	ISR	FSR	Ip_1	Ip_2	University	ER	AR	CPF
IFR	0	0	0.1511	0.2016	0.1949	0.2002	0	0.2662	0.2813
ISR	0.4850	0	0.0489	0.0861	0.0928	0.0875	0	0.0949	0.0797
FSR	0	0	0	0.2955	0.2955	0.2955	0	0	0
Ip_1	0.0509	0.0940	0.0533	0	0	0	0.1592	0.0582	0.0573
Ip_2	0.0084	0.0158	0.0092	0	0	0	0.0237	0.0100	0.0089
University	0.2048	0.4031	0.2222	0	0	0	0.8170	0.1933	0.1953
ER	0.2508	0.4871	0.2106	0.2138	0.2138	0.2138	0	0.1693	0.1693
AR	0	0	0.2257	0.1288	0.1288	0.1288	0	0	0.2081
CPF	0	0	0.0789	0.0742	0.0742	0.0742	0	0.2081	0

TABLE 3.14 Assignment.

Name of university	lp_1	lp_2	University	Class
A	0.0604	0.0095	0.2765	C_1
B	0.1062	0.0170	0.2464	C_1
C	0.2116	0.0321	0.1340	C_2
D	0.2910	0.0453	0.0439	C_3
E	0.3083	0.0481	0.0247	C_3

when the set of viable solutions is continuous, PROMETHEE V [15] for segmentation constraints problems, and PROMETHEE VI [16] for human brain representation.

As PROMETHEE I and PROMETHEE II are the foundations of other variants, their procedures are described briefly.

Step 1: Determine the weight of criteria.

In PROMETHEE II, the weight of criteria should be determined by decision makers completely.

Step 2: Calculate the deviations which present the difference between alternative a and b with respect to criterion j.

$$d_j(a, b) = g_j(a) - g_j(b) \tag{3.23}$$

where $g_j(a)$ and $g_j(b)$ refer to the performance of alternative a and b with respect to the jth criterion.

Step 3: Determine and apply the preference function.

The preference function is served to convert the deviations $d_j(a, b)$ obtained by two alternatives a and b into a preference degree ranging in [0, 1]. The preference of alternative a in comparison with alternative b with respect to criterion j can be obtained by Eq. (3.24).

$$P_j(a, b) = F_j[d_j(a, b)] \tag{3.24}$$

$p_j(a, b) \sim 0$ denotes weak preference of a over b.
$P_j(a, b) \sim 1$ denotes strong preference of a over b.
There are six common preference functions $F(d)$ proposed [17].
(1) Usual criterion (see Fig. 3.13)

$$F(d) = \begin{cases} 0, & if\ d \leq 0 \\ 1, & if\ d > 0 \end{cases} \tag{3.25}$$

TABLE 3.15 Limit supermatrix for university A.

	IFR	ISR	FSR	Ip_1	Ip_2	University	ER	AR	CPF
IFR	0.1198	0.1198	0.1198	0.1198	0.1198	0.1198	0.1198	0.1198	0.1198
ISR	0.1047	0.1047	0.1047	0.1047	0.1047	0.1047	0.1047	0.1047	0.1047
FSR	0.1024	0.1024	0.1024	0.1024	0.1024	0.1024	0.1024	0.1024	0.1024
Ip_1	0.0604	0.0604	0.0604	0.0604	0.0604	0.0604	0.0604	0.0604	0.0604
Ip_2	0.0095	0.0095	0.0095	0.0095	0.0095	0.0095	0.0095	0.0095	0.0095
University	0.2765	0.2765	0.2765	0.2765	0.2765	0.2765	0.2765	0.2765	0.2765
ER	0.1984	0.1984	0.1984	0.1984	0.1984	0.1984	0.1984	0.1984	0.1984
AR	0.0731	0.0731	0.0731	0.0731	0.0731	0.0731	0.0731	0.0731	0.0731
CPF	0.0551	0.0551	0.0551	0.0551	0.0551	0.0551	0.0551	0.0551	0.0551

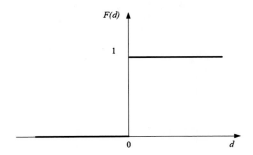

FIGURE 3.13 Usual criterion.

(2) U-shape criterion (see Fig. 3.14)

$$F(d) = \begin{cases} 0, \ if \ d \leq q \\ 1, \ if \ d > q \end{cases}$$ (3.26)

where q is the threshold of indifference, which refers to the largest d which can be negligible to decision makers.

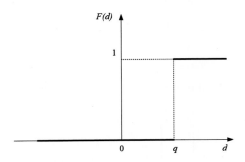

FIGURE 3.14 U-shape criterion.

(3) V-shape criterion (see Fig. 3.15)

$$F(d) = \begin{cases} 0, \ if \ d \leq 0 \\ \frac{d}{p}, \ if \ 0 < d \leq p \\ 1, \ if \ d > p \end{cases}$$ (3.27)

where p is the threshold of strict preference, which refers to the smallest d which is considered as full preference.

(4) Level criterion (see Fig. 3.16)

$$F(d) = \begin{cases} 0, \ if \ d \leq q \\ \frac{1}{2}, \ if \ q < d \leq p \\ 1, \ if \ d > p \end{cases}$$ (3.28)

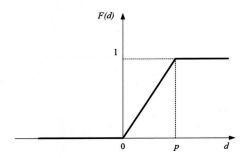

FIGURE 3.15 V-shape criterion.

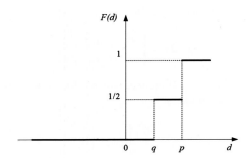

FIGURE 3.16 Level criterion.

(5) V-shape with indifference criterion (see Fig. 3.17)

$$F(d) = \begin{cases} 0, \ if \ d \leq q \\ \frac{d-p}{p-q}, \ if \ q < d \leq p \\ 1, \ if \ d > p \end{cases} \tag{3.29}$$

(6) Gaussian criterion (see Fig. 3.18)

$$F(d) = \begin{cases} 0, \ if \ d \leq 0 \\ 1 - e^{-\frac{d^2}{2\sigma^2}}, \ if \ d > 0 \end{cases} \tag{3.30}$$

Step 4: Calculate the global preference index $\pi(a, b)$ based on the weighted sum of $P_j(a, b)$ on each criterion.

$$\pi(a, b) = \sum_{j=1}^{k} P_j(a, b) w_j \tag{3.31}$$

Obviously, all $\pi(a, b) \in A$ satisfy the following properties:

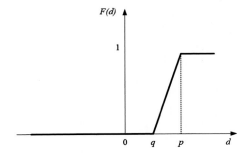

FIGURE 3.17 V-shape with indifference criterion.

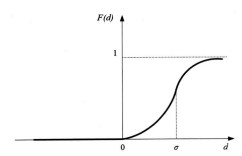

FIGURE 3.18 Gaussian criterion.

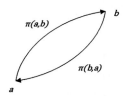

FIGURE 3.19 The flows between a and b.

(1) $\pi(a, a) = 0$;
(2) $0 \leq \pi(a, b) \leq 1$;
(3) $0 \leq \pi(b, a) \leq 1$; and
(4) $0 \leq \pi(a, b) + \pi(b, a) \leq 1$.

Step 5: Calculate the positive outranking flow (leaving flow) and negative outranking flow (entering flow). (See Fig. 3.19.)

$$\phi^+(a) = \frac{1}{n-1} \sum_{x \in A} \pi(a, x) \tag{3.32}$$

$$\phi^-(a) = \frac{1}{n-1} \sum_{x \in A} \pi(x, a) \tag{3.33}$$

where A refers to the set of alternatives. (See Figs. 3.20 and 3.21.)

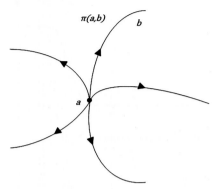

FIGURE 3.20 The positive outranking flow (leaving flow) of a.

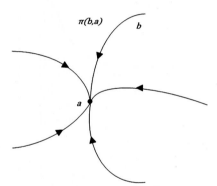

FIGURE 3.21 The negative outranking flow (entering flow) of a.

Step 6: Calculate the net outranking flow for each alternative on the basis of the positive flow and negative flow.

$$\phi(a) = \phi^+(a) - \phi^-(a) = \frac{1}{n-1} \sum_{j=1}^{k} \sum_{x \in A} [P_j(a, x) - P_j(x, a)] w_j \quad (3.34)$$

Step 7: Receive the complete ranking result according to the outranking flows. It is clear that the higher the positive flow and the lower the negative flow, the better the alternative.

In **PROMETHEE I**, there are three relations between a and b:

$$\text{If} \begin{cases} \phi^+(a) > \phi^+(b) \text{ and } \phi^-(a) < \phi^-(b), \text{ or} \\ \phi^+(a) = \phi^+(b) \text{ and } \phi^-(a) < \phi^-(b), \text{ or} \\ \phi^+(a) > \phi^+(b) \text{ and } \phi^-(a) = \phi^-(b) \end{cases}, a \text{ outranks } b \ (a P^I b).$$

If $\phi^+(a) = \phi^+(b)$ and $\phi^-(a) = \phi^-(b)$, a is indifferent to b (aI^Ib).

If $\begin{cases} \phi^+(a) > \phi^+(b) \text{ and } \phi^-(a) > \phi^-(b), \text{ or} \\ \phi^+(a) < \phi^+(b) \text{ and } \phi^-(a) < \phi^-(b) \end{cases}$, a is incomparable to b

(aR^Ib).

In **PROMETHEE II**, the following two rules based on the net outranking flows are considered:

If $\phi(a) > \phi(b)$, a outranks b ($aP^{II}b$).

If $\phi(a) = \phi(b)$, a is indifferent to b ($aI^{II}b$).

In real cases, both PROMETHEE I and PROMETHEE II have their advantages. The former considers the incomparability between alternatives which may help to make appropriate decisions, and the latter provides a complete ranking.

Due to the understandability and simplicity of PROMETHEE, it has been applied in various areas, such as environment management, business management, and energy management. Among these, environment management is regarded as the most popular topic in PROMETHEE applications, with large amounts of related papers [17].

Furthermore, to expand the application scope of PROMETHEE, it has been integrated with many other methods. In 1998, the PROMETHEE GDSS [18] was proposed for group decision-making problems. In addition, the analytic hierarchy process (AHP) is recommended for integration into PROMETHEE, mainly to deal with the shortage of the weight determination [19].

3.3.2 FlowSort and extensions

3.3.2.1 FlowSort

In 2008, FlowSort [20] was proposed as a PROMETHEE-based sorting method for assigning alternatives to predefined classes with either limiting profiles or central profiles. On the basis of the comparisons of all preference profiles, some assignment rules are provided to determine the category of alternatives. The procedure of FlowSort is as follows.

Step 1: Problem definition.

Define the $A = \{a_1, a_2, \cdots, a_i, \cdots, a_n\}$ as the set of n alternatives to be assigned to k categories $C = \{C_1, C_2, \cdots, C_h, \cdots, C_k\}$ based on the criteria set $G = \{g_1, g_2, \cdots, g_j, \cdots, g_m\}$ that have to be maximized.

The set of classes C are completely ordered as $C_1 \rhd C_2 \rhd \cdots \rhd C_k$, and it is described by limiting profiles $R_{lp} = \{lp_1, lp_2, \cdots lp_h, \cdots, lp_{k+1}\}$ or central profiles $R_{cp} = \{cp_1, cp_2, \cdots cp_h, \cdots, cp_k\}$. For example, category h can be defined by the higher profile lp_h and the lower profile lp_{h+1} or one single central profile cp_h.

Then the $R^* = \{r_1^*, r_2^*, \cdots, r_k^*\}$ is defined where there is no distinction between limiting profiles and central profiles.

Because the reference profiles define ordered classes, we shall assume condition 1:

Condition 1: $\forall r_h^*, r_l^* \in R^*$ *such that* $h < l$, $g_j(r_h^*) > g_j(r_l^*) \forall j \in 1, \cdots, m$.

Step 2: Further define the set $R_i^* = R^* \cup \{a_i\}$, where a_i is the alternative to be sorted.

Then calculate the preference degree $\pi(a, b)$ of alternative a over alternative b which presents the strength of preference ($\forall a, b \in R_i^*$). The preference degrees can be obtained as mentioned above in the PROMETHEE methodology. It can be computed for all alternatives of R_i^*.

The preference degree can be obtained as in PROMETHEE and it also satisfies conditions 2–6:

Condition 2: $0 \le \pi(x, y) \le 1$;
Condition 3: $\pi(x, y) + \pi(y, x) \le 1$;
Condition 4: $\pi(x, x) = 0$;
Condition 5: $\forall x', y' \in R_i^*$, *if* $\forall j : gj(x) - gj(y) \le gj(x') - gj(y')$, *then* $\pi(x, y) \le \pi(x', y')$;
Condition 6: $\forall r_h^*, r_l^* \in R_i^*$ *such that* $h < l$; $\pi(r_h^*, r_l^*) > 0$ *and* $\pi(r_l^*, r_h^*) = 0$.

Step 3: Calculate the positive (leaving) flow, negative (entering) flow and net flow of each alternative of R_i^*.

$$\phi_{R_i^*}^+(a) = \frac{1}{|R_i^*| - 1} \sum_{x \in R_i^*} \pi(a, x) \tag{3.35}$$

$$\phi_{R_i^*}^-(a) = \frac{1}{|R_i^*| - 1} \sum_{x \in R_i^*} \pi(x, a) \tag{3.36}$$

$$\phi_{R_i^*}(a) = \phi_{R_i^*}^+(a) - \phi_{R_i^*}^-(a) \tag{3.37}$$

For different alternative a_i to be assigned, the flow values of the preference profiles are different, but the flow order is invariant.

$$\forall h = 1, 2, \cdots, k, \begin{cases} \phi_{R_i}^+(r_h) > \phi_{R_i}^+(r_{h+1}) \\ \phi_{R_i}^-(r_h) < \phi_{R_i}^-(r_{h+1}) \\ \phi_{R_i}(r_h) > \phi_{R_i}(r_{h+1}) \end{cases} \tag{3.38}$$

On the basis of the rule, we can determine a category with the flow values.

Step 4: Assign the alternatives based on limiting profiles or central profiles.

(1) If the limiting profiles are defined, two different assignment rules can be defined as follows:

$$C_{\phi^+}(a_i) = C_h, \; if \; \phi_{R_i}^+(l p_h) \ge \phi_{R_i}^+(a_i) > \phi_{R_i}^+(l p_{h+1})$$

$$C_{\phi^-}(a_i) = C_h, \; if \; \phi_{R_i}^-(l p_h) < \phi_{R_i}^-(a_i) \le \phi_{R_i}^-(l p_{h+1})$$

Two different assignment results $C_{\phi^+}(a_i)$ and $C_{\phi^-}(a_i)$ can be obtained with positive flows and negative flows. We define the better category as $C_b(a_i)$ and the worse one as $C_w(a_i)$.

If the decision makers require a unique sorting result, the rule based on net flows can be taken into consideration.

$$C_\phi(a_i) = C_h, \; if \; \phi_{R_i}(lp_h) \geq \phi_{R_i}(a_i) > \phi_{R_i}(lp_{h+1})$$

Obviously, the result obtained with the net flows can be consistent with the results on the basis of the positive flows and negative flows:

$$\forall a_i \in A, C_b(a_i) \trianglerighteq C_\phi(a_i) \trianglerighteq C_w(a_i)$$

where $C \trianglerighteq \widetilde{C}$ denotes that $C \triangleright \widetilde{C}$ or $C = \widetilde{C}$.

As shown in Fig. 3.22, the point of a_2 lies in the rectangle of C_h defined by the points $\phi_{R_i}^+(lp_h)$, $\phi_{R_i}^-(lp_h)$, $\phi_{R_i}^+(lp_{h+1})$, and $\phi_{R_i}^-(lp_{h+1})$; therefore, it is assigned to the C_h on the basis of both positive and negative flows. However, the two flows classify a_1 and a_3 into different categories.

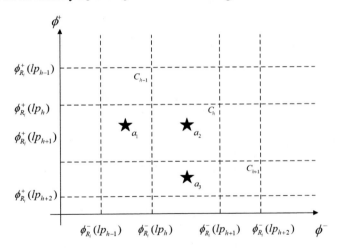

FIGURE 3.22 The assignment with limiting profiles.

(2) If we select central profiles to determine the category, the alternative should be assigned to the category whose central profile has the most similar flows. There are assignment rules according to positive flows and negative flows.

$$C_{\phi^+}(a_i) = C_h, \; if \; \forall l = 1, 2, \cdots, k:$$
$$\left| \phi_{R_i}^+(a_i) - \phi_{R_i}^+(cp_h) \right| \leq \left| \phi_{R_i}^+(a_i) - \phi_{R_i}^+(cp_l) \right|$$
$$C_{\phi^-}(a_i) = C_h, \; if \; \forall l = 1, 2, \cdots, k:$$
$$\left| \phi_{R_i}^-(a_i) - \phi_{R_i}^-(cp_h) \right| \leq \left| \phi_{R_i}^-(a_i) - \phi_{R_i}^-(cp_l) \right|$$

If there are several categories equally close to the alternative, we can assign it to the better class with an optimistic view or to the worse class with a pessimistic view.

In addition, we can also assign the alternative to the unique category on the basis of net flows:

$$C_\phi(a_i) = C_h, if \forall l = 1, 2, \cdots, k:$$
$$\left| \phi_{R_i}(a_i) - \phi_{R_i}(cp_h) \right| \le \left| \phi_{R_i}(a_i) - \phi_{R_i}(cp_l) \right|$$

As in the case of limiting profiles, the assignment based on central profiles can be described in Fig. 3.23.

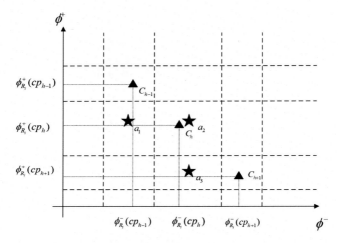

FIGURE 3.23   The assignment with central profiles.

3.3.2.2   Illustrative example

This is a numerical example to illustrate FlowSort with limiting profiles. In this case, we aim to assign five alternatives to five categories defined by six preference profiles based on five criteria. Assume that all the criteria need to be maximized.

The performances of the alternatives on each criterion are shown in Table 3.16 and the performances of limiting profiles are given in Table 3.17. The performances of the alternatives and limiting profiles are described in graphically in Fig. 3.24.

We select the usual preference function. This means that only when $d > 0$, $F(d) = 1$, otherwise $F(d) = 0$.

The performance degrees π of alternatives according to each limiting profile are shown in Table 3.18. From these preference degrees, we can obtain easily the positive flows, negative flows, and net flows (see Table 3.19).

TABLE 3.16 The performance of alternatives.

A	g_1	g_2	g_3	g_4	g_5
a_1	10	34	78	23	12
a_2	57	70	45	21	89
a_3	92	78	63	75	28
a_4	55	52	75	29	45
a_5	12	32	4	17	42

TABLE 3.17 The performance of limiting profiles.

lp	g_1	g_2	g_3	g_4	g_5
lp_1	100	100	100	100	100
lp_2	75	75	75	75	75
lp_3	50	50	50	50	50
lp_4	25	25	25	25	25
lp_5	0	0	0	0	0

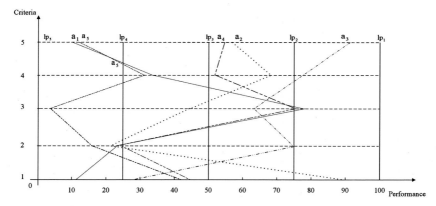

FIGURE 3.24 The performances of limiting profiles and alternatives.

From the value of the flows, we can find the sorting result of each alternative. According to the positive flow, a_1 which performs the same as lp_4 should be assigned to C_4, and considering negative flow, a_1 should be assigned to C_3. With regard to a_2, a_3, and a_4, they can be sorted to C_2 based on both positive and negative flows. a_5 should be assigned to C_4 unambiguously.

To clarify this further, the assignment result of a_1 is represented in Fig. 3.25.

TABLE 3.18 The preference degrees π between alternatives and limiting profiles.

	lp_1	lp_2	lp_3	lp_4	lp_5
$\pi(a_1, lp_h)$	0	0.2	0.2	0.4	1
$\pi(lp_h, a_1)$	1	0.8	0.8	0.6	0
$\pi(a_2, lp_h)$	0	0.6	0.6	0.8	1
$\pi(lp_h, a_2)$	1	0.4	0.4	0.2	0
$\pi(a_3, lp_h)$	0	0.4	0.8	1	1
$\pi(lp_h, a_3)$	1	0.4	0.2	0	0
$\pi(a_4, lp_h)$	0	0	0.6	1	1
$\pi(lp_h, a_4)$	1	0.8	0.4	0	0
$\pi(a_5, lp_h)$	0	0	0	0.4	1
$\pi(lp_h, a_5)$	1	1	1	0.6	0

TABLE 3.19 Flow values of alternatives and limiting profiles.

		lp_1	lp_2	lp_3	lp_4	lp_5	Flow value
a_1	ϕ^+	1	0.76	0.56	0.36	0	0.36
	ϕ^-	0	0.24	0.44	0.64	1	0.64
	ϕ	1	0.52	0.12	−0.28	−1	−0.28
a_2	ϕ^+	1	0.68	0.48	0.24	0	0.6
	ϕ^-	0	0.32	0.52	0.76	1	0.4
	ϕ	1	0.36	−0.04	−0.52	−1	0.2
a_3	ϕ^+	1	0.68	0.44	0.2	0	0.64
	ϕ^-	0	0.28	0.56	0.8	1	0.32
	ϕ	1	0.4	−0.12	−0.6	−1	0.32
a_4	ϕ^+	1	0.76	0.48	0.2	0	0.52
	ϕ^-	0	0.2	0.52	0.8	1	0.44
	ϕ	1	0.56	−0.04	−0.6	−1	0.08
a_5	ϕ^+	1	0.8	0.6	0.32	0	0.28
	ϕ^-	0	0.2	0.4	0.68	1	0.72
	ϕ	1	0.6	0.2	−0.36	−1	−0.44

3.3.2.3 FlowSort with imprecision

The FlowSort method has experienced several improvements which mostly focused on managing imperfect information. For instance, FlowSort was combined with interval theory [21], making it feasible to define imprecise input data by intervals rather than a single value.

Assume that there are some imprecisions in the performances of alternatives and preference profiles, which can be defined by interval values. $g_j(x)$ and $\overline{g_j}(x)$ denote the lower and upper bounds of the performance of x on the jth criterion. We suppose that the performances of all the alternatives of A are between

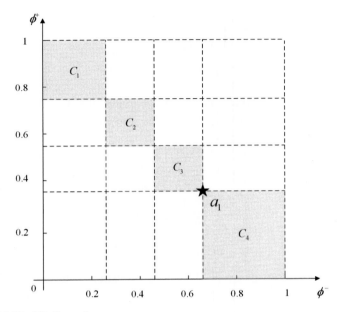

FIGURE 3.25 The flows of a_1.

the worst and best limiting profiles:

$$\forall a_i \in A, \forall g_j : \underline{g_j}(l\,p_{k+1}) \leq \underline{g_j}(a_i) \leq \overline{g_j}(a_i) \leq \overline{g_j}(l\,p_1)$$

One easy solution to deal with the interval value is to convert it into a single value, such as the mean value or median value. However, information will inevitably be lost due to conversion. Therefore, a new method was proposed to handle the problem.

The preference degree can be calculated with Eq. (3.39):

$$
\begin{aligned}
\hat{\pi}(a,b) &= \sum_{j=1}^{m} \widehat{P_j}(a,b) * w_j \\
&= \left[\sum_{j=1}^{m} \underline{P_j}(a,b) * w_j, \sum_{j=1}^{m} \overline{P_j}(a,b) * w_j \right] \\
&= [\underline{\pi}(a,b), \bar{\pi}(a,b)]
\end{aligned}
\tag{3.39}
$$

We choose the usual criterion as the preference function. The following properties of preference degrees can then be obtained, in which the latter property denotes that even though the performance of a is imprecise, the preference of a over a is 0.

$$\forall a, b \in R_i : 0 \leq \underline{\pi}(a, b) \leq \overline{\pi}(a, b) \leq 1$$
$$\forall a \in R_i : \underline{\pi}(a, a) = \overline{\pi}(a, a) = 0$$

The positive flow intervals $\widehat{\phi_{R_1}^+}(x)$, negative flow intervals $\widehat{\phi_{R_1}^-}(x)$, and net flows intervals $\widehat{\phi_{R_1}}(x)$ can be calculated based on the obtained preference degrees.

$$\widehat{\phi_{R_1}^+}(a) = \frac{1}{|R_i - 1|} * \sum_{x \in R_i} \widehat{\pi}(a, x) \tag{3.40}$$

$$\widehat{\phi_{R_1}^-}(a) = \frac{1}{|R_i - 1|} * \sum_{x \in R_i} \widehat{\pi}(x, a) \tag{3.41}$$

$$\widehat{\phi_{R_1}}(a) = \widehat{\phi_{R_1}^+}(a) - \widehat{\phi_{R_1}^-}(a) \tag{3.42}$$

Considering the positive flow, there are two relations between a and x. (See Fig. 3.26.)

CASE I:

a is ϕ^+- preferred to x: $aP^+x \Leftrightarrow \underline{\phi_{R_i}^+}(a) > \overline{\phi_{R_i}^+}(x)$

x is ϕ^+- preferred to a: $xP^+a \Leftrightarrow \underline{\phi_{R_i}^+}(x) > \overline{\phi_{R_i}^+}(a)$

CASE II:

a is ϕ^+- indifferent to x: $aI^+x \Leftrightarrow \overline{\phi_{R_i}^+}(a) \geq \underline{\phi_{R_i}^+}(x) \geq \underline{\phi_{R_i}^+}(a)$ or $\overline{\phi_{R_i}^+}(a) \geq \overline{\phi_{R_i}^+}(x) \geq \underline{\phi_{R_i}^+}(a)$

To distinguish the completely ordered preference profiles more clearly, we impose some conditions on the sorting method:

Condition 1:

$$\forall r_h, r_l \in R \text{ with } h < l,$$
$$\forall j \in \{1, \cdots, m\} : \underline{g_j}(r_h) \geq \overline{g_j}(r_l) \text{ and } \exists k : \underline{g_k}(r_h) > \overline{g_k}(r_l)$$

Condition 2:

$$\forall r_h, r_l \in R \text{ with } h < l : \underline{\pi}(r_h, r_l) > 0 \text{ and } \overline{\pi}(r_l, r_h) = 0$$

Based on these conditions, we can assign alternative a_i to the categories $\widehat{C_{\phi^+}}(a_i) = \left[\underline{C_{\phi^+}}(a_i), \overline{C_{\phi^+}}(a_i) \right]$. The assignment rules are as follows:

$$\overline{C_{\phi^+}}(a_i) = l, \Leftrightarrow \overline{\phi_{R_i}^+}(lp_l) > \underline{\phi_{R_i}^+}(a_i) \geq \overline{\phi_{R_i}^+}(lp_{l+1})$$

$$\underline{C_{\phi^+}}(a_i) = h, \Leftrightarrow \underline{\phi_{R_i}^+}(lp_h) > \overline{\phi_{R_i}^+}(a_i) \geq \underline{\phi_{R_i}^+}(lp_{h+1})$$

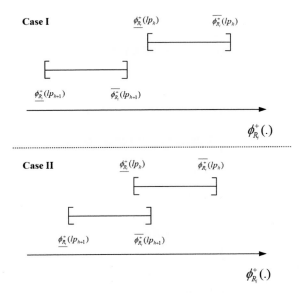

FIGURE 3.26 Two relations of consecutive limiting profiles.

With the assignment rules, the result may be unique or a set of consecutive classes. There are four situations depicted in Fig. 3.27: $\widehat{C_{\phi+}}(a_1) = [h-1,\ h]$, $\widehat{C_{\phi+}}(a_2) = [h-2,\ h]$, $\widehat{C_{\phi+}}(a_3) = [h-1,\ h]$, and $\widehat{C_{\phi+}}(a_4) = [h,\ h]$.

Similarly, with regard to negative flows, a_i should be assigned to $\widehat{C_{\phi-}}(a_i) = \left[\underline{C_{\phi-}(a_i)}, \overline{C_{\phi-}}(a_i)\right]$:

$$\overline{C_{\phi-}}(a_i) = l, \ \Leftrightarrow \phi_{R_i}^-(l\,p_{l+1}) > \overline{\phi_{R_i}^-}(a_i) \geq \phi_{R_i}^-(l\,p_l)$$

$$\underline{C_{\phi+}}(a_i) = h, \ \Leftrightarrow \overline{\phi_{R_i}^-}(l\,p_{h+1}) > \underline{\phi_{R_i}^-}(a_i) \geq \underline{\phi_{R_i}^-}(l\,p_h)$$

With the two assignment results, we can denote the best category $C_b(a_i) = \min\{\underline{C_{\phi-}}(a_i), \underline{C_{\phi+}}(a_i)\}$ and the worst category $C_w(a_i) = \max\{\overline{C_{\phi-}}(a_i),$ $\overline{C_{\phi+}}(a_i)\}$.

If a smaller set of categories is expected, we can apply the net flows to assignment. The result $\widehat{C_\phi}(a_i) = \left[\underline{C_\phi(a_i)}, \overline{C_\phi}(a_i)\right]$ can be obtained:

$$\overline{C_\phi}(a_i) = l, \ \Leftrightarrow \overline{\phi_{R_i}}(l\,p_l) > \overline{\phi_{R_i}}(a_i) \geq \overline{\phi_{R_i}}(l\,p_{l+1})$$

$$\underline{C_\phi}(a_i) = h, \ \Leftrightarrow \underline{\phi_{R_i}}(l\,p_h) > \overline{\phi_{R_i}}(a_i) \geq \underline{\phi_{R_i}}(l\,p_{h+1})$$

Because of the consistency of net-flow assignment, the following relation exists:

$$\forall a_i \in A, \ \widehat{C_\phi}(a_i) \subseteq [C_b(a_i),\ C_w(a_i)]$$

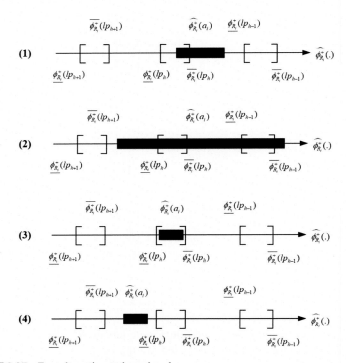

FIGURE 3.27 Four alternatives to be assigned.

3.3.2.4 FlowSort-GDSS

In 2015, a novel integrated method FlowSort-GDSS [22] for group decision was proposed based on the integration of FlowSort and group decision support systems (GDSS). Considering the different experience, expertise, and skills of different decision makers, we further define the weights of T decision makers as $W_d = \{w_{d1}, \cdots, w_{dt}, \cdots, w_{dT}\}$ and the weights of criteria as $W_g = \{w_{g1}, \cdots, w_{gj}, \cdots, w_{gm}\}$.

To characterize the k categories, $T \cdot (k+1)$ limiting profiles $R_r^j = \{r_1^{1,j}, \cdots, r_h^{1,j}, \quad \cdots, r_{k+1}^{1,j}, \cdots r_1^{t,j}, \cdots, r_h^{t,j}, \cdots, r_{k+1}^{t,j}, \cdots r_1^{T,j}, \quad \cdots, r_h^{T,j}, \cdots, r_{k+1}^{T,j}\}$ or $T \cdot k$ central profiles $R_r^j = \{r_1^{1,j}, \cdots, r_h^{1,j}, \cdots, r_k^{1,j}, \cdots r_1^{t,j}, \cdots, r_h^{t,j}, \cdots, r_k^{t,j}, \cdots r_1^{T,j}, \cdots, r_h^{T,j}, \cdots, r_k^{T,j}\}$ are defined on criterion j.

In order to avoid the overlapping of categories, the following condition is necessary.

$$r_k^{t,j} > r_{k+1}^{s,j}; \ \forall r_k^{t,j}, r_{k+1}^{s,j} \in R, \ \forall j = 1, \cdots, m \text{ and } \forall t, s = 1, \cdots, T$$

In FlowSort-GDSS, each $a_i \in A$ should be compared to all reference profiles of all decision makers. The net flow of a_i between -1 and 1 can be calculated as follows:

$$\phi_j(a_i) = \frac{1}{|R^j|} \sum_{r_h^{t,j} \in R^j} \left[P_j\left(a_i, r_h^{t,j}\right) - P_j\left(r_h^{t,j}, a_i\right) \right] \tag{3.43}$$

With the weight W_g, we can obtain the global net flow of a_i:

$$\phi(a_i) = \sum_{j=1}^{m} w_{gj} \phi_j(a_i) \tag{3.44}$$

The net flow of the reference profiles can be calculated through the comparisons with all preference profiles and the alternative to be assigned.

$$\phi_{j,i}(r_h^{t,j}) = \frac{1}{|R^j|+1} \sum_{r_l^{t,j} \in R^j} \left[P_j\left(r_h^{t,j}, r_l^{t,j}\right) - P_j\left(r_l^{t,j}, r_h^{t,j}\right) \right]$$
$$+ \frac{1}{|R^j|+1} \left[P_j\left(r_h^{t,j}, a_i\right) - P_j\left(a_i, r_h^{t,j}\right) \right] \tag{3.45}$$

$$\phi_i(r_h^t) = \sum_{j=1}^{m} w_{gj} \phi_{j,i}(r_h^{t,j}) \tag{3.46}$$

Then, we can assign the alternatives to the category on the basis of the net flow. Because the opinions of the group of the decision makers may be different, there are two cases: **unanimous assignment** and **nonunanimous assignment**.

If **limiting profiles** are selected, two different procedures of assignment are described as follows:

Unanimous assignment:
If $\exists h$, with $1 < h < k+1$, such that $\phi_i(r_h^t) \geq \phi(a_i) > \phi_i(r_{h+1}^t)$, $\forall t = 1, \cdots, T \Rightarrow C(a_i) = C_h$.
If $\phi(a_i) \geq \phi_i(r_1^t)$, $\forall t = 1, \cdots, T \Rightarrow C(a_i) = C_1$.
If $\phi(a_i) < \phi_i(r_{K+1}^t)$, $\forall t = 1, \cdots, T \Rightarrow C(a_i) = C_K$.

Nonunanimous assignment:
If there exists $\phi_i(r_h^t) \leq \phi(a_i) < \phi_i(r_h^s)$ where t and s are two different decision makers, it means that t assigns a_i to C_{h-1} and s assigns it to C_h.

To achieve the unique assignment result, the distance $d_i(h-1)$ and $d_i(h)$ between the net flow of a_i and the global limiting profiles of all decision makers should be obtained.

$$d_i(h-1) = \sum_{t:\phi(a_i) \geq \phi_i(r_h^t)} w_{dt} \left| \phi(a_i) - \phi_i(r_{h-1}^t) \right| \tag{3.47}$$

$$d_i(h) = \sum_{s:\phi(a_i) < \phi_i(r_h^s)} w_{ds} \left| \phi_i(r_h^s) - \phi(a_i) \right| \tag{3.48}$$

Compare with the two distances; the smaller one defines the final category. If the distances are equal, we can assign the alternative to the better class in an optimistic view and to the worse class in a pessimistic view.

If $d_i(h-1) - d_i(h) > 0 \Rightarrow C(a_i) = C_h$.

If $d_i(h-1) - d_i(h) < 0 \Rightarrow C(a_i) = C_{h-1}$.

If $d_i(h-1) - d_i(h) = 0 \Rightarrow C(a_i) = C_{h-1} \text{ or } C_h$.

If the categories are defined by **central profiles**, the two assignment procedures are distinguished.

Unanimous assignment:

If $\exists h$, with $1 \le h \le k$, such that $\left|\phi_i(r_h^t) - \phi(a_i)\right| < \left|\phi_i(r_l^t) - \phi(a_i)\right|$, $\forall t = 1, \cdots, T$ and $\forall l = 1, \cdots, k \Rightarrow C(a_i) = C_h$.

Nonunanimous assignment:

If $\left|\phi_i(r_h^t) - \phi(a_i)\right| \le \left|\phi_i(r_l^t) - \phi(a_i)\right|$, $\forall l = 1, \cdots, k$ and $\left|\phi_i(r_l^t) - \phi(a_i)\right| \le \left|\phi_i(r_h^t) - \phi(a_i)\right|$, $\forall h = 1, \cdots, k$, it means that at least two different decision makers (t and s) assign the alternative to different categories (h and l). And from the properties of the reference profiles, we can conclude that $h = l \pm 1$. Then the distance $d_i(h)$ and $d_i(l)$ between the a_i and the central profiles of C_h and C_l can be obtained.

$$d_i(h) = \sum_{t \in T_h} w_{dt} \left|\phi_i(r_h^t) - \phi(a_i)\right| \tag{3.49}$$

$$d_i(l) = \sum_{t \in T_l} w_{dt} \left|\phi_i(r_l^t) - \phi(a_i)\right| \tag{3.50}$$

Similarly, there are three assignment rules based on the distances of central profiles.

If $d_i(h) - d_i(l) > 0 \Rightarrow C(a_i) = C_l$.

If $d_i(h) - d_i(l) < 0 \Rightarrow C(a_i) = C_h$.

If $d_i(h) - d_i(l) = 0 \Rightarrow C(a_i) = C_h \text{ or } C_l$.

3.4 UTADIS (UTilités Additives DIScriminantes): a multi-criteria classification method

3.4.1 UTADIS

Multi-criteria decision analysis provides a variety of techniques to address sorting problems and often requires the decision maker to define specific information on parameters to develop the sorting model. The required information is usually complex, including the weights of the evaluation criteria, preference, indifference, and veto thresholds, etc. In this regard, it can be time-consuming and inaccurate to employ a direct procedure for estimating the global utility model.

Preference disaggregation analysis (PDA) overcomes this problem [23]. It disaggregates the judgment policy of the decision maker and then develops the criteria aggregation model that fits the preferences information with regression-based techniques. One of the representative methods is UTADIS [24], which employs the framework of PDA in developing an additive utility model indirectly for sorting purposes. This section provides a detailed introduction to the UTADIS method.

3.4.1.1 Principle and notation

Based on the methodological framework of PDA, the UTADIS method performs the classification through the development of an additive value function of the following general form:

$$U\left[g\left(a_j\right)\right] = \sum_{i=1}^{n} u_i\left[g_i\left(a_j\right)\right] \in [0, 1] \tag{3.51}$$

where $g_i\left(a_j\right)$ denotes the performance of alternative a_j on criterion g_i, $g\left(a_j\right)$ denotes the vector consisting of the performance of alternative a_j on all criteria g, and $U\left[g\left(a_j\right)\right]$ denotes the global utility of alternative a_j. In this way, the additive value function is simplified to the following form, which provides an aggregate score $U\left(g\right)$ for each alternative along all criteria:

$$U\left(g\right) = \sum_{i=1}^{n} u_i\left(g_i\right) \tag{3.52}$$

Obviously, both the marginal and the global value functions have the monotonicity property, and for any alternative a and b:

$$\begin{cases} U\left[g\left(a\right)\right] > U\left[g\left(b\right)\right] \Leftrightarrow a \succ b(\text{preference}) \\ U\left[g\left(a\right)\right] = U\left[g\left(b\right)\right] \Leftrightarrow a \sim b(\text{indifference}) \end{cases} \tag{3.53}$$

To estimate the actual marginal utility function of the criterion, it also has a piecewise linear form (see Fig. 3.28). Each criterion's range is divided into $b_i - 1$ intervals:

$$\left[g_i^p, g_i^{p+1}\right], p = 1, 2, \cdots, b_i - 1 \tag{3.54}$$

Then, the global utility $U\left(g\right)$ of every alternative a in which $g_i(a) \in \left[g_i^p, g_i^{p+1}\right]$ can be calculated by linear interpolation as follows:

$$U\left(g\right) = \sum_{i=1}^{n} \left(u_i\left(g_i^p\right) + \frac{g_i(a) - g_i^p}{g_i^{p+1} - g_i^p}\left[u_i\left(g_i^{p+1}\right) - u_i\left(g_i^p\right)\right]\right) \tag{3.55}$$

With the threshold of the global utility value, the alternatives can be assigned to the ordinal groups $C_1, C_2, \cdots, C_q$, where C_1 includes the most preferred

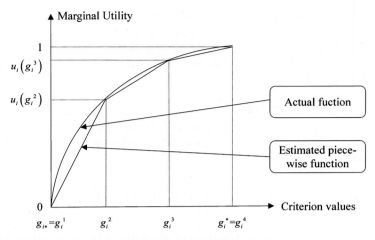

FIGURE 3.28 Piecewise linear form of marginal utility functions.

alternatives and C_q the least preferred ones:

$$\begin{cases} U\,(g) \geq u_1 \Rightarrow a \in C_1 \\ \qquad \cdots \\ u_k \leq U\,(g) < u_{k-1} \Rightarrow a \in C_k \\ \qquad \cdots \\ U\,(g) < u_q \Rightarrow a \in C_q \end{cases} \qquad (3.56)$$

Thus, the development of the sorting model through the UTADIS method requires the determination of the marginal utility functions to obtain the global utility function, as well as the careful selection of the thresholds u_k.

3.4.1.2 The UTADIS sorting model

In order to develop the utility model that can reproduce the decision maker's judgment policy, the reference set $A = \{a_1, a_2, \cdots, a_j\}$ may consist of:

- a set of past decision alternatives;
- a subset of the alternatives under consideration, such that $A' \in A$; and
- a set of reference alternatives, which can be easily judged by the decision maker to express his or her preference.

These alternatives can be regarded as training samples of the model. When the model uses them for classification, the following errors may occur:

$$\begin{cases} \sigma_j^+ = \max\left\{0, u_k - U\,(g_j)\right\}, \forall a_j \in C_k, k = 1, 2, \cdots, q - 1 \\ \sigma_j^- = \max\left\{0, U\,(g_j) - u_{k-1}\right\}, \forall a_j \in C_k, k = 2, 3, \cdots, q \end{cases} \qquad (3.57)$$

As Fig. 3.29 shows, errors σ_j^+ occur when the lower bound of group C_k is violated, whereas the errors σ_j^- occur when the upper bound of group C_k is violated.

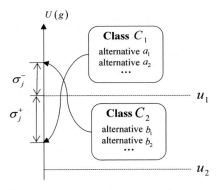

FIGURE 3.29 Classification errors.

In order to ensure that the model is as accurate as possible, linear programming is adopted as follows:

$$\min f = \sum_{k=1}^{q} \sum_{\forall a_j \in C_k} \left(\sigma_j^+ + \sigma_j^- \right) \tag{3.58}$$

s.t.

$$U\left(g_j\right) - u_1 + \sigma_j^+ \geq \delta_1, \forall a_j \in C_1 \tag{3.59}$$

$$\begin{cases} U\left(g_j\right) - u_k + \sigma_j^+ \geq \delta_1 \\ U\left(g_j\right) - u_{k-1} - \sigma_j^- \leq -\delta_2 \end{cases}, \forall a_j \in C_k, k = 2, 3, \cdots, q-1 \tag{3.60}$$

$$U\left(g_j\right) - u_{q-1} - \sigma_j^- \leq -\delta_2, \forall a_j \in C_q \tag{3.61}$$

$$\begin{cases} \sum_{i=1}^{n} u_i\left(g_i^*\right) = 1 \\ u_i\left(g_{i*}\right) = 0, \forall i = 1, 2, \cdots, n \end{cases} \tag{3.62}$$

$$u_k - u_{k+1} \geq s, \forall k = 1, 2, \cdots, q-2, \tag{3.63}$$

$$\sigma_j^+ \geq 0, \sigma_j^- \geq 0, s > \delta_1, \delta_2 \geq 0. \tag{3.64}$$

The objective of the above linear programming is to minimize the sum of the classification errors σ_j^+ and σ_j^- for the reference alternatives. Constraints (3.59) to (3.61) define the errors according to the classification rules in Eq. (3.56) and the piecewise utility function. $U\left(g_j\right)$ is the global utility of alternative a_j and u_k is the threshold that distinguishes the classes C_k and $C_k - 1$. Constraint (3.62) is the basis of utility function and constraint (3.63) ensures that the lower bound of C_k is absolutely higher than the lower bound of $C_k - 1$, thus ensuring the group is ordered from best to worst.

After the optimal solution f^* of this linear program is obtained, the stability analysis of the results is considered as a postoptimality analysis problem. This is a necessary stage in the model development process of the UTADIS method because, in most cases, the linear programming has other optimal or near-optimal solutions, which could provide a more consistent representation of the decision maker's preference. As Jacquet-Lagrèze and Siskos proposed in [25], the postoptimal solutions space can be defined as follows:

$$\begin{cases} f \leq f^* + k(f^*) \\ \text{all the constraint of LP} \end{cases} \tag{3.65}$$

where $k(f^*)$ is a small proportion of f^*.

In this way, a range is determined for both the marginal utilities and the utility thresholds that is representative of their stability. Once the appropriate additive utility model has been developed, it can easily be used for the evaluation of any alternatives.

3.4.2 PREFDIS: decision support system for sorting problems

In order to achieve higher discriminating and predicting ability, Doumpos and Zopounidis proposed three variants of the UTADIS method, namely UTADIS I, UTADIS II, and UTADIS III, and incorporated them into the PREFDIS (**PREF**erence **DIS**crimination) multi-criteria decision support system [26]. Decision makers can develop interactively powerful additive utility models to assign a set of alternatives into predefined classes with the help of this application. However, it is more valuable to focus on its theoretical basis than the instruction manual of the system. Therefore, a detailed description of the family of UTADIS method is presented as follows.

3.4.2.1 UTADIS I

In addition to the case of misclassification, UTADIS I also consider the distance from the utility threshold of the correctly classified alternatives into the model, which has to be maximized to achieve the most significant distinction possible. Under the circumstance, the utility values of alternatives can be placed as far as possible from the threshold and avoid overlapping with it. The formulation of UTADIS I is as follows:

$$\min f = p_1 \sum_{k=1}^{q} \sum_{\forall a_j \in C_k} \left(\sigma_j^+ + \sigma_j^- \right) - p_2 \sum_{k=1}^{q} \sum_{\forall a_j \in C_k} \left(d_j^+ + d_j^- \right) \tag{3.66}$$

s.t.

$$U\left(g_j\right) - u_1 + \sigma_j{}^+ - d_j^+ = 0, \forall a_j \in C_1$$

$$\begin{cases} U\left(g_j\right) - u_k + \sigma_j{}^+ - d_j^+ = 0 \\ U\left(g_j\right) - u_{k-1} - \sigma_j{}^- + d_j^- = -\delta \end{cases}, \forall a_j \in C_k, k = 2, 3, \cdots, q-1$$

$$U\left(g_j\right) - u_{q-1} - \sigma_j{}^- + d_j^- = -\delta, \forall a_j \in C_q \qquad (3.67)$$

$$\begin{cases} \sum_{i=1}^{n} u_i \left(g_i{}^*\right) = 1 \\ u_i \left(g_{i*}\right) = 0, \forall i = 1, 2, \cdots, n \end{cases}$$

$$u_k - u_{k+1} \geq s, \forall k = 1, 2, \cdots, q-2,$$

$$\sigma_j{}^+ \geq 0, \sigma_j{}^- \geq 0, d_j^+ \geq 0, d_j^- \geq 0, s > 0, \delta > 0.$$

where p_1 and p_2 are weighting parameters of the two objectives that involve the minimization of classification errors and the maximization of the distances of the global utility value of the correctly classified alternatives from the utility thresholds.

Notice that these parameters must be set such that $p_1 > p_2$, otherwise the classification error variables $\sigma_j{}^+$ and $\sigma_j{}^-$ will be pushed toward their upper bound to allow the increase of the distance variables d^+ and d^-, leading to the development of a meaningless additive utility function.

3.4.2.2 UTADIS II

In some cases, using the magnitude of the deviations from the utility threshold as the discrimination criterion may lead to suboptimal discrimination results. Consider a simple example concerning a dichotomous classification problem, where three alternatives are misclassified and their deviations from the utility threshold are $[0.1, 0.1, 0.1]$. The overall error is 0.3 and every error of misclassified alternative is relatively small. However, the result could not be the optimal one, because the case that a single alternative with misclassified error of 0.3 will be better.

Therefore, UTADIS II is based on a mixed-integer programming formulation in order to minimize the number of misclassifications instead of their magnitude. The formulation of UTADIS II is as follows:

$$\min f = \sum_{k=1}^{q} \sum_{\forall a_j \in C_k} \left(M_j^+ + M_j^-\right) \qquad (3.68)$$

s.t.

$$U\left(g_j\right) - u_1 + M_j^+ \geq 0, \forall a_j \in C_1$$

$$\begin{cases} U\left(g_j\right) - u_k + M_j^+ \geq 0 \\ U\left(g_j\right) - u_{k-1} - M_j^- \leq -\delta \end{cases}, \forall a_j \in C_k, k = 2, 3, \cdots, q-1,$$

$$U\left(g_j\right) - u_{q-1} - M_j^- \leq -\delta, \forall a_j \in C_q,$$ (3.69)

$$\begin{cases} \sum_{i=1}^{n} u_i\left(g_i^*\right) = 1, \\ u_i\left(g_{i*}\right) = 0, \forall i = 1, 2, \cdots, n, \end{cases}$$

$$u_k - u_{k+1} \geq s, \forall k = 1, 2, \cdots, q - 2,$$

$$M_j^+, M_j^- \in \{0, 1\}, s > 0, \delta > 0.$$

where M_j^+ and M_j^- are binary variables indicating the misclassification of an alternative. If $M_j^+ = 1$ or $M_j^- = 1$, then the alternative is misclassified.

3.4.2.3 UTADIS III

UTADIS III combines UTADIS I and UTADIS II, and aims to maximize the distance of alternatives from utility thresholds and minimize the number of misclassfications. The formulation of UTADIS III is as follows:

$$\min f = \sum_{k=1}^{q} \sum_{\forall a_j \in C_k} \left(M_j^+ + M_j^-\right) - \sum_{k=1}^{q} \sum_{\forall a_j \in C_k} \left(d_j^+ + d_j^-\right)$$ (3.70)

s.t.

$$U\left(g_j\right) - u_1 + M_j^+ - d_j^+ = 0, \forall a_j \in C_1,$$

$$\begin{cases} U\left(g_j\right) - u_k + M_j^+ - d_j^+ = 0 \\ U\left(g_j\right) - u_{k-1} - M_j^- + d_j^- = -\delta \end{cases}, \forall a_j \in C_k, k = 2, 3, \cdots, q - 1,$$

$$U\left(g_j\right) - u_{q-1} - M_j^- + d_j^- = -\delta, \forall a_j \in C_q,$$ (3.71)

$$\begin{cases} \sum_{i=1}^{n} u_i\left(g_i^*\right) = 1, \\ u_i\left(g_{i*}\right) = 0, \forall i = 1, 2, \cdots, n, \end{cases}$$

$$u_k - u_{k+1} \geq s, \forall k = 1, 2, \cdots, q - 2,$$

$$M_j^-, M_j^- \in \{0, 1\}, d_j^+ \geq 0, d_j^- \geq 0, s > 0, \delta > 0.$$

The constraints of UTADIS III are similar to UTADIS I and UTADIS II, thus there is no further elaboration. Further details of how combined UTADIS methods to develop utility models to support decisions are described in [27,28].

3.4.3 UTADIS GMS–GROUP

Although there are a variety of methods for selecting the utility function, none of them takes into account all compatible value functions. Therefore, Greco, Mousseau, and Slowinski proposed robust ordinal regression (ROR) in [29] with the aim of using the whole set of compatible general additive value functions as a preference model. The first robust ordinal regression method has been the generalization of the Utility Additive (UTA) method, called UTA^{GMS} [30]. Furthermore, this approach has been extended to the UTADIS^{GMS} method [31] to deal with sorting problems.

The family of methods has been originally designed to deal with preferences expressed by a single decision-maker. However, group decision-making is also important and frequently encountered in companies and organizations. Typical examples of such problems can be found in management and business, e.g., evaluation of consumer preferences, personnel selection, or allocation of priorities to projects. In order to deal with preferences expressed by a set of decision-makers, UTA^{GMS}−GROUP and UTADIS^{GMS}−GROUP were proposed for ranking and sorting decision problems, respectively [32].

In this section, the UTADIS^{GMS} sorting method for group decisions is introduced in detail and a simple example is provided to show how the methodology can be applied in decision support.

3.4.3.1 UTADIS GMS

The sorting problem involves the assignment of a set of alternatives into predefined homogeneous classes, which are ordered from best to worst. We denote them by $C_1, C_2, \cdots, C_p$, where $C_h + 1$ is preferred to C_h, $h = 1, 2, \cdots, p - 1$. Both threshold-based and example-based value driven sorting procedures by UTADIS^{GMS} are proposed in [31]. The example-based one is more widely used, because the comparisons of alternatives are more intuitive and much easier than determination of threshold parameters for the decision-maker under normal circumstances.

On the basis of the UTADIS method, the following concepts are introduced in UTADIS^{GMS}:

(1) Preference information: the decision maker (DM) is asked to provide a set of assignment examples to express his or her preference. Each assignment example consists of an alternative $a \in A^R \in A$ and its desired assignment $a \rightarrow [C_{L(a)}, C_{R(a)}]$, where $[C_{L(a)}, C_{R(a)}]$ is an interval of contiguous classes, $C_{L(a)} \leq C_{R(a)}$, where $L(a)$ and $R(a)$ are the indices of the worst class and best class to which alternative a is assigned by value function U.

(2) Compatibility of a value function with the preference information: for a value function U, the preference information is said to be consistent with U iff:

$$\forall a, b \in A^R, L(a) > R(b) \Rightarrow U(a) > U(b) \qquad (3.72)$$

which is equivalent to:

$$\forall a, b \in A_{dr}, U(a) \geq U(b) \Rightarrow R(a) \geq L(a) \qquad (3.73)$$

In other words, it uses a value function U to decide the assignments in such a way that if $U(a) \geq U(b)$, then a is assigned to the class not worse than b.

(3) Possible and necessary assignments: for a set of preference information A^R and a corresponding set of compatible value function U_{A^R}, the *possible assignments* $C_P(a)$ determines the set of indices h of classes C_h for which there exists at least one compatible value function $U \in U_{A^R}$ assigning a to C_h:

$$
\begin{aligned}
C^P(a) &= \left[L_P^U(a), R_P^U(a) \right] \\
&= \left\{ h \in H : \exists U \in U_{A^R} \text{ for which } h \in \left[L^U(a), R^U(a) \right] \right\}
\end{aligned}
\tag{3.74}
$$

and the *necessary assignments* specifies the set of indices h of classes C_h for which all compatible value functions $U \in U_{A^R}$ assigning a to C_h:

$$
\begin{aligned}
C^N(a) &= \left[L_N^U(a), R_N^U(a) \right] \\
&= \left\{ h \in H : \forall U \in U_{A^R} \text{ for which } h \in \left[L^U(a), R^U(a) \right] \right\}
\end{aligned}
\tag{3.75}
$$

The *possible assignment* specifies the range of classes to which the alternative can be assigned considering any compatible value function individually, while the *necessary assignment* considers all compatible value functions simultaneously.

The procedure consists of six steps, which starts with the elicitation of preference information, leads through the statement of ordinal regression problems and calculation of the relations between any two alternatives on the set of all, and ends with the computation of possible and necessary class assignments. The detailed steps of the example-based sorting procedure of the UTADIS^{GMS} method are as follows [33]:

Step 1: Ask the DM for preference information in the form of a set of assignment examples.

Step 2: Formulate the ordinal regression problem to verify that the set of compatible value functions U_{A^R} is not empty. A general additive compatible value function is an additive value function $U(g) = \sum_{i=1}^{n} u_i(g_i)$ satisfying the following set of constraints, including monotonicity and normalization:

$$
\left.
\begin{aligned}
&\sum_{i=1}^{n} u_i(g_i^*) = 1 \\
&u_i(g_{i*}) = 0, \forall i = 1, 2, \cdots, n \\
&u_k - u_{k-1} \geq s, \forall k = 1, 2, \cdots, q - 2
\end{aligned}
\right\}
\left(E_{base}^{A^R} \right)
\tag{3.76}
$$

In order to verify that the set of all compatible value functions U_{A^R} is not empty, it is sufficient to check whether ε has an option value $\varepsilon^* > 0$, where:

$$
\varepsilon^* = \max \varepsilon
\tag{3.77}
$$

s.t.

$$\left. \begin{array}{l} U\,(a) \geq U\,(b) + \varepsilon, \forall a, b \in A^R : L\,(a) > R\,(b) \\ E_{base}^{AR} \end{array} \right\} \left(E^{A^R} \right) \qquad (3.78)$$

If there is no value function compatible with the preference information, i.e., $\varepsilon^* \leq 0$, the DM should decide whether to accept that some exemplary assignments of reference alternatives will not be reproduced by any value function, or to identify reasons of incompatibility in order to remove it. Dealing with the incompatibility issue is discussed in detail in [34].

Step 3: Calculate the necessary and the possible relations $a \succ \sim^N a^*$, $a \succ \sim^P a^*$, $a^* \succ \sim^N a$ and $a^* \succ \sim^P a$ with $a^* \in A^R$ and $a \in A$. In order to check the *truth* or *falsity* of the necessary and the possible relations, the following linear programs need to be solved:

$$a \succ \sim^N b \Leftrightarrow \varepsilon_* \leq 0 \qquad (3.79)$$

where:

$$\varepsilon_* = \max \varepsilon$$
$$\left\{ \begin{array}{l} U\,(b) \geq U\,(a) + \varepsilon \\ E^{A^R} \end{array} \right. \qquad (3.80)$$

and:

$$a \succ \sim^P b \Leftrightarrow \varepsilon^* > 0 \qquad (3.81)$$

where:

$$\varepsilon^* = \max \varepsilon$$
$$\left\{ \begin{array}{l} U\,(a) \geq U\,(b) \\ E^{A^R}. \end{array} \right. \qquad (3.82)$$

Step 4: Calculate for each alternative $a \in A$ the indices of the worst class and best class, which are defined as follows:

(1) minimum class of possible assignment

$$L_P^U(a) = Max \left\{ \{1\} \cup \left\{ L(a^*) : \forall U \in U_{A^R} : U(a) \geq U(a^*) \right\} \right\}$$
$$= Max \left\{ \{1\} \cup \left\{ L(a^*) : a \succ \sim^N a^* \right\} \right\} \qquad (3.83)$$

(2) minimum class of necessary assignment

$$L_N^U(a) = Max \left\{ \{1\} \cup \left\{ L(a^*) : \exists U \in U_{A^R} : U(a) \geq U(a^*) \right\} \right\}$$
$$= Max \left\{ \{1\} \cup \left\{ L(a^*) : a \succ \sim^P a^* \right\} \right\} \qquad (3.84)$$

(3) maximum class of necessary assignment

$$R_N^U(a) = Min \left\{ \{p\} \cup \left\{ R(a^*) : \exists U \in U_{AR} : U(a^*) \geq U(a) \right\} \right\}$$
$$= Min \left\{ \{p\} \cup \left\{ R(a^*) : a^* \succ \sim^P a \right\} \right\} \tag{3.85}$$

(4) maximum class of possible assignment

$$R_P^U(a) = Min \left\{ \{p\} \cup \left\{ R(a^*) : \forall U \in U_{AR} : U(a^*) \geq U(a) \right\} \right\}$$
$$= Min \left\{ \{p\} \cup \left\{ R(a^*) : a^* \succ \sim^N a \right\} \right\} \tag{3.86}$$

Step 5: Assign to each alternative a to its *possible assignment* $C^P(a)$.

Step 6: Assign to each alternative a to its *necessary assignment* $C^N(a)$ in case $L_N^U(a) \leq R_N^U(a)$, otherwise $C^N(a) = \emptyset$.

3.4.3.2 UTADIS^{GMS}–GROUP

The robust ordinal regression model had been introduced to the case of group decision making [32], which refers to several decision-makers (DMs) cooperating to make a collective decision, namely UTA^{GMS}–GROUP and UTADIS^{GMS}–GROUP. The model required DMs to offer individual preference information, and then robust ordinal regression is used to develop the collective preference model and achieve a consensus solution.

This method can be divided into two phases. In the first phase, each DM $d_r \in D$ is considered individually, and the possible and the necessary assignments of his or her preference information are identified, which is consistent with the UTADIS^{GMS} method. In the second phase, spaces of consensus are investigated for subsets of DMs. This is achieved by introduction of a second level of certainty, which refers to how DMs confirm the specific result. In other words, it checks whether these necessary and possible assignments are provided by at least one or all DMs in D. Consequently, the method provides results of four different types:

(1) Necessary Necessary (N, N) consists of the necessary assignments which is confirmed by all DMs in D:

$$C_D^{N,N}(a) = \cap_{d_r \in D} C_{d_r}^N(a) \tag{3.87}$$

It represents assignments to classes which hold when considering simultaneously all compatible instances of a preference model for all DMs. Therefore, the Necessary Necessary results can be referred to as "absolutely sure" preference statements.

(2) Necessary Possible (N, P) consists of the necessary assignments which are confirmed by at least one DM in D:

$$C_D^{N,P}(a) = \cup_{d_r \in D} C_{d_r}^N(a) \tag{3.88}$$

This result can indicate the extents of certainty about the specific result expressed by any DM. In addition, it is important to investigate the subsets of DMs who agree or differ with respect to the given outcome. In this way, we are able to state whether the definite result is "almost sure," "sure on average," or "barely sure" against the set D. Such analysis may help a single DM to change his or her opinion in the following iterations to reach the consistent solution.

(3) Possible Necessary (P, N) consists of the possible assignments which is confirmed by all DMs in D:

$$C_D^{P,N}(a) = \cap_{d_r \in D} C_{d_r}^{P}(a) \qquad (3.89)$$

It reflects the full conviction of the set of DMs that a specific outcome may be true. Similarly, the Possible Necessary results can persuade some DMs to change the *possible* into *necessary* by enrichment of the Necessary Possible and Necessary Necessary results in the following iterations.

(4) Possible Possible (P, P) consists of the possible assignments which is confirmed by at least one DM in D:

$$C_D^{P,P}(a) = \cup_{d_r \in D} C_{d_r}^{P}(a) \qquad (3.90)$$

It refers to the most normal situation, which can be obtained when considering individually any compatible model of any DM. Notice that if Possible Possible relation or assignment is true, one needs to treat it as an indication with the lowest level of certainty, which is accounted for by the method.

In the UTADIS^{GMS}–GROUP method, there is a new iteration t when any DM $d_r \in D'$ adds, removes, or makes more precise exemplary assignments of reference alternatives. Obviously, for all $a \in A$, $C_{t,D'}^{N,N}(a)$, $C_{t,D'}^{P,N}(a)$, $C_{t,D'}^{N,P}(a)$, and $C_{t,D'}^{P,P}(a)$ can be calculated, and recommendations can be given for DMs that corresponds to the different confidence levels. Generally, for all $a \in A$ and $D' \in D$:

$$C_{D'}^{N,N}(a) \subseteq C_{D'}^{N}(a) \subseteq C_{D'}^{P}(a) \subseteq C_{D'}^{P,N}(a) \subseteq C_{D'}^{P,P}(a) \qquad (3.91)$$

Detailed proof can be found in [34].

3.4.3.3   *Illustrative example*

In this section, we illustrate how a decision-aiding process can be supported by UTADIS^{GMS}–GROUP in a simple example.

There is a sorting problem with a set of alternatives $A = \{a_1, a_2, \cdots, a_8\}$ and a criteria vector $G = \{g_1, g_2, g_3\}$. The problem is about sorting alternatives into five classes $C = \{C_1, C_2, C_3, C_4, C_5\}$, where C_{h+1} is preferred to C_h, $h = 1, 2, 3, 4$. The performance matrix is presented in Table 3.20.

The preference information provided by three decision makers $D = \{d_1, d_2, d_3\}$ is presented in Table 3.21. For example, d_1 provides assignment examples

TABLE 3.20 The performance matrix.

	a_1	a_2	a_3	a_4	a_5	a_6	a_7	a_8
g_1	2	6	7	5	5	8	4	6
g_2	3	7	9	3	5	9	2	8
g_3	4	5	3	1	2	6	5	3

TABLE 3.21 Preference information provided by three decision makers.

$A_{d_1}^R$	$C_L^{d_1}$	$C_R^{d_1}$	$A_{d_2}^R$	$C_L^{d_2}$	$C_R^{d_2}$	$A_{d_3}^R$	$C_L^{d_3}$	$C_R^{d_3}$
a_1	C_1	C_1	a_2	C_3	C_4	a_5	C_2	C_3
a_3	C_4	C_4	a_5	C_2	C_2	a_7	C_1	C_2
a_5	C_2	C_3	a_6	C_4	C_5	a_8	C_4	C_4

for actions from the reference set $A_{d_1}^R = \{a_1, a_3, a_5\}$ and d_1 feels confident that a_1 should be assigned to C_1, i.e., $a_1 \to [C_1, C_1]$, while a_5 is not worse than class C_2 and not better than class C_3, i.e., $a_5 \to [C_2, C_3]$. Obviously, the set of compatible value functions is not empty.

Calculation results of necessary and possible relations for all alternative according to d_1 are given in Tables 3.22 and 3.23. "T" and "F" stand for true and false of the relation $\succ \sim^P$ or $\succ \sim^N$, respectively, whereas "-" means that the relation does not need to be computed for this pair of nonreference alternatives, because the result of necessary and possible assignments is irrelevant to it.

TABLE 3.22 Matrices of possible relation $\succ \sim^P$ between alternatives.

	a_1	a_2	a_3	a_4	a_5	a_6	a_7	a_8
a_1	T	F	F	T	T	F	T	F
a_2	T	T	T	–	T	–	–	–
a_3	T	T	T	T	T	F	T	T
a_4	T	–	F	T	T	–	–	–
a_5	T	F	F	T	T	F	T	F
a_6	T	–	T	–	T	T	–	–
a_7	T	–	F	–	T	–	T	–
a_8	T	–	T	–	T	–	–	T

We calculate the boundary assignment indices following rules (3.84)–(3.86). The computational process of possible and necessary assignments of a_4 is as

TABLE 3.23 Matrices of necessary relation $\succ \sim^N$ between alternatives.

	a_1	a_2	a_3	a_4	a_5	a_6	a_7	a_8
a_1	T	F	F	T	F	F	F	F
a_2	T	T	F	–	T	–	–	–
a_3	T	T	T	T	T	F	T	T
a_4	T	–	F	T	F	–	–	–
a_5	T	F	F	T	T	F	T	F
a_6	T	–	T	–	T	T	–	–
a_7	T	–	F	–	F	–	T	–
a_8	T	–	F	–	T	–	–	T

follows:

$$L^P_{d_1}(a_4) = \max\{1, L_{d_1}(a_1) = 1\} = 1$$
$$R^P_{d_1}(a_4) = \min\{5, R_{d_1}(a_1) = 1, R_{d_1}(a_3) = 4, R_{d_1}(a_5) = 3\} = 1$$
$$L^N_{d_1}(a_4) = \max\{1, L_{d_1}(a_1) = 1, L_{d_1}(a_5) = 2\} = 2 \tag{3.92}$$
$$R^N_{d_1}(a_4) = \min\{5, R_{d_1}(a_1) = 1, R_{d_1}(a_3) = 4, R_{d_1}(a_5) = 3\} = 1$$

In this case, $L^N_{d_1}(a_4) > R^N_{d_1}(a_4)$, and consequently, $C^N_{d_1}(a_4) = \emptyset$. The resulting possible and necessary assignments for the rest of the alternatives in set A are given in Table 3.24.

TABLE 3.24 Possible and necessary assignments based on preference information provided by d_1.

	$L^P_{d_1}$	$R^P_{d_1}$	$L^N_{d_1}$	$R^N_{d_1}$
a_1	C_1	C_1	C_1	C_1
a_2	C_2	C_4	C_4	C_4
a_3	C_4	C_4	C_4	C_4
a_4	C_1	C_1		
a_5	C_2	C_3	C_2	C_3
a_6	C_4	C_5	C_4	C_5
a_7	C_1	C_3		
a_8	C_2	C_4	C_4	C_4

In the same way, for every DM d_r in D, we can calculate the possible and necessary assignments based on his or her provided preference information. The results are shown in Tables 3.25 and 3.26.

Then, the preference model provided by every d_r can be combined by the framework of UTADIS^{GMS}–GROUP to achieve a conjunct solution. In other

TABLE 3.25 Possible and necessary assignments based on preference information provided by d_2.

	$L_{d_2}^P$	$R_{d_2}^P$	$L_{d_2}^N$	$R_{d_2}^N$
a_1	C_1	C_2	C_2	C_2
a_2	C_3	C_4	C_3	C_4
a_3	C_3	C_5	C_4	C_4
a_4	C_1	C_2	C_2	C_2
a_5	C_2	C_2	C_2	C_2
a_6	C_4	C_5	C_4	C_5
a_7	C_1	C_2	C_1	C_2
a_8	C_2	C_4		

TABLE 3.26 Possible and necessary assignments based on preference information provided by d_3.

	$L_{d_1}^P$	$R_{d_1}^P$	$L_{d_1}^N$	$R_{d_1}^N$
a_1	C_1	C_2	C_1	C_2
a_2	C_4	C_5	C_4	C_4
a_3	C_4	C_5	C_4	C_5
a_4	C_1	C_2	C_1	C_2
a_5	C_2	C_3	C_2	C_3
a_6	C_2	C_5	C_4	C_5
a_7	C_1	C_2	C_1	C_2
a_8	C_4	C_4	C_4	C_4

words, the confidence levels of all decision makers' judgment policies will be computed as rules (3.88)–(3.90). The results are provided in Table 3.27.

TABLE 3.27 Necessary Necessary and Possible Necessary assignments.

$C_D^{N,N}$	Alternatives	$C_D^{P,N}$	Alternatives
C_1	$\emptyset$	C_1	a_1, a_4, a_7
C_2	a_5	C_2	a_5, a_7
C_3	$\emptyset$	C_3	$\emptyset$
C_4	a_2, a_3, a_6	C_4	a_2, a_3, a_6, a_8
C_5	a_6	C_5	a_6

It should be noted that in the initial iterations, preference information is poor. Usually several empty sets of necessary assignments exist. In addition, some alternatives may be assigned in multiple groups due to the inaccuracy of preference information. In that case, the result is too general to be decisive enough.

However, this approach is intended to be used interactively, so that the DMs could either add some new assignments of reference alternatives or revise the previous judgments. In the process of iteration, the preference information provided by a group of DMs will achieve consensus and robustness, and finally aid decision making.

3.5 ELECTRE TRI: a sorting method based on ELECTREE

3.5.1 ELECTRE III

In recent decades, the ELECTRE method [35] has become a very popular research field of MCDM which refuses to the total compensation among the performances of alternatives. In 1966, the first ELECTRE method was proposed [36]; during the following 20 years, ELECTRE II, ELECTRE III, ELECTRE IV, and ELECTRE TRI were developed successively [37].

In this section, the outranking method ELECTRE III [38] is introduced, which was proposed for the sake of ranking alternatives from the best to the worst based on pseudo-criteria. In this method, the key point is the pairwise comparisons between every two alternatives on each criterion.

The procedure is described in detail as follows.

Step 1: Fundamental definition.

We define the set of alternatives as $A = \{a, b, ..., n\}$ and the set of criteria as $G = \{g_1, g_2, ..., g_m\}$ with the weight $W = (w_1, w_2, ..., w_m)^T$. The performance of alternative a on criteria can be evaluated as $g(a) = \{g_1(a), g_2(a), ..., g_m(a)\}$.

In this method, the value of $g_j(a)$ is not exact because of the imprecision, indetermination, or uncertainty:

(1) Imprecision: there is difficulty of determination even without random fluctuation.

(2) Indetermination: the value is obtained from the relatively arbitrary choice among several possible definitions.

(3) Uncertainty: the value may vary over time.

To handle the problem, we set the indifference threshold q_j and preference threshold p_j on each criterion g_j to establish the set of pseudo-criteria. The indifference threshold denotes the maximum difference value between two alternatives which is considered as no difference, and the preference threshold denotes the minimum difference value between them which is considered as strong difference.

Step 2: Calculate the threshold value for each alternative.

The definition of threshold value should satisfy the following conditions:

Condition 1:

$$g(a) > g(b)$$
$$\rightarrow g(a) + q(g(a)) > g(b) + q(g(b)),$$
$$g(a) + p(g(a)) > g(b) + p(g(b))$$

Condition 2: for all criteria G, $p(g) > q(g)$.

The threshold value can be calculated with the subsequent equations, where the values of α and β can be determined in three ways:

$$p_j(g_j(a)) = \alpha_p + \beta_p g_j(a) \qquad (3.93)$$

$$q_j(g_j(a)) = \alpha_q + \beta_q g_j(a) \qquad (3.94)$$

(1) $\beta = 0$ and α has to be determined: constant.
(2) $\alpha = 0$ and β has to be determined: proportional to $g_j(a)$.
(3) Both α and β have to be determined: combine the two above.

If $g(a) \geq g(b)$, there are three relations between two alternatives:

$$g(a) > g(b) + p(g(b)) \Leftrightarrow a\ P\ b$$

$$g(b) + q(g(b)) < g(a) \leq g(b) + p(g(b)) \Leftrightarrow a\ Q\ b$$

$$g(b) \leq g(a) \leq g(b) + q(g(b)) \Leftrightarrow a\ I\ b$$

where P refers to strong preference of a on b, Q means weak preference, and I means indifference.

Step 3: Calculate the concordance index and discordance index.

With regard to two arbitrary alternatives a and b, the concordance index $c(a,\ b) \in [0,\ 1]$ expresses the strength of the affirmation "alternative a at least as good as b," and it is computed by:

$$c(a, b) = \frac{1}{W} \sum_{j=1}^{m} w_j c_j(a, b) \qquad (3.95)$$

$$W = \sum_{j=1}^{m} w_j \qquad (3.96)$$

We can determine the outranking degree $c_j(a, b)$ with the following two rules:

$$c_j(a, b) = 0, \ if \ g_j(b) - g_j(a) > p_j(g_j(a))$$

$$0 < c_j(a, b) \leq 1, \ if \ q_j(g_j(a)) < g_j(b) - g_j(a) \leq p_j(g_j(a))$$

$$c_j(a, b) = 1, \ if \ g_j(b) - g_j(a) \leq q_j(g_j(a))$$

where $q_j(g_j(a)) < g_j(b) - g_j(a) \leq p_j(g_j(a))$.

Then we obtain the discordance index $d_j(a, b) \in [0,\ 1]$, which refers to the strength of the opposition to the affirmation "alternative a is at least as good as b." In the following equations, the veto threshold v_j defines the minimum threshold of difference between two alternatives having a total different preference.

$$v_j(g_j(a)) = \alpha_v + \beta_v g_j(a) \qquad (3.97)$$

$$d_j(a, b) = 0, \ if \ g_j(b) - g_j(a) \le p_j(g_j(a))$$
$$0 < d_j(a, b) \le 1, \ if \ p_j(g_j(a)) < g_j(b) - g_j(a) \le v_j(g_j(a))$$
$$d_j(a, b) = 1, \ if \ g_j(b) - g_j(a) > v_j(g_j(a))$$

Step 4: Obtain the degree of outranking.

The outranking degree $S(a, b)$ is defined as:

$$S(a, b) = \begin{cases} c(a, b), \ if \ \forall j, \ d_j(a, b) \le c(a, b) \\ c(a, b) \times \prod_{j \in J(a,b)} \frac{1 - d_j(a,b)}{1 - c(a,b)}, \ otherwise \end{cases} \quad (3.98)$$

where $J(a, b)$ refers to the set of criteria where $d_j(a, b) > c(a, b)$.

Step 5: Exploitation ranking procedure.

We should construct complete preorders Z_1 and Z_2 by the descending distillation procedure and ascending distillation procedure, respectively.

In the descending distillation procedure, determine the maximum value of the credibility index λ_{max} and set $\lambda^* = \lambda_{max} - (0.3 - 0.15\lambda)$. Then determine the λ-length and λ-weakness of each alternative. The former refers to the number of alternatives to which the alternative is λ-preferred with $\lambda = \lambda^*$. The latter refers to the number of alternatives which are λ-preferred to the alternative with $\lambda = \lambda^*$. Now we can obtain the qualification which is its λ-length minus its λ-weakness. The set of alternatives with the largest qualification is defined as the first distillate D_1. If D_1 has more than one alternative, repeat the process with D_1 until all alternatives have been classified. Then continue with the original set minus D1 and repeat until all alternatives have been classified.

In the ascending distillation procedure, Z_2 can be obtained in the similar way as in the descending distillation procedure. The only point that needs to be mentioned is that the set of alternatives having the lowest qualification forms the first distillate.

The final order can be obtained with $Z = \frac{1}{2}(Z_1 + Z_2)$.

3.5.2 ELECTRE TRI and extensions

3.5.2.1 ELECTRE TRI

Based on the ELECTRE III method, the ELECTRE TRI method [39] was proposed to assign alternatives to completely ordered categories.

The description of ELECTRE TRI is presented as follows.

Step 1: Problem definition.

On the basis of the fundamental definition in ELECTRE III, we further define the set of ordered categories C_i, $i = 1, \cdots, k$, where C_k denotes the best (highest) category and C_1 denotes the worst (lowest) one.

The k category can be defined by $(k-1)$ reference profiles r_i, $i = 1, \cdots, k - 1$, where r_i refers to the upper limit of C_{i+1} and the lower limit of C_i (see Fig. 3.30).

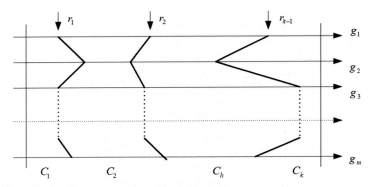

FIGURE 3.30 Reference profiles and categories in ELECTRE TRI.

Step 2: Calculate the concordance index and discordance index.

With the preference threshold $p_j(r_i)$ and indifference threshold $q_j(r_i)$, the concordance index can be obtained (see Fig. 3.31):

$$c_j(a, r_i) = \frac{p_j(r_i) - [g_j(r_i) - g_j(a)]}{p_j(r_i) - q_j(r_i)} \tag{3.99}$$

$$\begin{cases} \textit{If } g_j(a) < g_j(r_i) - p_j(r_i), \textit{ then } c_j(a, r_i) = 0 \\ \textit{If } g_j(r_i) - p_j(r_i) < g_j(a) \leq g_j(r_i) - q_j(r_i), \textit{ then } 0 < c_j(a, r_i) \leq 1 \\ \textit{If } g_j(a) > g_j(r_i) - q_j(r_i), \textit{ then } c_j(a, r_i) = 1 \end{cases}$$

$$\tag{3.100}$$

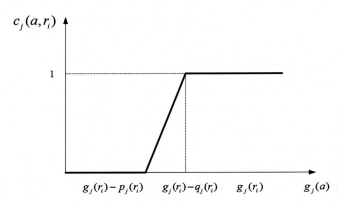

FIGURE 3.31 The value of the concordance index.

For the comparison of the alternative and reference profiles on all criteria, the global concordance index needs to be calculated:

$$C(a, r_i) = \frac{\sum\limits_{j=1}^{m} w_j \cdot c_j(a, r_i)}{\sum\limits_{j=1}^{m} w_j} \tag{3.101}$$

The discordance index can be obtained in a similar way with veto threshold $v_j(r_i)$ (see Fig. 3.32):

$$d_j(a, r_i) = \frac{v_j(r_i) - g_j(a) - p_j(r_i)}{v_j(r_i) - p_j(r_i)} \tag{3.102}$$

$$\begin{cases} If\ g_j(a) > g_j(r_i) - p_j(r_i),\ then\ d_j(a, r_i) = 0 \\ If\ g_j(r_i) - v_j(r_i) < g_j(a) \leq g_j(r_i) - p_j(r_i),\ then\ 0 < d_j(a, r_i) \leq 1 \\ If\ g_j(a) \leq g_j(r_i) - v_j(r_i),\ then\ d_j(a, r_i) = 1 \end{cases}$$

$$\tag{3.103}$$

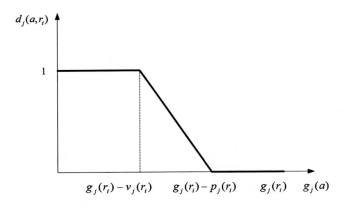

FIGURE 3.32 The value of the discordance index.

Step 3: Obtain the credibility index.

The credibility index $\sigma_s(a, r_i)$ refers to the strength of the affirmation "alternative a outranks reference profile r_j on all criteria." To calculate it, we should further define the $\bar{G}(a, r_i) = \{\forall j = 1, \cdots, m : d_j(a, r_i) > c_j(a, r_i)\}$ as the set of the criteria where the discordance index value is greater than the global concordance value. If $\bar{G}(a, r_i)$ is empty, the credibility index is $c_j(a, r_i)$. Otherwise, it can be calculated as follows:

$$\sigma_s(a, r_i) = \begin{cases} C(a, r_i),\ if\ \bar{G}(a, r_i) = \emptyset \\ C(a, r_i) \cdot \prod\limits_{j \in G} \frac{1 - d_j(a, r_i)}{1 - C(a, r_i)},\ if\ \bar{G}(a, r_i) \neq \emptyset \end{cases} \tag{3.104}$$

Step 4: Determine the relations between the alternative and the preference profile.

With the credibility index, the outranking relations (S) can be determined.

$$\sigma_s(a, r_i) \geq \lambda \Leftrightarrow aSr_i$$

where $\lambda \in [0.5, 1]$ refers to the outranking cut level.

Then we can determine the preference (P), indifference (I), and incomparability (R) relations between a and r_i.

$$aIr_i \Leftrightarrow \quad áSr_i \text{ and } \quad r_iSa$$
$$aPr_i \Leftrightarrow \quad aSr_i \text{ and no } r_iSa$$
$$r_iPa \Leftrightarrow no\, aSr_i \text{ and } \quad r_iSa$$
$$aRr_i \Leftrightarrow no\, aSr_i \text{ and no } r_iSa$$

Step 5: Assign the alternative to a category.

With regard to the relations between a and r_i, there are two assignment rules:

(1) If aPr_i and $r_{i+1}Pa$ or aIr_{i+1}, a_i should be assigned to C_{i+1}.

(2) If aPr_i and $aRr_{i+1}, aRr_{i+2}, \cdots, aRr_{i+k}, r_{i+k+1}Ra$, a_i should be sorted to C_{i+1} with a pessimistic view or to C_{i+k+1} with an optimistic view.

Throughout these procedures, we can find that the parameter λ defined by decision makers can influence the sorting result to some extent by changing the relations between alternatives and reference profiles. In addition, information should be provided for the preference thresholds, indifference thresholds, veto thresholds, and the weights of criteria.

To illuminate the procedures of ELECTRE TRI, here is a simple numerical example. In this case, there are five alternatives assigned to four categories defined by three limiting profiles based on five criteria. The performances of alternatives and limiting profiles are presented in Tables 3.28 and 3.29. The weight of criteria, the preference threshold, indifference threshold, and veto threshold are determined (see Table 3.30).

To ensure the accuracy and the confidence of the result, we set $\lambda=0.75$. After calculation, the concordance index, discordance index, and credibility index are obtained (see Tables 3.31–3.35). Eventually, with the assignment rules, the final sorting results in a pessimistic view and optimistic view are presented in Table 3.36.

3.5.2.2 ELECTRE TRI-C

On the basis of ELECTRE TRI, ELECTRE TRI-C [40] is a method first proposed in 2009 for sorting problems where the set of completely ordered categories is defined by a single characteristic reference profile defined as b_h, $h = 1, \cdots, k$. The assignment result is a range of successive categories of each alternative based on the outranking credibility index λ.

There are two joint rules for assignment:

TABLE 3.28 The performances of alternatives.

A	g_1	g_2	g_3	g_4	g_5
a_1	90	30	50	40	80
a_2	90	80	70	80	40
a_3	80	70	45	60	30
a_4	50	20	30	50	80
a_5	50	20	30	20	10

TABLE 3.29 The performances of limiting profiles.

R	g_1	g_2	g_3	g_4	g_5
r_1	80	85	90	70	65
r_2	75	70	78	50	45
r_3	40	55	48	35	30

TABLE 3.30 The values of weights and thresholds determined.

	g_1	g_2	g_3	g_4	g_5
q	5	5	5	5	5
p	10	10	10	10	10
v	30	30	30	30	30
w	1	1	1	1	1

TABLE 3.31 The concordance index $c(a, r)$.

	g_1	g_2	g_3	g_4	g_5	$C(a, r)$
$c(a_1, r_3)$	1	0	0	0	1	0.4
$c(a_2, r_3)$	1	1	0	1	0	0.6
$c(a_3, r_3)$	1	0	0	0	0	0.2
$c(a_4, r_3)$	0	0	0	0	0	0
$c(a_5, r_3)$	1	0	0	0	1	0.4
$c(a_1, r_2)$	1	1	0.4	1	1	0.88
$c(a_2, r_2)$	1	1	0	1	0	0.6
$c(a_3, r_2)$	0	0	0	1	1	0.4
$c(a_4, r_2)$	0	0	0	0	0	0
$c(a_5, r_2)$	1	0	1	1	1	0.8
$c(a_1, r_1)$	1	0	0	0	1	0.4
$c(a_2, r_1)$	1	1	1	1	1	1
$c(a_3, r_1)$	1	1	1	1	1	1
$c(a_4, r_1)$	1	0	0	1	1	0.6
$c(a_5, r_1)$	1	0	0	0	0	0.2

TABLE 3.32 The concordance index $c(r, a)$.

	g_1	g_2	g_3	g_4	g_5	$C(r, a)$
$c(r_3, a_1)$	1	1	1	1	0	0.8
$c(r_3, a_2)$	0	1	1	0	1	0.6
$c(r_3, a_3)$	1	1	1	1	1	1
$c(r_3, a_4)$	1	1	1	1	0	0.8
$c(r_3, a_5)$	1	1	1	1	1	1
$c(r_2, a_1)$	1	1	1	1	0	0.8
$c(r_2, a_2)$	0	0	1	0	1	0.4
$c(r_2, a_3)$	1	1	1	0	1	0.8
$c(r_2, a_4)$	1	1	1	1	1	1
$c(r_2, a_5)$	0	1	1	1	0	0.6
$c(r_1, a_1)$	0	1	1	1	0	0.6
$c(r_1, a_2)$	0	0	0	0	0	0
$c(r_1, a_3)$	0	0	1	0	1	0.4
$c(r_1, a_4)$	0	1	1	0	0	0.4
$c(r_1, a_5)$	0	1	1	1	1	0.8

TABLE 3.33 The discordance index $d(a, r)$.

	g_1	g_2	g_3	g_4	g_5
$d(a_1, r_3)$	0	1	1	1	0
$d(a_2, r_3)$	0	0	0.5	0	0.75
$d(a_3, r_3)$	0	0.25	1	0	1
$d(a_4, r_3)$	1	1	1	0.5	0
$d(a_5, r_3)$	1	1	1	1	1
$d(a_1, r_2)$	0	1	0.9	0	0
$d(a_2, r_2)$	0	0	0	0	0
$d(a_3, r_2)$	0	0	1	0	0.25
$d(a_4, r_2)$	0.75	1	1	0	0
$d(a_5, r_2)$	0.75	1	1	1	1
$d(a_1, r_1)$	0	0.75	0	0	0
$d(a_2, r_1)$	0	0	0	0	0
$d(a_3, r_1)$	0	0	0	0	0
$d(a_4, r_1)$	0	1	0.4	0	0
$d(a_5, r_1)$	0	1	0.4	0.25	0.5

(1) Descending rule:

Select an outranking credibility index $\lambda \in [0.5, 1]$ and then decrease h from $(k + 1)$ until the first value h which satisfies $\sigma(a, b_h) \geq \lambda$.

(1) For $h = k$, C_k is considered as a possible category for alternative a.

(2) For $0 < h < k$, if $\rho(a, b_h) > \rho(a, b_{h+1})$, C_h can be perceived as a possible sorting result; otherwise, we select C_{h+1}.

TABLE 3.34 The discordance index $d(r, a)$.

	g_1	g_2	g_3	g_4	g_5
$d(r_3, a_1)$	0	0	0	0	0.25
$d(r_3, a_2)$	0	0	0	0	0
$d(r_3, a_3)$	0	0	0	0	0
$d(r_3, a_4)$	0	0	0	0	0.25
$d(r_3, a_5)$	0	0	0	0	0
$d(r_2, a_1)$	0	0	0	0	1
$d(r_2, a_2)$	0.25	0	0	1	0
$d(r_2, a_3)$	0	0	0	0	0
$d(r_2, a_4)$	0	0	0	0	1
$d(r_2, a_5)$	0	0	0	0	0
$d(r_1, a_1)$	1	0	0	0	1
$d(r_1, a_2)$	1	0.75	0.6	1	0
$d(r_1, a_3)$	1	0.25	0	0.75	0
$d(r_1, a_4)$	0	0	0	0.25	1
$d(r_1, a_5)$	0	0	0	0	0

TABLE 3.35 The credibility index $\sigma(a, r)$ and $\sigma(r, a)$.

	$\sigma(a, r)$		$\sigma(r, a)$
$\sigma(a_1, r_3)$	0	$\sigma(r_3, a_1)$	0.8
$\sigma(a_2, r_3)$	0.375	$\sigma(r_3, a_2)$	0.6
$\sigma(a_3, r_3)$	0	$\sigma(r_3, a_3)$	1
$\sigma(a_4, r_3)$	0	$\sigma(r_3, a_4)$	0.8
$\sigma(a_5, r_3)$	0	$\sigma(r_3, a_5)$	1
$\sigma(a_1, r_2)$	0	$\sigma(r_2, a_1)$	0
$\sigma(a_2, r_2)$	0.88	$\sigma(r_2, a_2)$	0
$\sigma(a_3, r_2)$	0	$\sigma(r_2, a_3)$	0.8
$\sigma(a_4, r_2)$	0	$\sigma(r_2, a_4)$	0
$\sigma(a_5, r_2)$	0	$\sigma(r_2, a_5)$	1
$\sigma(a_1, r_1)$	0.8	$\sigma(r_1, a_1)$	0
$\sigma(a_2, r_1)$	1	$\sigma(r_1, a_2)$	0
$\sigma(a_3, r_1)$	1	$\sigma(r_1, a_3)$	0
$\sigma(a_4, r_1)$	0	$\sigma(r_1, a_4)$	0
$\sigma(a_5, r_1)$	0	$\sigma(r_1, a_5)$	0.8

(3) For $h = 1$, we select C_1 as a possible category for a.

(2) Ascending rule:

Select an outranking credibility index $\lambda \in [0.5, 1]$ and then increase h from 0 until the first value h which satisfies $\sigma(b_h, a) \geq \lambda$.

(1) For $h = 1$, choose C_1 as a possible category for a.

TABLE 3.36 The assignment result.

A	Pessimistic category	Optimistic category
a_1	C_3	C_2
a_2	C_2	C_1
a_3	C_3	C_3
a_4	C_4	C_2
a_5	C_4	C_4

(2) For $1 < h < (k + 1)$, if $rho(a, b_h) > \rho(a, b_{h-1})$, select C_h as a possible class; otherwise, select C_{h-1}.

(3) For $h = (k + 1)$, select C_k as a possible result.

In the two rules above, the selecting function $\rho(a, b_h)$ is aimed to select a suitable sorting result for a between two consecutive categories.

$$\rho(a, b_h) = \min \{s(a, b_h), s(b_h, a)\} \tag{3.105}$$

Both the descending rule and ascending rule provide one single possible category for alternative a. We can make use of them jointly to determine the highest possible category and the lowest possible category. Then the range of the possible assignment result can be obtained. The two possible limits of assignment can be the same.

To receive the final exact category, the decision maker can choose:

(1) a single category when the two possible categories from two different rules are the same;

(2) one of the two possible categories when the two selected categories are consecutive; or

(3) one of the two possible categories or one of the intermediate categories when the two categories are not consecutive.

3.5.2.3 ELECTRE TRI-nC

In 2012, on the basis of ELECTRE TRI-C, a novel sorting method ELECTRE TRI-nC [41] was developed with each category characterized by several reference profiles, which can assist decision makers in defining the categories in a collaborative decision-making process.

The ELECTRE TRI-nC assignment procedure also consists of two conjoint assignment rules (descending rule and ascending rule) with a categorical credibility index instead of a credibility index as in ELECTRE TRI-C. The categorical credibility index $\sigma(\{a\}, B_h)$, which refers to the categorical outranking degrees of the alternative a over the set of reference profiles $B_h = \{b_h^r, r = 1, \cdots, m_h\}$ of C_h, can be calculated using the following equation:

$$\sigma(\{a\}, B_h) = \max_{r=1,\cdots,m_h} \{\sigma(a, b_h^r)\} \tag{3.106}$$

Similarly, we can obtain the categorical credibility index $\sigma(B_h, \{a\})$ as follows:

$$\sigma(B_h, \{a\}) = \max_{s=1,\cdots,m_h} \left\{ \sigma(b_h^s, a) \right\} \qquad (3.107)$$

There are four axioms of the categorical credibility index:

- If $B_h = \{b_h^1\}$, then for any alternative a, $\sigma(\{a\}, B_h) = \sigma(\{a\}, b_h^1)$.
- If $B_h = \{b_h^1\}$, then for any alternative a, $\sigma(a, B_h) = \sigma(b_h^1, a)$.
- If $|B_h| \geq 2$ and there exists $b_h^r \in B_h$ such that $\sigma(a, b_h^r) \leq \sigma(\{a\}, B_h)$, then for any alternative a, $\sigma(\{a\}, B_h \setminus b_h^r) = \sigma(\{a\}, B_h)$.
- If $|B_h| \geq 2$ and there exists $b_h^r \in B_h$ such that $\sigma(b_h^r, a) \leq \sigma(B_h, \{a\})$, then for any alternative a, $\sigma(B_h \setminus b_h^r, \{a\}) = \sigma(B_h, \{a\})$.

(1) Descending rule:

Select an outranking credibility index $\lambda \in [0.5, 1]$ and then decrease h from $(k + 1)$ until the first value h which satisfies $\sigma = (\{a\}, B_h) \geq \lambda$. We consider C_h as the descending preselected category.

(1) For $h = k$, C_k is considered as a possible category for alternative a.

(2) For $0 < h < k$, if $rho(\{a\}, B_h) > \rho(\{a\}, b_{h+1})$, C_h can be perceived as a possible sorting result; otherwise, we select C_{h+1}.

(3) For $h = 1$, we select C_1 as a possible category for a.

(2) Ascending rule:

Select an outranking credibility index $\lambda \in [0.5, 1]$ and then increase h from 0 until the first value h which satisfies $\sigma(b_h, \{a\}) \geq \lambda$. We consider C_h as the ascending preselected category.

(1) For $h = 1$, choose C_1 as a possible category for a.

(2) For $1 < h < (k+1)$, if $\rho(\{a\}, B_h) > \rho(\{a\}, B_{h-1})$, select C_h as a possible class; otherwise, select C_{h-1}.

(3) For $h = (k + 1)$, select C_k as a possible result.

In both joint rules above, the following selecting function is suggested to apply:

$$\rho(\{a\}, B_h) = \min \left\{ \sigma(\{a\}, B_h), \sigma(B_h, \{a\}) \right\} \qquad (3.108)$$

The ELECTRE TRI-nC method also provides a range of categories of a with the lowest category and highest category. There are again three possible cases of the result, as follows:

(1) one single category if the two possible categories are the same;

(2) two categories if the two possible categories are consecutive; or

(3) a range of more than two categories if the two possible categories are not consecutive.

3.6 TOPSIS-Sort: a sorting method based on TOPSIS

3.6.1 TOPSIS

TOPSIS (Technique of Order Preference Similarity to the Ideal Solution) is one of the most popular MCDM methods [42]. Used for ranking problems, the TOPSIS method only needs a small amount of input from users, and its output is easy to understand. The only parameter that requires human participation is the weights of criteria. Before introducing the algorithm, some notations that will be used here are as follows.

Define $A = (a_1, a_2, ..., a_m)^T$ as a set of m alternatives and let $G = (g_1, g_2, ..., g_n)^T$ be the set of n criteria. $W = (w_1, w_2, ..., w_n)^T$ is a vector of weights with n elements, where w_j is the weight of criterion g_j. G^+ and G^- are the subsets of beneficial and cost criteria, respectively. Let $a_{i,j}$ be the performance of alternative a_i under criterion g_j.

The TOPSIS method includes six steps.

Step 1: Normalize the decision matrix $X = [a_{i,j}]_{m \times n}$, which represents the alternatives' performances of different criteria. The purpose of this step is to unify dimensions (e.g., years, centimeters). There are several normalization methods that are suitable for TOPSIS:

(1) The distributive normalization. The formula is defined as follows:

$$r_{i,j} = \frac{a_{i,j}}{\sqrt{\sum_{i=1}^{m} a_{i,j}^2}}, i = 1, 2, ..., m, j = 1, 2, ..., n. \tag{3.109}$$

(2) The ideal normalization. For the beneficial criteria, each performance is divided by the highest value in each column of $X = [a_{i,j}]_{m \times n}$. As for the cost criteria, each performance is divided by the lowest score in each column of X.

$$r_{i,j} = \frac{x_{i,j}}{u_j^+}, i = 1, 2, ..., n, j = 1, 2, ..., m. \tag{3.110}$$

$$r_{i,j} = \frac{x_{i,j}}{u_j^-}, i = 1, 2, ..., n, j = 1, 2, ..., m. \tag{3.111}$$

where u_i^+ and u_i^- are the highest value and lowest value, respectively, in the jth column of X.

After normalization, a new decision matrix $R = [r_{i,j}]_{m \times n}$ is obtained.

Step 2: Calculate the decision matrix $V = [v_{i,j}]_{m \times n}$.

$$v_{i,j} = w_j \cdot r_{i,j} \tag{3.112}$$

where $\sum_{j=1}^{n} w_j = 1$.

Step 3: Determine the ideal and antiideal solutions. There are three disparate ways of defining these solutions.

(1) The ideal solutions are the best performance on each criterion of the decision matrix V. Correspondingly, the antiideal solutions are the worst performance on each criterion of V.

$$v^+ = [v_1^+, v_2^+, ..., v_n^+], v_j^+ = \begin{cases} \max_i v_{i,j}, g_j \in G^+ \\ \min_i v_{i,j}, g_j \in G^- \end{cases} \quad (3.113)$$

$$v^- = [v_1^-, v_2^-, ..., v_n^-], v_j^- = \begin{cases} \min_i v_{i,j}, g_j \in G^+ \\ \max_i v_{i,j}, g_j \in G^- \end{cases} \quad (3.114)$$

where v^+ and v^- represent the ideal solution vector and antiideal solution vector, respectively.

(2) If the action a of the decision problem is not considered in the definition, the ideal and antiideal solutions could be assumed as $v^+ = [1, 1, ..., 1]$ and $v^- = [0, 0, ..., 0]$.

(3) Decision makers (DMs) could choose the ideal solutions and antiideal solutions by themselves. The value of ideal solutions and antiideal solutions in each criterion must be between the value calculated with both methods mentioned above. It should be noted that this method is not commonly used because it requires the users to input data.

Step 4: Calculate the Euclidian distances between each alternative for the ideal and antiideal solutions.

$$d_{a_i}^+ = \sqrt{\sum_{j=1}^{n} (v_{i,j} - v_j^+)^2}, i = 1, 2, ..., m. \quad (3.115)$$

$$d_{a_i}^- = \sqrt{\sum_{j=1}^{n} (v_{i,j} - v_j^-)^2}, i = 1, 2, ..., m. \quad (3.116)$$

where $d_{a_i}^+$ and $d_{a_i}^-$ are the Euclidian distances of each alternative from the ideal and anti-ideal solutions. This method of calculating distances is the most popular and practical.

Step 5: Calculate the relative closeness coefficient of each alternative from the ideal solution on the basis of the Euclidian distances obtained above.

$$Cl(a_i) = \frac{d_{a_i}^-}{d_{a_i}^+ + d_{a_i}^-}, i = 1, 2, ..., m, \quad (3.117)$$

where $Cl(a_i) \in [0, 1]$ is the closeness coefficient. If the alternative a_i is close to the ideal solution, $Cl(a_i)$ is close to 1, whereas if the alternative a_i is close to the antiideal solution, $Cl(a_i)$ is close to 0.

Step 6: Rank the alternatives in descending order according to the closeness coefficient.

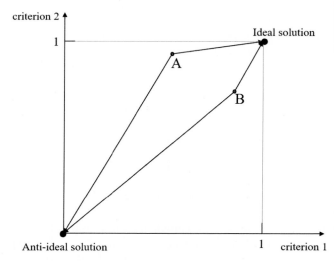

FIGURE 3.33 A simple example of TOPSIS.

The basic idea of TOPSIS is that the best solution is the solution with the shortest distance from the ideal solution and the longest distance from the anti-ideal solution [43,44].

In Fig. 3.33, in the TOPSIS method, the alternative B is a better solution than A. This is because in the case that both criteria are to be maximized, B is closer to the ideal solution and farther from the antiideal solution than A is.

3.6.2 TOPSIS-Sort and extensions

To solve sorting problems, in 2016, Sabokbar, Hosseini, Banaitis, and Banaitiene presented the TOPSIS-Sort approach [45]. However, unsolved problems remain in the TOPSIS-Sort method. For example, ranking reversal may occur. For example, if some external alternatives are added, the allocation result of specific alternatives may change. In addition, working with characteristic profiles is more practical than determining boundary profiles. For these reasons, in 2020, the TOPSIS-Sort-B method and the TOPSIS-Sort-C method were proposed to address the remaining problems [46].

3.6.2.1 TOPSIS-Sort

There is an assumption that should be considered prior to applying the TOPSIS-Sort method.

Assumption 1: Classes are defined in advance, and the classes are ordered by preference as follows:

$$C_1 \succ C_2 \succ ... \succ C_q \tag{3.118}$$

Let $C = (C_1, C_2, ..., C_q)^T$ be a set of q predefined ordered classes and $P = (P_1, P_2, ..., P_q)^T$ be a set of q profiles. Define $P_k = (\overline{P_k}, \underline{P_k})$, among which $\overline{P_k}$ is the upper limit of class C_k and $\underline{P_k}$ is the lower limit of class C_k. Refer to Section 3.6.1 for definitions of other symbols.

Step 1: Establish the decision matrix $X = [a_{i,j}]_{m \times n}$.

Step 2: Determine a set of q profiles $P = \{(\overline{P_1}, \underline{P_1}), (\overline{P_2}, \underline{P_2}), ..., (\overline{P_q}, \underline{P_q})\}$.

Step 3: Add the profiles to the decision matrix to obtain $M = [M_{i,j}]_{(m+q-1) \times n}$.

Step 4: Normalize the decision matrix M by Eq. (3.119). For the beneficial criteria, each performance is divided by the highest value in each column of M.

$$r_{i,j} = \frac{M_{i,j}}{\max\limits_{1 \le i \le (m+q-1)} M_{i,j}}, i = 1, 2, ..., (m+q-1), j = 1, 2, ..., n. \quad (3.119)$$

As for the cost criteria, the normalization equation is as follows:

$$r_{i,j} = \frac{\min\limits_{1 \le i \le (m+q-1)} M_{i,j}}{M_{i,j}}, i = 1, 2, ..., (m+q-1), j = 1, 2, ..., n. \quad (3.120)$$

Step 5: Calculate the weighted normalized decision matrix $V = [v_{i,j}]_{m \times n}$.

$$v_{i,j} = w_j \cdot r_{i,j} \quad (3.121)$$

where $\sum_{j=1}^n w_j = 1$.

Step 6: Determine the ideal and antiideal solutions. The ideal solutions are the best performance on each criterion of the decision matrix V. Correspondingly, the antiideal solutions are the worst performance on each criterion of V.

$$v^+ = [v_1^+, v_2^+, ..., v_n^+], v_j^+ = \begin{cases} \max\limits_i v_{i,j}, g_j \in G^+ \\ \min\limits_i v_{i,j}, g_j \in G^- \end{cases} \quad (3.122)$$

$$v^- = [v_1^-, v_2^-, ..., v_n^-], v_j^- = \begin{cases} \min\limits_i v_{i,j}, g_j \in G^+ \\ \max\limits_i v_{i,j}, g_j \in G^- \end{cases} \quad (3.123)$$

where v^+ and v^- represent the ideal solution vector and antiideal solution vector, respectively.

Step 7: Calculate the Euclidian distances of each alternative or limit of the criteria for the ideal and antiideal solutions.

$$d_{a_i}^+ = \sqrt{\sum\nolimits_{j=1}^n (v_{i,j} - v_j^+)^2}, i = 1, 2, ..., m \quad (3.124)$$

$$d_{a_i}^- = \sqrt{\sum\nolimits_{j=1}^n (v_{i,j} - v_j^-)^2}, i = 1, 2, ..., m \quad (3.125)$$

where $d_{a_i}^+$ and $d_{a_i}^-$ are the Euclidian distances of each alternative or limits to the ideal and antiideal solutions.

Step 8: Calculate the relative closeness coefficient of each alternative or limit from the ideal solution on the basis of the Euclidian distances obtained above.

$$Cl(a_i) = \frac{d_{a_i}^-}{d_{a_i}^+ + d_{a_i}^-}, i = 1, 2, ..., m \qquad (3.126)$$

Here, the closeness coefficients of each alternative $Cl(a_i)$, upper limit profile $Cl(\overline{P_k})$, and lower limit profile $Cl(\underline{P_k})$ are determined.

Step 9: Compare the closeness coefficients $Cl(a_i)$ of each alternative with those of the upper limits $Cl(\overline{P_k})$ and lower limits $Cl(\underline{P_k})$, and allocate the alternatives to the classes according to the assignment rules as follows:

$$a_i \in C_k \; if \; Cl(\overline{P_k}) < Cl(a_i) < Cl(\underline{P_k}), i = 1, 2, ..., m, k = 1, 2, ..., q. \quad (3.127)$$

From the procedure above, we could find out that the lower limit of the profile is equal to the upper level of the subsequent profile. In other words, $Cl(\underline{P_k}) = Cl(\overline{P_{k+1}})$. Furthermore, the upper limit profile for the most preferred class and the lower limit profile for the least preferred class make no sense. Another issue that should be considered is that a ranking reversal involving an alternative and a profile may occur when an alternative is added or removed. To settle the problems above, TOPSIS-Sort-B was proposed [46].

3.6.2.2 TOPSIS-Sort-B

TOPSIS-Sort-B is similar to TOPSIS-Sort, but there are three extra assumptions which should be highlighted.

Assumption 2: Based on the largest (a_j^+) and smallest (a_j^-) possible value of each criterion in the decision matrix, the criterion domain could be determined by experts.

Assumption 3.1: The boundary profile is defined as the limit of the two predefined classes. For example, the boundary profile P_k is both the upper limit of the class C_{k+1} and the lower limit of the class C_k (see Fig. 3.34). $P_{k,j}$ is the limit value between two predefined classes C_k and C_{k+1} for criterion g_j.

Assumption 4: The profile P_k dominates the profile P_{k+1}, which means that $P_{k,j} \succ P_{k+1,j}$. The strict preference $(\succ)$ holds for at least one criterion.

Let $P = (P_1, P_2, ..., P_{q-1})^T$ be a set of $(q-1)$ profiles, where P_k defines the limit between C_k and C_{k+1}.

Step 1: Establish the decision matrix $X = [a_{i,j}]_{m \times n}$.

Step 2: Determine a set of $q - 1$ profiles $P = [P_{k,j}]_{(q-1) \times n}$.

Step 3: Establish the criterion domain, which is represented by

$$D = \begin{bmatrix} a_1^+ & \cdots & a_j^+ & \cdots & a_n^+ \\ a_1^- & \cdots & a_j^- & \cdots & a_n^- \end{bmatrix}.$$

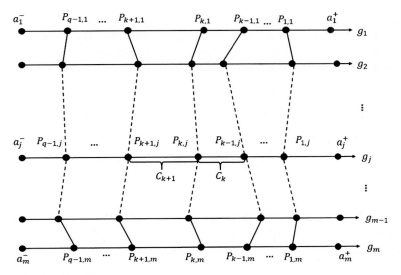

FIGURE 3.34 Boundary profiles.

Step 4: Determine a new decision matrix $M = [M_{i,j}]_{(m+q+1)\times n} = \begin{bmatrix} X \\ P \\ D \end{bmatrix}$.

Step 5: Normalize the decision matrix M.

There are two options:

(1) Normalize the decision matrix M by the following equations. For the beneficial criteria, each performance is divided by a_j^+.

$$r_{i,j} = \frac{M_{i,j}}{a_j^+}, i = 1, 2, ..., (m + q + 1), j = 1, 2, ..., n. \qquad (3.128)$$

As for the cost criteria, the normalization equation is as follows:

$$r_{i,j} = \frac{M_{i,j}}{a_j^-}, i = 1, 2, ..., (m + q + 1), j = 1, 2, ..., n \qquad (3.129)$$

(2) Min-max normalization

$$r_{i,j} = \frac{M_{i,j} - a_j^-}{a_j^+ - a_j^-}, i = 1, 2, ..., (m + q + 1), j = 1, 2, ..., n. \qquad (3.130)$$

Step 6: Calculate the weighted normalized decision matrix $V = [v_{i,j}]_{(m+q+1)\times n}$.

$$v_{i,j} = w_j \cdot r_{i,j}, i = 1, 2, ..., (m + q + 1), j = 1, 2, ..., n. \qquad (3.131)$$

where $\sum_{j=1}^{n} w_j = 1$.

Step 7: Determine the ideal and antiideal solutions. The ideal solutions are the best performance on each criterion of the decision matrix V. Correspondingly, the antiideal solutions are the worst performance on each criterion of V.

$$v^+ = [v_1^+, v_2^+, ..., v_n^+], v_j^+ = \begin{cases} \max_i v_{i,j}, g_j \in G^+ \\ \min_i v_{i,j}, g_j \in G^- \end{cases} \tag{3.132}$$

$$v^- = [v_1^-, v_2^-, ..., v_n^-], v_j^- = \begin{cases} \min_i v_{i,j}, g_j \in G^+ \\ \max_i v_{i,j}, g_j \in G^- \end{cases} \tag{3.133}$$

Step 8: Calculate the Euclidian distances of each alternative and profile of the criteria or the ideal and antiideal solutions.

$$d_{a_i}^+ = \sqrt{\sum_{j=1}^{n} (v_{i,j} - v_j^+)^2}, i = 1, 2, ..., m \tag{3.134}$$

$$d_{a_i}^- = \sqrt{\sum_{j=1}^{n} (v_{i,j} - v_j^-)^2}, i = 1, 2, ..., m \tag{3.135}$$

$$d_{P_k}^+ = \sqrt{\sum_{j=1}^{n} (v_{i,j} - v_j^+)^2}, k = 1, 2, ..., (q - 1), i = k + m \tag{3.136}$$

$$d_{P_k}^- = \sqrt{\sum_{j=1}^{n} (v_{i,j} - v_j^-)^2}, k = 1, 2, ..., (q - 1), i = k + m \tag{3.137}$$

where $d_{a_i}^+$ and $d_{a_i}^-$ are the Euclidian distances of each alternative from the ideal and antiideal solutions, and $d_{P_k}^+$ and $d_{P_k}^-$ are the Euclidian distances of each profile from the ideal and antiideal solutions.

Step 9: Calculate the relative closeness coefficient of each alternative and profile from the ideal solution on the basis of the Euclidian distances obtained above.

$$Cl(a_i) = \frac{d_{a_i}^-}{d_{a_i}^+ + d_{a_i}^-}, i = 1, 2, ..., m \tag{3.138}$$

$$Cl(P_k) = \frac{d_{P_k}^-}{d_{P_k}^+ + d_{P_k}^-}, k = 1, 2, ..., (q - 1) \tag{3.139}$$

Step 10: Compare the closeness coefficients $Cl(a_i)$ of each alternative with those of the profiles $Cl(P_k)$ and allocate the alternatives to the classes according to the following equation:

$$a_i \in C_1 \; if \; Cl(a_i) \geq Cl(P_1) \tag{3.140}$$

$$a_i \in C_k \; if \; Cl(P_{k-1}) > Cl(a_i) \geq Cl(P_k),$$

$$i = 1, 2, \ldots, m, k = 2, 3, \ldots, (q - 1) \tag{3.141}$$

$$a_i \in C_q \; if \; Cl(a_i) < Cl(P_{q-1}) \tag{3.142}$$

There are two main ways in which TOPSIS-Sort-B improves TOPSIS-Sort.

(1) It changes the number of profiles. TOPSIS-Sort requires $2q$ profiles while in TOPSIS-Sort-B, only $(q - 1)$ are required.

(2) It introduces a new decision matrix D in **Step 4** to address the problem of ranking reversal. The domain of each criterion has been determined by DMs as the matrix D, which means that the range of acceptable values for the application has been set in this step. Therefore, adding or removing any alternatives will not affect the domain. In other words, the ideal and antiideal solutions will not change and ranking reversals are avoided.

3.6.2.3 TOPSIS-Sort-C

For experts, defining a class by using a characteristic profile rather by defining two boundary profiles is easier. For example, when experts aim to define whether the environmental quality of an area is good or bad, they could compare the characteristics of the area with those of other areas in good or bad environments. In addition, the process of defining boundary profiles is sometimes intuitive. Therefore, using characteristic profiles to sort alternatives is practical, which is the dominant idea of TOPSIS-Sort-C.

There is an extra assumption which should be highlighted in TOPSIS-Sort-C.

Assumption 3.2: The characteristic profile is defined as the representative alternative of the class. For instance, the characteristic profile P_k represents the typical features of class C_k (see Fig. 3.35). $P_{k,j}$ is the central profile of class C_k for criterion g_j.

Let $P = \{P_1, P_2, \ldots, P_q\}$ be a set of q profiles, where P_k defines the typical feature of C_k.

Step 1: Establish the decision matrix $X = [a_{i,j}]_{m \times n}$.

Step 2: Determine a set of q profiles $P = [P_{k,j}]_{q \times n}$.

Step 3: Establish the domain of each criterion, which is represented by $D =$
$$\begin{bmatrix} a_1^+ & \cdots & a_j^+ & \cdots & a_n^+ \\ a_1^- & \cdots & a_j^- & \cdots & a_n^- \end{bmatrix}.$$

Step 4: Determine a new decision matrix $M = [M_{i,j}]_{(m+q+2) \times n} = \begin{bmatrix} X \\ P \\ D \end{bmatrix}.$

Step 5: Normalize the decision matrix M.

There are two options:

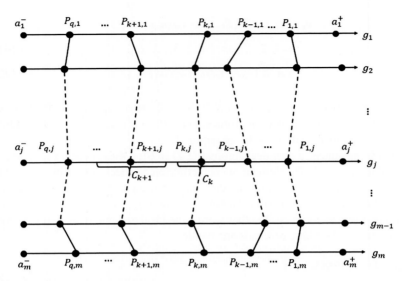

FIGURE 3.35 Characteristic profiles.

(1) Normalize the decision matrix M by Eq. (3.143). For the beneficial criteria, each performance is divided by a_j^+.

$$r_{i,j} = \frac{M_{i,j}}{a_j^+}, i = 1, 2, ..., (m + q + 2), j = 1, 2, ..., n. \tag{3.143}$$

As for the cost criteria, the normalization equation is as follows:

$$r_{i,j} = \frac{M_{i,j}}{a_j^-}, i = 1, 2, ..., (m + q + 2), j = 1, 2, ..., n \tag{3.144}$$

(2) Min-max normalization

$$r_{i,j} = \frac{M_{i,j} - a_j^-}{a_j^+ - a_j^-}, i = 1, 2, ..., (m + q + 2), j = 1, 2, ..., n. \tag{3.145}$$

Step 6: Calculate the weighted normalized decision matrix $V = [v_{i,j}]_{(m+q+1) \times n}$.

$$v_{i,j} = w_j \cdot r_{i,j}, i = 1, 2, ..., (m + q + 2), j = 1, 2, ..., n \tag{3.146}$$

where $\sum_{j=1}^{n} w_j = 1$.

Step 7: Determine the ideal and antiideal solutions. The ideal solutions are the best performance on each criterion of the decision matrix V. Correspondingly, the antiideal solutions are the worst performance on each criterion of V.

$$v^+ = [v_1^+, v_2^+, ..., v_n^+], v_j^+ = \begin{cases} \max_i v_{i,j}, g_j \in G^+ \\ \min_i v_{i,j}, g_j \in G^- \end{cases} \quad (3.147)$$

$$v^- = [v_1^-, v_2^-, ..., v_n^-], v_j^- = \begin{cases} \min_i v_{i,j}, g_j \in G^+ \\ \max_i v_{i,j}, g_j \in G^- \end{cases} \quad (3.148)$$

Step 8: Calculate the Euclidian distances of each alternative and profile on the criteria to the ideal and antiideal solutions.

$$d_{a_i}^+ = \sqrt{\sum_{j=1}^n (v_{i,j} - v_j^+)^2}, i = 1, 2, ..., m \quad (3.149)$$

$$d_{a_i}^- = \sqrt{\sum_{j=1}^n (v_{i,j} - v_j^-)^2}, i = 1, 2, ..., m \quad (3.150)$$

$$d_{P_k}^+ = \sqrt{\sum_{j=1}^n (v_{i,j} - v_j^+)^2}, k = 1, 2, ..., q, i = k + m \quad (3.151)$$

$$d_{P_k}^- = \sqrt{\sum_{j=1}^n (v_{i,j} - v_j^-)^2}, k = 1, 2, ..., q, i = k + m \quad (3.152)$$

where $d_{a_i}^+$ and $d_{a_i}^-$ are the Euclidian distances of each alternative to the ideal and antiideal solutions, and $d_{P_k}^+$ and $d_{P_k}^-$ are the Euclidian distances of each profile to the ideal and antiideal solutions.

Step 9: Calculate the relative closeness coefficient of each alternative and profile to the ideal solution on the basis of the Euclidian distances obtained above.

$$Cl(a_i) = \frac{d_{a_i}^-}{d_{a_i}^+ + d_{a_i}^-}, i = 1, 2, ..., m \quad (3.153)$$

$$Cl(P_k) = \frac{d_{P_k}^-}{d_{P_k}^+ + d_{P_k}^-}, k = 1, 2, ..., (q) \quad (3.154)$$

Step 10: Compare the closeness coefficients $Cl(a_i)$ of each alternative with those of the profiles $Cl(P_k)$ and classify the alternatives. Unlike TOPSIS-Sort-B, TOPSIS-Sort-C allocates alternatives to classes with the most similar closeness coefficient value to their own.

$$a_i \in C_1 \text{ if } |Cl(a_i) - Cl(P_1)| \le |Cl(a_i) - Cl(P_2)|, i = 1, 2, ..., m \quad (3.155)$$

$$a_i \in C_k \, if \begin{cases} |Cl(a_i) - Cl(P_k)| < |Cl(a_i) - Cl(P_{k-1})| \\ |Cl(a_i) - Cl(P_k)| \leq |Cl(a_i) - Cl(P_{k+1})| \\ i = 1, 2, \ldots, m, \, k = 2, 3, \ldots, q - 1 \end{cases}, \tag{3.156}$$

$$a_i \in C_q \, if \, |Cl(a_i) - Cl(P_q)| < |Cl(a_i) - Cl(P_{q-1})|, \, i = 1, 2, \ldots, m \tag{3.157}$$

3.6.2.4 Illustrative example

In this section, to illustrate the TOPSIS-Sort-B method, we use a numerical example. We allocate five alternatives $A = (a_1, a_2, a_3, a_4, a_5)^T$ to three classes $C = (C_1, C_2, C_3)^T$ under four beneficial criteria $g = (g_1, g_2, g_3, g_4)^T$.

Step 1: Establish the decision matrix $X = [a_{i,j}]_{5 \times 4}$.

$$X = \begin{bmatrix} 7 & 9 & 9 & 8 \\ 8 & 7 & 8 & 7 \\ 9 & 6 & 7 & 12 \\ 6 & 11 & 8 & 6 \\ 5 & 9 & 6 & 10 \end{bmatrix} \tag{3.158}$$

Step 2: Determine a set of $(q - 1)$ profiles $P = [P_{k,j}]_{2 \times 4}$.

$$P = \begin{bmatrix} 8 & 9 & 8 & 10 \\ 6 & 7 & 7 & 7 \end{bmatrix} \tag{3.159}$$

Step 3: Establish the domain of each criterion.

$$D = \begin{bmatrix} 15 & 15 & 15 & 15 \\ 0 & 0 & 0 & 0 \end{bmatrix} \tag{3.160}$$

Step 4: After **Steps 1–3**, we could derive a new decision matrix M.

$$M = [M_{i,j}]_{9 \times 4} = \begin{bmatrix} 7 & 9 & 9 & 8 \\ 8 & 7 & 8 & 7 \\ 9 & 6 & 7 & 12 \\ 6 & 11 & 8 & 6 \\ 5 & 9 & 6 & 10 \\ 8 & 9 & 8 & 10 \\ 6 & 7 & 7 & 7 \\ 15 & 15 & 15 & 15 \\ 0 & 0 & 0 & 0 \end{bmatrix} \tag{3.161}$$

Step 5: Normalize the decision matrix M.

$$R = [r_{i,j}]_{9 \times 4} = \begin{bmatrix} 0.467 & 0.600 & 0.600 & 0.533 \\ 0.533 & 0.467 & 0.533 & 0.467 \\ 0.600 & 0.400 & 0.467 & 0.800 \\ 0.400 & 0.733 & 0.533 & 0.400 \\ 0.333 & 0.600 & 0.400 & 0.667 \\ 0.533 & 0.600 & 0.533 & 0.667 \\ 0.400 & 0.467 & 0.467 & 0.467 \\ 1.000 & 1.000 & 1.000 & 1.000 \\ 0.000 & 0.000 & 0.000 & 0.000 \end{bmatrix} \qquad (3.162)$$

Step 6: Calculate the weighted normalized decision matrix $V = [v_{i,j}]_{9 \times 4}$. Here, we assume that the weight vector is $W = (0.1, 0.4, 0.3, 0.2)^T$.

$$V = [v_{i,j}]_{9 \times 4} = \begin{bmatrix} 0.047 & 0.240 & 0.180 & 0.107 \\ 0.053 & 0.187 & 0.160 & 0.093 \\ 0.060 & 0.160 & 0.140 & 0.160 \\ 0.040 & 0.293 & 0.160 & 0.080 \\ 0.033 & 0.240 & 0.120 & 0.133 \\ 0.053 & 0.240 & 0.160 & 0.133 \\ 0.040 & 0.187 & 0.140 & 0.093 \\ 0.100 & 0.400 & 0.300 & 0.200 \\ 0.000 & 0.000 & 0.000 & 0.000 \end{bmatrix} \qquad (3.163)$$

Step 7: Determine the ideal and antiideal solutions.

$$v^+ = [\ 0.1 \quad 0.4 \quad 0.3 \quad 0.2\ ] \qquad (3.164)$$

$$v^- = [\ 0 \quad 0 \quad 0 \quad 0\ ] \qquad (3.165)$$

Step 8: Calculate the Euclidian distances of each alternative and profile of the criteria for the ideal and antiideal solutions.

$$A = \begin{matrix} & \begin{matrix} d_i^+ & \ d_i^- \end{matrix} \\ \begin{matrix} a_1 \\ a_2 \\ a_3 \\ a_4 \\ a_5 \\ P_1 \\ P_2 \end{matrix} & \begin{bmatrix} 0.227 & 0.322 \\ 0.280 & 0.268 \\ 0.294 & 0.273 \\ 0.221 & 0.346 \\ 0.259 & 0.301 \\ 0.228 & 0.322 \\ 0.293 & 0.254 \end{bmatrix} \end{matrix} \qquad (3.166)$$

Step 9: Calculate the relative closeness coefficient of each alternative and profile to the ideal solution on the basis of the Euclidian distances obtained above.

$$A = \begin{array}{c} \\ a_1 \\ a_2 \\ a_3 \\ a_4 \\ a_5 \\ P_1 \\ P_2 \end{array} \begin{array}{ccc} d_i{}^+ & d_i{}^- & Cl_i \\ \left[\begin{array}{ccc} 0.227 & 0.322 & 0.586 \\ 0.280 & 0.268 & 0.489 \\ 0.294 & 0.273 & 0.481 \\ 0.221 & 0.346 & 0.610 \\ 0.259 & 0.301 & 0.538 \\ 0.228 & 0.322 & 0.586 \\ 0.293 & 0.254 & 0.464 \end{array}\right] \end{array} \qquad (3.167)$$

Step 10: Compare the closeness coefficients $Cl(a_i)$ of each alternative with those of the profiles $Cl(P_k)$ and allocate the alternatives to the classes.

$$A = \begin{array}{c} \\ a_1 \\ a_2 \\ a_3 \\ a_4 \\ a_5 \\ P_1 \\ P_2 \end{array} \begin{array}{cccc} d_i{}^+ & d_i{}^- & Cl_i & class \\ \left[\begin{array}{cccc} 0.227 & 0.332 & 0.586 & 1 \\ 0.280 & 0.268 & 0.489 & 2 \\ 0.294 & 0.273 & 0.481 & 2 \\ 0.221 & 0.346 & 0.610 & 1 \\ 0.259 & 0.301 & 0.538 & 2 \\ 0.228 & 0.322 & 0.586 & - \\ 0.293 & 0.254 & 0.464 & - \end{array}\right] \end{array} \qquad (3.168)$$

Finally, we get the sorting results of five alternatives. a_1 and a_4 are allocated to the first class, while a_2, a_3, and a_5 are assigned to the second class. There is no alternative in the third class.

3.7   VIKORSort: a sorting method based on VIKOR

3.7.1   VIKOR

As the MCDM tools have been developed to help decision makers (DMs) to evaluate and select the best compromise alternatives, Vlsekriterijumska Optimizacija I KOmpromisno Resenje (VIKOR) [47] has received more and more attention.

The VIKOR method was developed by Opricovic [47], and later was applied to multi-criteria optimization of complicated systems and complex problems [48,49]. In other words, this method focuses on ranking and alternatives when there are conflicting criteria. Like TOPSIS, it introduces multi-criteria ranking index on the basis of closeness to the ideal solutions.

Some of the notations that will be used in the chapter are as follows.

Define $A = (a_1, a_2, ..., a_m)^T$ as a set of m alternatives and let $K = (k_1, k_2, ..., k_n)^T$ be the set of n criteria. $W = (w_1, w_2, ..., w_n)^T$ is a vector of weights with n elements, where w_j is the weight of criterion k_j. For alternative a_i, the value under criterion k_j is denoted by f_{ij}.

The $L_p - metric$ is the start of the VIKOR method.

$$L_{p,j} = \left\{ \sum_{i=1}^{n} \left[\frac{w_i(f_i^+ - f_{ij})}{(f_i^+ - f_i^-)} \right]^p \right\}^{\frac{1}{p}}, 1 \le p \le \infty, j = 1, 2, ..., m \quad (3.169)$$

The VIKOR method involves the following steps.

Step 1: Determine the best values of all criterion functions as f_j^+ and the worst values of all criterion functions as f_j^-. For beneficial criteria, $f_j^+ = \max f_{ij}$, $f_j^- = \min f_{ij}$, $j = 1, 2, ..., n$. For cost criteria, $f_j^+ = \min f_{ij}$, $f_j^- = \max f_{ij}$, $j = 1, 2, ..., n$.

Step 2: Compute the values S_j and R_j, which are utility measure and regret measure, respectively. The formulas are as follows:

$$S_i = \sum_{j=1}^{n} \frac{w_j(f_j^+ - f_{ij})}{(f_j^+ - f_j^-)} \quad (3.170)$$

$$R_i = \max_j \left[\frac{w_j(f_j^+ - f_{ij})}{(f_j^+ - f_j^-)} \right] \quad (3.171)$$

The minimum S_i expresses the minimization of the average sum of the individual regrets and the minimum R_i represents the minimization of the maximum individual regrets for prioritizing the improvement. In other words, the minimum S_i emphasizes the maximum group utility, while the minimum R_i stresses selecting the minimum among the maximum individual regrets.

The obtained solution is compromised by the minimum S_i of the majority, and a minimum of the individual regret represented by the minimum R_i of the opponent.

Step 3: Calculate the values Q_j, $j=1,2,...,m$, using the following relations:

$$Q_i = \frac{v(S_i - S^+)}{S^- - S^+} + (1 - v)\left(\frac{R_j - R^+}{R^- - R^+} \right) \quad (3.172)$$

$$S^+ = \max_i S_i \quad (3.173)$$

$$S^- = \min_i S_i \quad (3.174)$$

$$R^+ = \max_i R_i \quad (3.175)$$

$$R^- = \min_i R_i \quad (3.176)$$

where $\frac{(S_i - S^-)}{S^+ - S^-}$ represents the closeness to the ideal solution, while $\frac{(S_i - R^-)}{R^+ - R^-}$ is the closeness to the antiideal solution.

Where v is the weight of the strategy of maximum group utility, $0 \leq v \leq 1$. $1 - v$ is the weight of the individual regret. In other words, if $v > 0.5$, then the decision-making process could use the strategy of the maximum group utility, while if $v \approx 0.5$, the process should use the consensus strategy. In addition, when $v < 0.5$, the strategy should include a veto.

Step 4: Rank the alternatives, sorting by the values S_i, R_i, and Q_i in decreasing order. Since VIKOR was established to resolve decision-making problems that feature noncommensurable and incompatible criteria, it applies the two conditions "acceptable advantage" and "acceptable stability" to determine the maximum group utility of the majority and the minimum individual regret of the opponent in providing such a compromise solution.

(1) Acceptable advantage

$$Q(A_2) - Q(A_1) \geq \left(\frac{1}{m-1}\right) \tag{3.177}$$

where A_1 is the best-ranked alternative by Q. A_2 is the alternative in the second position in the ranking list by Q.

(2) Acceptable stability in decision making

A_1 is the best-ranked alternative not only by Q, but also by S or/and R.

If neither of the conditions are met, a set of compromise solutions is proposed as follows:

- Alternatives A_1 and A_2, if only condition (2) is not satisfied.
- Alternatives A_1, A_2,..., A_m, if condition (1) is not satisfied. A_m is determined by the relation $Q(A_m) - Q(A_1) < (\frac{1}{m-1})$ for maximum m (the positions of these alternatives are "in closeness").

VIKOR is used to find a compromise solution that satisfies the maximized utility of the entire group. The compromise solution is shown in Fig. 3.36.

VIKOR is a very useful multi-criteria decision-making tool when DMs cannot or do not know how to express their preferences at the beginning of system design. The compromise solutions could be used as the basis of negotiation, involving the preferences of DMs according to the criteria weights.

3.7.2   VIKORSort

Among the literature, it seems that the VIKOR method has presented more realistic results and is easy to apply in strategic decision making [50]. Therefore, in 2018, the VIKORSort method was proposed, in which DMs could take a pessimistic or optimistic attitude when expressing their opinions.

3.7.2.1   Methodology

Here, we introduce the procedure of VIKORSort.

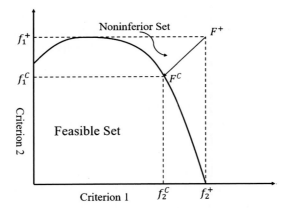

FIGURE 3.36 Ideal and compromise solutions.

Let $G = \{g_1, g_2, \ldots, g_n\}$ be a set of h predefined ordered groups.

Step 1: Conduct **Steps 1–3** of the VIKOR method (see Section 3.7). Determine the best values and the worst values of all criterion functions, which are represented by f_j^+ and f_j^-, respectively. Next, compute the values of S_j and R_j. Finally, calculate the value Q_j.

Step 2: For the initial assignment, alternative a must satisfy the following two conditions:

(1) Acceptable advantage

Employ the following expression to check if the alternative with the smallest Q value (A_1) has an acceptable advantage.

$$Q(A_2) - Q(A_1) \geq \left(\frac{1}{m-1}\right) \qquad (3.178)$$

Considering limiting profiles (l), the expression was modified as follows:

$$Q(l) - Q(a) \geq \left(\frac{1}{m-1}\right) \qquad (3.179)$$

(2) Acceptable stability

In VIKOR, if the alternative with the smallest Q value also has the minimum S and/or R values, then acceptable stability is achieved. In VIKORSort, if the alternative has acceptable stability, then the R and/or S values are smaller than those of the limit profile, which could be expressed as $R, S(a) < R, S(l)$.

The alternative is allocated into a group when it meets both conditions above. We assume that $g_1 > g_2 > \ldots > g_h$ and $l_1 > l_2 > \ldots > l_{h-1}$. Similar to VIKOR, three disparate situations exist during the assignment process.

(a) The alternative satisfies both conditions. If the DMs hold optimistic attitudes, the comparison process starts with the best limit profile (l_1). Then, the alternative is allocated directly to g_1. The process continues until all alternatives are assigned. If the alternative is compared with the worst limit profile (l_{h-1}) in a pessimistic situation, it cannot be assigned directly to g_{h-1}. The pairwise comparison process continues, comparing alternatives with better (high-level) limit profiles. Finally, the alternative is allocated to the best of the two groups separated by the last compared limit profile.

(b) **The alternative does not satisfy both conditions.** If the DMs hold optimistic attitudes, the comparison process starts with the best limit profile (l_1). Then, the alternative cannot be allocated directly to g_2. The pairwise comparison process continues, comparing alternatives with worse (low-level) limit profiles. Finally, the alternative is allocated to the worst of the two groups separated by the last compared limit profile. If the alternative is compared with the worst limit profile (l_{h-1}) in a pessimistic situation, it is possible to say that the alternative is worse than the compared limit profile. Therefore, the alternative is assigned directly to g_h.

(c) **The alternative satisfies only one of the conditions.** In this situation, no matter whether the DMs hold pessimistic or optimistic attitudes, the allocation of alternatives cannot be determined. The alternative is assigned firstly to the "unassigned alternatives group" and then to one of the two groups separated by a limit profile, using the final assignment rules in **Step 3**.

Step 3: VIKORSort final assignment

After **Steps 1 and 2**, some alternatives may not be allocated to any of the groups because of the following situations:

- $Q(a) = Q(l)$ and $S(a) = S(l)$ or
  $Q(a) = Q(l)$ and $R(a) = R(l)$

- $Q(l) - Q(a) \geq \left(\frac{1}{m-1}\right)$ and $R, S(a) > R, S(l)$ or
  $Q(l) - Q(a) \leq \left(\frac{1}{m-1}\right)$ and $R, S(a) < R, S(l)$

In these situations, the assignment of alternative a was according to the following procedure.

Step 3.1: Determine the two closest groups to a by comparing the Q values of a and limit profiles.

Step 3.2: For each group, calculate the mean distances between the Q values of the group members and a. The distances are calculated by dividing the total distance by the number of group members.

Step 3.3: The alternative a is allocated to the group with the closest mean distance.

3.7.2.2   Illustrative example

Suppose that we are sorting the excellence levels of all employees in a company. The company has 20 employees and 10 evaluation criteria (see Table 3.37). We establish the weights of all criteria as shown in Table 3.38. The number of

TABLE 3.37 Criteria values for employees and limiting profiles.

Employees	k_1	k_2	k_3	k_4	k_5	k_6	k_7	k_8	k_9	k_{10}
a_1	67	70	75	70	72	30	62	12	75	50
a_2	40	31	22	13	31	28	16	7	24	33
a_3	58	62	71	70	69	66	58	7	51	59
a_4	63	70	66	51	49	58	71	20	55	62
a_5	21	19	32	18	25	34	47	8	30	32
a_6	50	59	66	72	58	36	49	30	60	53
a_7	47	54	63	57	48	55	63	15	57	42
a_8	27	41	33	21	18	25	30	10	30	40
a_9	99	62	79	73	51	6	68	30	79	90
a_{10}	58	69	58	80	99	51	66	25	90	70
a_{11}	61	55	65	48	30	52	53	30	53	63
a_{12}	13	45	39	13	33	29	26	8	45	30
a_{13}	58	61	49	63	49	74	62	27	57	63
a_{14}	59	63	70	69	40	65	59	8	52	58
a_{15}	22	36	34	41	17	14	9	8	25	20
a_{16}	46	58	61	56	53	66	71	8	54	42
a_{17}	83	76	88	79	72	86	81	24	63	81
a_{18}	19	30	21	30	23	26	19	10	24	23
a_{19}	79	83	86	84	74	78	65	7	67	60
a_{20}	55	63	62	60	54	51	66	30	63	48
l_1	30	35	40	50	40	50	30	25	25	30
l_2	65	70	80	90	70	80	70	7	65	60

groups is three (good, moderate, and bad), which means that two limit profiles are defined (l_1 and l_2).

Step 1: Determine the best and worst values for all criterion functions shown in Table 3.39. After that, R, S, and Q values for employees and limit profiles are calculated. These values are listed in ascending order in Table 3.40.

Steps 2 and 3: We choose employee 1 and employee 4 as an example.

- From the results above, we could find that employee 1 satisfies both conditions. Therefore, they should be allocated to the best group (g_1).
- When compared with l_2, employee 4 does not meet any of the conditions, so they were compared with l_1. In that case, employee 4 satisfies both conditions. Therefore, this employee should be assigned to the moderate group.

The final sorting results are shown in Table 3.41.

DEASort [51] is combined with AHP, the output of which is used to take into account the expertise of the decision-makers in calculating the weights. This weight constraint is then added to the DEASort model.

TABLE 3.38 Criteria and weights.

Criteria	Weights
k_1	0.1
k_2	0.1
k_3	0.15
k_4	0.1
k_5	0.1
k_6	0.05
k_7	0.1
k_8	0.1
k_9	0.15
k_{10}	0.05

TABLE 3.39 f_j^+ and f_j^- values.

Criteria	f_j^+	f_j^-
k_1	99	13
k_2	83	19
k_3	88	21
k_4	90	13
k_5	99	17
k_6	86	6
k_7	81	9
k_8	7	30
k_9	90	24
k_{10}	90	20

3.7.2.3 Methodology

The method classifies I items based on J criteria by K decision-makers, using the six steps described here.

Step 1: Normalization of item scores

The measured score v_{ij} of each item i for each criterion j (e.g., frequency of issue, annual usage value) is normalized on a 0–1 scale to make them comparable via the following expression:

$$v_{i,j}^* = \frac{v_{i,j} - \min_{i=1,2,...,I} v_{i,j}}{\max_{i=1,2,...,I} v_{i,j} - \min_{i=1,2,...,I} v_{i,j}} \qquad \forall i = 1, 2, ..., I \qquad (3.180)$$

TABLE 3.40 R, S, and Q values for employees and limit profiles.

Employees	S_j	R_j	Q_j	Ascending order list		
a_1	0.291	0.037	0.069	4	1	2
a_2	0.793	0.15	0.973	21	21	21
a_3	0.365	0.089	0.357	7	11	6
a_4	0.43	0.08	0.369	9	7	8
a_5	0.761	0.136	0.887	18	17	18
a_6	0.497	0.1	0.513	13	12	14
a_7	0.474	0.075	0.384	11	5	11
a_8	0.748	0.136	0.877	17	17	17
a_9	0.317	0.1	0.368	6	12	7
a_{10}	0.307	0.078	0.264	5	6	5
a_{11}	0.534	0.1	0.543	15	12	15
a_{12}	0.707	0.11	0.725	16	16	16
a_{13}	0.512	0.087	0.469	14	10	12
a_{14}	0.401	0.086	0.375	8	9	9
a_{15}	0.784	0.148	0.956	20	19	20
a_{16}	0.434	0.082	0.382	10	8	10
a_{17}	0.261	0.074	0.208	3	4	4
a_{18}	0.826	0.15	1	22	21	22
a_{19}	0.205	0.052	0.067	1	2	1
a_{20}	0.485	0.1	0.504	12	12	13
l_1	0.763	0.148	0.939	19	19	19
l_2	0.25	0.057	0.123	2	3	3

TABLE 3.41 Sorting results.

Groups	Employees
g_1 (good group)	a_1, a_{19}
g_2 (moderate group)	$a_1, a_3, a_4, a_5, a_6, a_7, a_8, a_9, a_{11}, a_{12}, a_{13}, a_{14}, a_{16}, a_{17}, a_{20}$
g_3 (bad group)	a_2, a_{15}, a_{18}

Step 2: Criteria weight evaluation

Criteria weights are evaluated separately via AHP by K decision-makers. For this purpose, the J criteria are pairwise compared in a matrix on a 1–9 scale. Weights are found by calculating the eigenvector. It should be noted that the consistency of the evaluations entered by the decision-maker can be tested using the consistency ratio (CR).

Step 3: Weight bounding

In order to limit the range of possible weights, a lower bound and upper bound are defined for each weight. The lower bound of the weight for criterion

j is given by the minimum evaluation score among K experts:

$$w_{LBj} = min_{k=1,2,...,K}\{w_{j,k}\} \tag{3.181}$$

The upper bound of the weight for criterion j is given by the maximum evaluation score among K experts:

$$w_{UBj} = max_{k=1,2,...,K}\{w_{j,k}\} \tag{3.182}$$

Step 4: Calculation of the item priority

For each specific item o under evaluation, the mathematical program in Eq. (3.183) inspired by data envelopment analysis (DEA) is solved. This method improves on the previous DEA models by introducing the weight constraints, corresponding to the last line of Eq. (3.183).

$$\max\ P_o = \sum_{j=1}^{n} w_{o,k} v_{o,k}$$

$$\text{s.t.}\quad \sum_{j=1}^{n} w_{o,k} v_{o,k} \leq 1 \qquad i = 1, 2, ..., I$$
$$w_{oj} \geq 0 \qquad\qquad i = 1, 2, ..., I \tag{3.183}$$
$$w_{LBj} < w_{oj} < w_{UBj}$$

A weight bounding in the model may result in its infeasibility, and thus lead to zero or negative priorities; therefore, the weight bounding needs to be re-assessed.

Step 5: Definition of classes

The number of classes must be set and the classes defined. In general, three classes C_c corresponding to $C_1 = A$, $C_2 = B$, and $C_3 = C$ are chosen. In order to define these classes, each expert k is asked to select L reference items that she or he knows very well and that belong to each class. The item with priority P_{ckl} is then calculated for each reference item. A decision tree [52] is trained on the reference items, the inputs being the item priorities P_{ckl} and the outputs being their relative classes. The decision tree uses Gini's diversity index as a splitting criterion. The number of thresholds is equal to the number of classes minus one. The classification tree is able to work with multiple reference items and is robust to misclassified reference items.

Step 6: Sorting into classes

Item z is assigned to class C_l, which has its threshold th_l just below the item priority P_z.

$$P_z \geq th_1 \qquad\qquad \Longrightarrow\ z \in C_1$$
$$th_2 \leq P_z \leq th_1 \quad \Longrightarrow\ z \in C_2$$
$$\cdots \tag{3.184}$$
$$P_z < th_{n-1} \qquad\quad \Longrightarrow\ z \in C_n$$

Note that **Steps 2 and 3** are optional. If no information on the weights is known beforehand, then **Step 4** can be directly used after **Step 1** and the last line of Eq. (3.183) can be removed for calculation of the priority items.

3.7.2.4 Illustrative example

Suppose that we are sorting 10 items into classes A, B, and C according three criteria c_1, c_2, and c_3.

Step 1: Normalization of item scores

The values of the three criteria were normalized for each item using Eq. (3.180) (see Table 3.42.)

Step 2: Criteria weight evaluation

Two decision-makers (DMs) were asked to compare pairwise the importance of the three criteria. The results of this process are given in Table 3.43.

TABLE 3.42 Data on each criterion for all alternatives.

Items	c_1	c_2	c_3
1	25	42	36
2	30	25	43
3	42	46	45
4	78	27	24
5	47	50	60
6	76	42	49
7	45	10	54
8	68	75	72
9	52	57	78
10	79	43	46

TABLE 3.43 Criteria weights estimated by the two DMs.

Criteria	DM 1	DM 2
c_1	0.33	0.4
c_2	0.33	0.2
c_3	0.33	0.4

Step 3: Weight bounding

The range of weights permissible in DEA for each criterion was obtained by setting the lowest Eq. (3.181) and highest Eq. (3.182) values from Table 3.43. The results of this procedure are displayed in Table 3.44.

Step 4: Calculation of the item priorities

TABLE 3.44 Range of permissible weights.		
Criteria	Lower bound	Upper bound
c_1	0.33	0.4
c_2	0.2	0.33
c_3	0.33	0.4

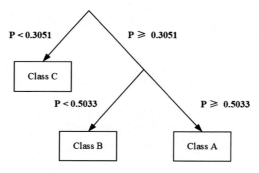

FIGURE 3.37 Trained decision tree.

TABLE 3.45 Priorities of typical items.		
Class	DM_1	DM_2
A	$p_8 = 0.6054$	$p_2 = 0.4252$
B	$p_5 = 0.3745$	$p_4 = 0.4470$
C	$p_1 = 0.2356$	$p_7 = 0.5324$

The algorithm in Eq. (3.184) was implemented and the item priority P_k was calculated for each item.

Step 5: Definition of classes

The two DMs selected a typical item for each class; their item priorities are listed in Table 3.45. This training set (Table 3.45) was fed into the classification tree algorithm in MATLAB® to train the decision tree described in Fig. 3.37.

Step 6: Assignment to classes

Table 3.46 lists the items assigned to classes A, B, and C. Three items were found to have a score above the limiting profile of class A and were therefore assigned to this class. Four items were assigned to class B, with their scores falling between the limiting profiles of class A and class B. Three items scored below the limiting profile of class C and were therefore assigned to class C.

TABLE 3.46 Items assigned to classes A, B, and C.

Items	p_k	Class
1	0.235641	C
2	0.425239	B
3	0.484815	B
4	0.446966	B
5	0.374487	C
6	0.543615	A
7	0.53235	A
8	0.605362	A
9	0.369946	C
10	0.458333	B

3.8 CODAS-SORT: a new CODAS-based method for sorting problems

3.8.1 CODAS

In this section, a new method is introduced that was proposed by Keshavarz Ghorabaee et al. [53] to deal with multi-criteria decision problems: **CO**mbinative **D**istance-based **AS**sessment (CODAS).

In this method, the desirability of alternatives is determined by two distance-based measures. The main and primary measure is related to the Euclidean distance of alternatives from the negative-ideal point, which requires an l^2–$norm$ indifference space for criteria. If several alternatives are incomparable by the former metric, the Taxicab distance is used as secondary measure, which is related to the l^1–$norm$ indifference space. It is obvious that the alternative which has greater distance from the negative-ideal solution is preferred. Although the l^2–$norm$ indifference space is preferred in the CODAS, two types of indifference space could be considered in its process.

To describe the proposed method, Keshavarz Ghorabaee et al. [53] use a simple situation with seven alternatives and two criteria. Suppose that weighted performance values have been calculated, which are dimensionless and normalized between 0 and 1. Fig. 3.38 illustrates the position of all alternatives according to these values.

As can be seen in this figure, $ns = [0.1, 0.1]$ is the negative-ideal point. The Euclidean distances of alternatives from this point are as follows:

$$E_1 = \sqrt{(0.1 - 0.1)^2 + (0.3 - 0.1)^2} = 0.2$$
$$E_2 = \sqrt{(0.5473 - 0.1)^2 + (0.5 - 0.1)^2} = 0.6$$

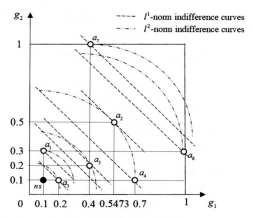

FIGURE 3.38 A simple graphical example with two criteria.

$$E_3 = \sqrt{(0.2 - 0.1)^2 + (0.1 - 0.1)^2} = 0.1$$

$$E_4 = \sqrt{(0.7 - 0.1)^2 + (0.1 - 0.1)^2} = 0.6$$

$$E_5 = \sqrt{(0.4 - 0.1)^2 + (0.2 - 0.1)^2} = 0.3162$$

$$E_6 = \sqrt{(1 - 0.1)^2 + (0.3 - 0.1)^2} = 0.9220$$

$$E_7 = \sqrt{(0.4 - 0.1)^2 + (1 - 0.1)^2} = 0.9487$$

Therefore, the order of these alternatives can be obtained according to the Euclidean distance:

$$a_3 \prec a_1 \prec a_5 \prec a_2 = a_4 \prec a_6 \prec a_7$$

However, in this l^2–*norm* indifference space, we cannot find the difference between a_2 and a_4. Thus the Taxicab distance, which measures the l^1–*norm* indifference space, is used in this case. The Taxicab distance between alternatives and the negative-ideal point is calculated as follows:

$$T_2 = |0.5473 - 0.1| + |0.5 - 0.1| = 0.8473$$
$$T_4 = |0.7 - 0.1| + |0.1 - 0.1| = 0.6$$

Due to the Taxicab distance value of a_2 being greater than a_4, it can be found that a_4 is preferred to a_2, thus the final order of all alternatives is:

$$a_3 \prec a_1 \prec a_5 \prec a_4 \prec a_2 \prec a_6 \prec a_7$$

This fact can be obtained intuitively from Fig. 3.38.

3.8.2 CODAS-SORT

Based on CODAS, Ouhibi and Frikha [54] proposed a new sorting method called CODAS-SORT. The assignment rules are based on the use of two measures. The first measure is related to the Euclidean distance, and the second to the Taxicab distance. The assignment rules are based on the difference between the two distances. The steps of the proposed method are as follows.

Step 1: Construct the decision-making matrix (X) with n alternatives and m criteria, as follows:

$$X = [x_{ij}]_{n*m} = \begin{bmatrix} x_{11} & x_{12} & \cdots & x_{1m} \\ x_{21} & x_{22} & \cdots & x_{2m} \\ \vdots & \vdots & \vdots & \vdots \\ x_{n1} & x_{n2} & \cdots & x_{nm} \end{bmatrix} \quad (3.185)$$

where x_{ij} denotes the performance value of alternative a_i on the criterion g_j.

Step 2: Construct the matrix (Y) with l limits and m criteria.

$$Y = [y_{kj}]_{l*m} = \begin{bmatrix} y_{11} & y_{12} & \cdots & y_{1m} \\ y_{21} & y_{22} & \cdots & y_{2m} \\ \vdots & \vdots & \vdots & \vdots \\ y_{l1} & y_{n2} & \cdots & y_{lm} \end{bmatrix} \quad (3.186)$$

where y_{kj} denotes the performance value of limit b_k on the criterion g_j.

Step 3: Determine the negative-ideal solution as follows:

$$ns_j = \min_i x_{ij}$$
$$ms_j = \min_k y_{kj} \quad (3.187)$$

Step 4: Calculate the Euclidean and Taxicab distances of the alternatives and limits from the negative-ideal solution, as follows:

$$E_{a_i} = \sqrt{\sum_{j=1}^{m} (x_{ij} - ns_j)^2} \quad (3.188)$$

where E_{a_i} denotes the Euclidean distance between the alternatives a_j and the negative-ideal solution ns_j.

$$E_{b_k} = \sqrt{\sum_{j=1}^{m} (y_{kj} - ms_j)^2} \quad (3.189)$$

where E_{b_k} denotes the Euclidean distance between the limit b_k and the negative-ideal solution ms_j.

$$T_{a_i} = \sum_{j=1}^{m} \left| x_{kj} - ns_j \right| \tag{3.190}$$

where T_{a_i} denotes the Taxicab distance between the alternative a_i and the negative-ideal solution ns_j.

$$T_{b_k} = \sum_{j=1}^{m} \left| y_{kj} - ms_j \right| \tag{3.191}$$

where T_{b_k} denotes the Taxicab distance between the limit b_k and the negative-ideal solution ms_j.

Step 5: Construct the relative assessment matrix, as follows:

$$h(a_i, b_k) = \left[E_{a_i} - E_{b_k} \right] + (\psi \left[E_{a_i} - E_{b_k} \right] * \left[T_{a_i} - T_{b_k} \right]) \tag{3.192}$$

where ψ denotes a threshold function to recognize the equality of the Euclidean distances of alternatives, and is defined as follows:

$$\psi(x) = \begin{cases} 1, \text{if} \left| E_{a_i} - E_{b_k} \right| < \tau \\ 0, \text{if} \left| E_{a_i} - E_{b_k} \right| \geq \tau \end{cases} \tag{3.193}$$

The value of τ can be set by the decision-maker. If the difference of Euclidean distances between alternatives is less than τ, then these two alternatives are also compared by the Taxicab distance.

Step 6: Assign alternatives to categories. To assign an alternative a_i to one of the predefined categories, there are two ways that depend on the type of available profile provided by the decision maker:

(1) Central profiles

If central profiles have been defined, the alternative a_i is assigned to the class C_k which has the smallest $|h(a_i, b_k)|$.

(2) Limiting profiles

If limiting profiles have been defined and $|h(a_i, b_k)|$ is the smallest, then there are two cases:

- If $h(a_i, b_k) \geq 0$ then the alternative a_i is assigned to the class C_k.
- If $h(a_i, b_k) < 0$ then the alternative a_i is assigned to the class C_{k-1}.

3.8.2.1   Illustrative example

This section gives a numerical example to illustrate how this method solves the sorting problem. Suppose that 12 alternatives need to be assigned into five ordinal classes, where C_{h+1} is preferred to C_h, according to six criteria. The performance matrix is shown in Table 3.47.

The limiting profiles are given in Table 3.48. Each reference b_k bounds the lower part of the category C_{k+1} and the upper part of the category C_k.

TABLE 3.47 The performance of each alternative on all criteria.

	g_1	g_2	g_3	g_4	g_5	g_6
a_1	1	4	6	4.3	2.7	5.5
a_2	1	5	2	5	1.3	8.2
a_3	3	4.5	3	4.4	9.7	6
a_4	1	3.5	7	4.1	4.7	6.5
a_5	1	2	7	4.9	3.7	8.2
a_6	3	6.5	5	5.2	12	8
a_7	3	5.5	5	8.7	12.2	8.9
a_8	3	7	1	5.4	1.9	5.9
a_9	2	4	6	5.2	11.6	4.9
a_10	3	3	9	3.5	2.8	8.2

TABLE 3.48 Limiting profiles.

	g_1	g_2	g_3	g_4	g_5	g_6
b_1	1	3	3	4	2	5
b_2	1	4	4	5	5	6
b_3	2	5	6	5	7	8
b_4	3	7	8	6	3	8

Then, we calculate the Euclidean and Taxicab distances of alternatives and limits from the negative-ideal solution. The results are presented in Tables 3.49 and 3.50.

TABLE 3.49 The Euclidean and Taxicab distances of alternatives.

Alternatives	E_{a_k}	T_{b_k}
a_1	5.65	9.8
a_2	4.81	8.8
a_3	9.32	16.9
a_4	7.26	13.1
a_5	7.39	13.1
a_6	12.93	26
a_7	13.93	29.6
a_8	5.83	10.5
a_9	11.79	20
a_10	9.26	15.8

TABLE 3.50 The Euclidean and Taxicab distances of limitings.

Alternatives	E_{a_k}	T_{b_k}
b_1	0	0
b_2	3.61	7
b_3	7	15
b_4	10.34	23

In this example, the value of τ is set as 0.3, then the $h(a_i, b_k)$ is calculated following the rule (3.192). The results are given in Table 3.51.

TABLE 3.51 Relative evaluation matrix.

	b_1	b_2	b_3	b_4
a_1	5.65	**2.05**	5.66	57.23
a_2	4.81	**1.20**	11.39	73.04
a_3	9.32	5.71	**2.32**	5.23
a_4	9.32	3.66	**−0.24**	27.43
a_5	7.26	3.78	**0.39**	26.29
a_6	7.39	9.33	5.93	**2.59**
a_7	12.93	10.33	6.93	**3.59**
a_8	5.83	**2.22**	4.10	51.93
a_9	11.79	8.18	4.79	**1.44**
a_{10}	9.06	5.46	**2.06**	7.94

We can then obtain the sorting results. For example, in Table 3.51, $h(a_1, b_2) \geq 0$ is the smallest value in $h(a_1, b_k), k = 1, 2, 3, 4$, thus a_1 is assigned to C_2; $h(a_4, b_3) < 0$ is the smallest value in $h(a_4, b_k), k = 1, 2, 3, 4$, thus a_4 is assigned to C_2. The final assignments are presented in Table 3.52.

TABLE 3.52 The final assignments of all alternatives.

Categories	Alternatives
C_1	∅
C_2	a_1, a_2, a_4, a_8
C_3	a_3, a_5, a_{10}
C_4	a_6, a_7, a_9

3.9 MACBETHSort: a multiple-criteria decision-aid procedure for sorting problems

3.9.1 MACBETH

MACBETH (Measuring Attractiveness by a Categorical-Based Evaluation TecHnique) is a multi-criteria decision analysis approach that requires only qualitative judgments about differences of attractiveness to help a decision maker quantify the relative value of options [55]. MACBETH is supported by an algorithm based on linear programming models.

Let X be a finite set of elements; different options are under evaluation. $v(x)$ is defined as a numerical score of the attractiveness of the element x of X:

(1) $\forall x, y \in X : x$ is more attractive than $y(x P y) \Rightarrow v(x) > v(y)$.

(2) $\forall x, y \in X : x$ is as attractive as $y(x I y) \Rightarrow v(x) = v(y)$.

When x is more attractive than y, the decision maker is asked to give a qualitative judgment about the difference of attractiveness between x and y, on the seven semantic scales shown in Table 3.53.

TABLE 3.53 Semantic scales.

Semantic scale	Equivalent numerical level	Categories
No	0	C_0
Very weak	1	C_1
Weak	2	C_2
Moderate	3	C_3
Strong	4	C_4
Very strong	5	C_5
Extreme	6	C_6

When the decision maker hesitates to give an exact qualitative judgment, he or she also has the right to choose more than one consecutive categories. Each time that a qualitative judgment is entered in the upper triangular matrix, M-MACBETH tests the consistency of all the judgments made by the decision maker. Then linear program (LP-MACBETH) is used to convert the ordinal performance scales into cardinal scales, where x^+ is at least as attractive as any other element x of X and x^- is at most as attractive as any other element x of X. The linear optimization of LP-MACBETH is as follows:

$$\text{Min} \left[v \left(x^+ \right) - v \left(x^- \right) \right] \tag{3.194}$$

$$\begin{cases} v(x) - v(y) = 0, \quad \forall x, y \in C_0. \\ v(x) - v(y) \geq i, \quad \forall x, y \in C_i \cup \cdots \cup C_s \\ \text{with } i, s \in \{1, 2, 3, 4, 5, 6\} \quad \text{and} \quad i \leq s \\ v(x) - v(y) \geq v(w) - v(z) + i - s', \quad \forall x, y \in C_i \cup \cdots \cup C_s \\ \text{and } \forall w, z \in C_{i'} \cup \cdots \cup C_{s'} \quad \text{with } i, s, i', s' \in \{1, 2, 3, 4, 5, 6\}, \\ i \leq s, \quad i' \leq s' \quad \text{and} \quad i > s'. \end{cases}$$

MACBETH uses the given qualitative judgment on attractiveness to generate the value scores and weights of options through linear programming. Take the following example to better understand MACBETH: consider k criteria for which the cardinal MACBETH score is generated with four performance levels: M_1, M_2, M_3, M_4. The performance levels for that criterion are arranged in a matrix form according to descending order of their importance from left to right and top to bottom, as shown in Table 3.54. Assume that the preference of importance for the performance levels is $M_2 > M_1 > M_3 > M_4$. Therefore, if $v(M_2)$, $v(M_1)$, $v(M_3)$, and $v(M_4)$ are the quantified MACBETH scores for levels M_1, M_2, M_3, and M_4, respectively, then $v(M_2) = 100$, $v(M_4) = 0$, and $v(M_2) > v(M_1) > v(M_3) > v(M_4)$.

TABLE 3.54 Strengths of performance levels for k^{th} criterion.

Performance levels	M_2	M_1	M_3	M_4
M_2	No	Very strong	P	P
M_1		No	Moderate	P
M_3			No	Weak
M_4				No

The next step is to convert the ordinal performance scales into cardinal scale. If the decision maker prefers the performance of M_1 over M_3 with a strength $h \in \{0, 1, \ldots, 6\}$, then $v(M_1) - v(M_3) = h\alpha$, where α is a coefficient necessary to meet the condition that $v(M_1)$ and $v(M_2) \in [0, 100]$. When the strengths of performance levels are provided, the quantified MACBETH scores can be obtained from the matrix of judgments by solving a linear program (LP-MACBETH). From the judgments provided in Table 3.54, the following system of equations can be extracted:

$$v(M_2) - v(M_1) = 5\alpha \tag{3.195}$$

$$v(M_1) - v(M_3) = 3\alpha \tag{3.196}$$

$$v(M_3) - v(M_4) = 2\alpha \tag{3.197}$$

Considering $v(M_2) = 100$ and $v(M_4) = 0$, the solutions can be obtained by solving Eqs. (3.195)–(3.197), where $\alpha = 10$, $v(M_1) = 50$, and $v(M_3) = 20$. As for the quantification of performance levels of other remaining criteria, this can be done by the same procedure. Entering the relevant data into M-MACBETH software, the global attractive scores are obtained to rank the considered alternatives.

$$V(X_i) = \sum_{j=1}^{n} v_j \cdot w_j \qquad (3.198)$$

with $\sum_{j=1}^{n} w_j = 1$, $w_j > 0$ and $\begin{cases} v_j\left(x_j^+\right) = 100 \\ v_j\left(x_j^-\right) = 0 \end{cases}$ where w_j is the weight for

the jth criterion. Based on the value of $V(X_i)$, the final ranking of alternatives can be obtained.

3.9.2 MACBETHSort

As introduced in Section 3.9.1, MACBETH uses only qualitative judgments of difference in attractiveness to generate value scores for options and weights. MACBETH has been used widely for ranking problems [56], and also for sorting problems [55,57]. The MACBETHSort method was proposed by Alessio Ishizaka [58] in order to assign products into ordered and predefined characterized classes.

3.9.2.1 Methodology

The sorting steps of the MACBETHSort method are as follows.

Step 1: Define the goal, criteria c_j, $j = 1, 2, \ldots, m$, and options o_k, $k = 1, 2, \ldots, l$.

Step 2: Define the sorting classes C_i, $i = 1, 2, \ldots, n$, where the classes are ordered and usually in a descending order (e.g., Class A, Class B, Class C or good, medium, bad).

Step 3: Define the local limiting profiles lp_{ij} or local central profiles cp_{ij} of each class. The local limiting profile lp_{ij} means that the minimum performance needed on criterion c_j belongs to a class C_i and the local central profile cp_{ij} is given by a typical example of an element belonging to the class C_i on the criterion c_j. In order to define each class, we need $m \cdot (n-1)$ limiting profiles lp_{ij} or $m \cdot n$ central profiles cp_{ij}.

The definition of the profile is a very critical step, which determines the boundary of the classification. Depending on the expertise of the decision-maker, there are three situations:

(1) In the simplest case, the decision-maker is an expert in this field and can give a clear definition of the limiting profiles.

(2) A slightly more complicated situation is where the decision-maker has limited expertise, and we need to help him or her to make the most of his or

her knowledge. We have to investigate each criterion, set the score of the investigated criterion at the lowest level, and gradually increase the score until the decision-maker thinks that the option should be assigned to a higher class, and the corresponding score is the limiting profile. We can also use the top-down method.

(3) When the decision-maker has little expertise and only provides a typical example for each class, we can only use central profiles to determine the boundary of the classification.

Step 4: When comparing the importance of the two criteria, the decision-maker is asked for a qualitative judgment after being presented with seven categories, which are shown in Table 3.53.

Derive the weights $w_j = \Phi(c_j)$ of criterion c_j by solving the linear program as in MACBETH, where c^+ is at least as attractive as any other element c_j and c^- is at most as attractive as any other element c_j.

$$\text{Min}[\Phi\left(c^+\right) - \Phi\left(c^-\right)] \tag{3.199}$$

$$\begin{cases} \Phi\left(c^-\right) = 0 \text{ (arbitrary assignment)} \\ \Phi\left(c_x\right) - \Phi\left(c_y\right) = 0 \ \forall c_x, c_y \in C_0 \\ \Phi\left(c_x\right) - \Phi\left(c_y\right) \geq i \ \forall c_x, c_y \in C_i \cup \ldots \cup C_s \\ \text{with } i, s \in \{1, 2, \ldots, 6\} \text{ and } i \leq s \\ \Phi\left(c_x\right) - \Phi\left(c_y\right) \geq \Phi\left(c_w\right) - \Phi\left(c_z\right) + i - s' \ \forall c_x, c_y \in C_i \cup \ldots \cup C_s \\ \text{and } \forall c_w, c_z \in C_{i'} \cup \ldots \cup C_{s'} \text{ with } i, s, i', s' \in \{1, 2, \ldots, 6\}, i' \leq s' < i \leq s \end{cases}$$

Step 5: In the judgment matrix, we compare pairwise the difference in importance between a single option and each limiting profile lp_{ij} or central profile cp_{ij} for each criterion c_j. We calculate the local attractiveness a_{kj} of the option o_k and the local attractiveness p_{ij} of the limiting profiles lp_{ij} or central profile cp_{ij} with the linear program (3.199).

Step 6: We calculate the overall attractiveness a_k for the option o_k by aggregating the weighted local attractiveness and the overall attractiveness lp_i for the limiting profiles or cp_i for central profiles.

$$a_k = \sum_{j=1}^{m} a_{kj} \cdot w_j \tag{3.200}$$

$$lp_i \text{ or } cp_i = \sum_{j=1}^{m} a_{ij} \cdot w_j \tag{3.201}$$

Step 7: We assign the option o_k to a class C_i by comparing a_k with lp_i or cp_i. However, the different types of profile determine different kinds of assignment algorithm used to define classes:

(1) Limiting profiles:
If choosing limiting profiles, the process of assigning option o_k to class C_i requires lp_i just below the overall attractiveness a_k.

$$
\begin{aligned}
a_k \geq lp_1 & \Rightarrow o_k \in C_1 \\
lp_2 \leq a_k < lp_1 & \Rightarrow o_k \in C_2 \\
\ldots \\
a_k < lp_{n-1} & \Rightarrow o_k \in C_n
\end{aligned}
\tag{3.202}
$$

(2) Central profiles:
As reported in Section 3.9.1, the central profile is less precise than the limiting profile because it is only used when the decision-maker cannot define a limiting profile. In this case, a typical example of each class can be defined, which corresponds to the central profiles cp_i. The limiting profiles are deduced by $(cp_i + cp_{i+1})/2$. The option o_k is assigned to the class C_i which has the nearest central profiles, the optimistic assignment allocates o_k to the upper class, and the pessimistic assignment vision allocates o_k to the lower class.

$$
\begin{aligned}
a_k \geq cp_1 & \Rightarrow o_k \in C_1 \\
cp_2 \leq a_k < cp_1 \text{ AND } (cp_1 - a_k) < (cp_2 - a_k) & \Rightarrow o_k \in C_1 \\
cp_2 \leq a_k < cp_1 \text{ AND } (cp_1 - a_k) = (cp_2 - a_k) & \Rightarrow o_k \in C_2 (\text{optimistic}) \\
cp_2 \leq a_k < cp_1 \text{ AND } (cp_1 - a_k) = (cp_2 - a_k) & \Rightarrow o_k \in C_2 (\text{pessimistic}) \\
cp_2 \leq a_k < cp_1 \text{ AND } (cp_1 - a_k) > (cp_2 - a_k) & \Rightarrow o_k \in C_2 \\
\ldots \\
a_k < cp_n & \Rightarrow o_k \in C_n
\end{aligned}
\tag{3.203}
$$

3.9.2.2 Illustrative example

In order to verify the validity of the method, the complete steps of MACBETH-Sort are conducted in the following case study.

Step 1: Problem description
A glass company is chosen for this case study and it provides five products that need to be classified according to their strategic importance. Then the manager of the company selects four criteria: *time consuming, return, market share, productivity*. For convenience, we denote the products as $X_k (k = 1, 2, \ldots, 5)$.

Step 2: Class definition
Three classes have been defined:
(1) The products of class A always need to be in stock to satisfy the actual demand.
(2) The products of class B need to be in stock to satisfy 80% of the actual demand.
(3) The products of class C do not need to be in stock.
Step 3: Limiting profiles definition (see Table 3.55)

TABLE 3.55 Limiting profiles in case study.

Criteria	Limiting profiles	
Time consuming	A: 2 weeks	B: 4 weeks
Benefits	A: $4	B: $2
Market share	A: 8%	B: 5%
Productivity	A: 60%	B: 30%

TABLE 3.56 Pairwise comparisons and weights.

	Market	Productivity	Benefits	Time	All lower
Market	No	Weak-mod	Weak	Strong	Positive
Productivity		No	Weak-str	Strong	Positive
Benefits			No	Moderate	Positive
Time				No	Positive
All lower					no

TABLE 3.57 Scores for all glass products.

	X_5	Upper	Lower	Current scale
X_5	No	Strong	Strong	200
Upper		No	Strong	100
Lower			No	0

Step 4: Criteria weight assessment

The manager of the company was asked to give the qualitative judgment of the two arbitrary criteria. By entering the relative data into M-MACBETH, the weights of criteria can be obtained.

Step 5: Compare options to limiting profiles

As for each criterion, the value of each product should also be compared with the limiting profiles of Class A and Class B. Table 3.57 shows the comparison results of the limiting profile of class A (called upper) and the limiting profile of class B (called lower) in terms of productivity of option X_5.

Step 6: Score calculation

Scores for all products after being calculated by linear optimization in Eq. (3.199) are shown in Tables 3.56 and 3.58.

Step 7: Sorting into classes

We compare each score of the product with the limiting profile of Class A and Class B, and sort each product into the corresponding class using Eq. (3.202). The sorting results are obtained and given in Table 3.59.

TABLE 3.58 Scores for all glass products.

	Time consuming (0.0476)	Benefits (0.3333)	Market share (0.4286)	Productivity (0.1905)	Overall score
X_1	63.65	−25	133.33	−5.26	50.84045
X_2	−45.46	87.5	−100	−52.63	−25.8862
X_3	200	−100	0	−100	−42.86
X_4	−19.19	200	200	42.11	159.4885
X_5	−100	12.5	66.67	200	66.08101

TABLE 3.59 Sorting results of glass products.

Class	Product	Overall score
A	X_4	159.4885
B	X_5	66.08101
	X_1	50.84045
C	X_2	−16.02
	X_3	−66.78

3.10 DEASort: data envelopment analysis based on sorting

3.10.1 DEA

Data envelopment analysis (DEA) is a multi-criteria ranking method that can rank items by importance. DEASort, as an extension of DEA, is aimed at sorting items into ordered classes. This section introduces DEA models and the DEASort method.

DEA is a date-oriented method used to evaluate the relative efficiency of a set of decision-making units with multiple input and multiple output indexes. Initiated by Charnes et al. [59], it has been applied to a variety of areas such as ecology, finance, efficiency assessment, and environment. This section introduces the Charnes–Cooper–Rhodes (CCR) model and discusses the effectiveness of the DEA method.

3.10.1.1 CCR model

The CCR model is the most basic DEA model and has two significant advantages. First, the CCR model takes the weight coefficient of multiindex input and output as the decision variables to evaluate in the sense of optimization, which avoids the determination of the index weight coefficient in the sense of statistical average. Secondly, due to the mutual connection and restriction between input and output, there is no need to determine any expression of their relationship in the CCR model, which has the characteristics of a black box type of research method.

The above assumes that there are n decision-making units (DMUs) with s outputs and m inputs. Using vector notations of outputs $y_j = (y_{1j}, y_{2j}, \cdots, y_{sj})$ and inputs $x_j = (x_{1j}, x_{2j}, \cdots, x_{mj})$, let $u_r = (u_1, u_2, \cdots, u_s)^T$, $v_i = (v_1, v_2, \cdots, v_m)^T$ be the vector of weights for outputs and inputs. The input-oriented CCR model in multiplier form is as follows:

$$max \quad h_o = \frac{u^T y_o}{v^T x_o}$$

$$\text{s.t.}$$

$$\begin{cases} \frac{u^T y_j}{v^T x_j} \leq 1 \, (j = 1, 2, \cdots, n) \\ u \geq 0, w \geq 0 \end{cases} \tag{3.204}$$

The above equation is fractional programming, which can be transformed into an equivalent linear programming model $(\bar{p})$:

$$t = \frac{1}{v^T x_o}, \omega = tv, \mu = tu$$

$$max \quad V_p = \mu^T y_o$$

$$\text{s.t.}$$

$$\begin{cases} \omega^T x_j - \mu^T y_j \geq 0 \\ \omega^T x_o = 1 \\ \omega \geq 0, \mu \geq 0 \end{cases} \tag{3.205}$$

Its dual model (D) can be expressed as follows:

$$min \quad V^D = \theta$$

$$\text{s.t.}$$

$$\begin{cases} \sum_{j=1}^n x_j \lambda_j + s^- = \theta x_o \\ \sum_{j=1}^n y_j \lambda_j - s^+ = y_o \\ \lambda_j \geq 0, s^{+ \geq 0}, s^- \geq 0 \end{cases} \tag{3.206}$$

where $s^+ = (s_1^+, s_2^+, \cdots, s_m^+)^T$ and $s^- = (s_1^-, s_2^-, \cdots, s_m^-)^T$ are slack variables.

3.10.1.2 Effectiveness of the DEA method

The DEA method can not only calculate the efficiency of decision-making units, but also consider their effectiveness evaluation.

Definition. If the optimal solution w^o, μ^o of the linear programming model $\bar{p}$ satisfies

$$V_p = \left(\mu^o\right) y_o \tag{3.207}$$

then the unit o is a weakly efficient element.

Definition. If the optimal solution w^o, μ^o of the linear programming model $\bar{p}$ satisfies

$$V_p = \left(\mu^o\right) y_o \tag{3.208}$$

in which $w^o \geq 0$, $w^o \geq 0$, then the unit o is a strongly efficient element.

Some basic properties of the linear programming model $\bar{p}$ and the dual model D are given here.

Theorem. *Both linear programming $\bar{p}$ and its dual model D have feasible solutions, so they both have optimal solutions, and the optimal values are as follows:*

$$V_P = V_D \leq 1 \tag{3.209}$$

According to the duality theory of linear programming, the duality model D can be used to determine the validity of the corresponding decision units:

(1) If the optimal value $V_D < 1$, the unit j_o is invalid and vice versa.

(2) If the optimal value $V_D = 1$, the unit j_o is weakly efficient and vice versa.

(3) If the optimal value $V_D = 1$, meanwhile $s^{o+} = 0$, $s^{o-} = 0$, the unit j_o is strongly efficient and vice versa.

The above definitions and theorem can be used to determine the effectiveness of DEA, but the implementation of the above judgment methods is relatively complicated. In practical applications, in order to judge DEA effectiveness more easily, Charnes and Cooper [59] introduced the concept of the non-Archimedes infinitesimal and transformed it into a linear programming problem. The CCR model D_ε with non-Archimedes infinitesimal quantities can be expressed as follows:

$$max\, V_p = \mu^T y_o$$

$$\text{s.t.}$$

$$\begin{cases} \omega^T x_j - \mu^T y_j \geq 0 \\ \omega^T x_o = 1 \\ \mu^T \geq \varepsilon \hat{e}^T \\ \omega^T \geq \varepsilon e^T \end{cases} \tag{3.210}$$

where $e^T = (1, 1, \cdots, 1)$ is an m-dimension vector and $e^T = (1, 1, \cdots, 1)$ is a p-dimension vector. The validity of decision-making units in this model is determined as follows:

Theorem. *If the optimal solution $\theta^o = 1$, the unit j_o is weakly efficient. Moreover, if it satisfies $s^{o+} = 0$, $s^{o-} = 0$, the unit j_o is strongly efficient.*

3.10.2 DEASort

DEASort [51] is a variant of DEA aimed at sorting problems. Its output is used to take into account the expertise of decision-makers in calculating the weights. This weight constraint is then added to the DEASort model.

3.10.2.1 Methodology

According to the number of decision-makers, this method can be applied to individual and group decision-making problems.

- **Individual decision-making**

The method classifies I items based on J criteria by only one decision-maker, using the four steps described here.

Step 1: Normalization of item scores

The measured score $v_{i,j}$ of each item i for each criterion j is normalized on a 0–1 scale to make them comparable via the following expression:

$$v_{i,j}^* = \frac{v_{i,j} - \min_{i=1,2,\dots,I} v_{i,j}}{\max_{i=1,2,\dots,I} v_{i,j} - \min_{i=1,2,\dots,I} v_{i,j}} \qquad \forall i = 1, 2, \dots, I \qquad (3.211)$$

Step 2: Calculation of the item priority

For each specific item o under evaluation, the mathematical program in Eq. (3.212) inspired by DEA is solved.

$$\max P_o = \sum_{j=1}^{n} w_{o,k} v_{o,k}$$

$$\text{s.t.} \quad \sum_{j=1}^{n} w_{o,k} v_{o,k} \leq 1 \quad i = 1, 2, \dots, I$$
$$w_{oj} \geq 0 \qquad\qquad i = 1, 2, \dots, I$$

(3.212)

Step 3: Definition of classes

The number of classes must be set and the classes defined. In order to define these classes, the decision-maker is asked to select L reference items that she or he knows very well and that belong to each class. The item with priority P_{ckl} is then calculated for each reference item.

Step 4: Sorting into classes

Item z is assigned to class C_I which has its threshold th_I just below the item priority P_z.

$$P_z \geq th_1 \qquad\qquad \Longrightarrow z \in C_1$$
$$th_2 \leq P_z \leq th_1 \quad \Longrightarrow z \in C_2$$
$$\dots$$
$$P_z < th_{n-1} \qquad \Longrightarrow z \in C_n$$

(3.213)

- **Group decision-making**

If there are K decision-makers and information on the weights is known beforehand, then the method classifies I items based on J criteria using the six steps described here.

Step 1: Normalization of item scores

This is similar to **Step 1** in individual decision-making.

Step 2: Criteria weight evaluation

Criteria weights are evaluated separately via AHP by K decision-makers. For this purpose, the J criteria are pairwise compared in a matrix on a 1–9 scale. Weights are found by calculating the eigenvector. It should be noted that the consistency of the evaluations entered by the decision-maker can be tested using the consistency ratio (CR).

Step 3: Weight bounding

In order to limit the range of possible weights, a lower bound and upper bound are defined for each weight. The lower bound of the weight for criterion j is given by the minimum evaluation score among K experts:

$$w_{LBj} = min_{k=1,2,...,K}\{w_{j,k}\} \tag{3.214}$$

The upper bound of the weight for criterion j is given by the maximum evaluation score among K experts:

$$w_{UBj} = max_{k=1,2,...,K}\{w_{j,k}\} \tag{3.215}$$

Step 4: Calculation of the item priority

This method improves on the previous DEA models by introducing the weight constraints, corresponding to the last line of Eq. (3.216).

$$
\begin{aligned}
\max\ P_o &= \sum_{j=1}^{n} w_{o,k} v_{o,k} \\
\text{s.t.}\ \ \sum_{j=1}^{n} w_{o,k} v_{o,k} &\leq 1 \qquad i = 1, 2, ..., I \\
w_{oj} &\geq 0 \qquad\quad i = 1, 2, ..., I \\
w_{LBj} &< w_{oj} < w_{UBj}
\end{aligned} \tag{3.216}
$$

A weight bounding in the model may result in its infeasibility, and thus lead to zero or negative priorities; therefore, the weight bounding needs to be reassessed.

Step 5: Definition of classes

The number of classes must be set and the classes defined. In order to define these classes, each expert k is asked to select L reference items that she or he knows very well and that belong to each class. The item with priority P_{ckl} is then calculated for each reference item. A decision tree [52] is trained on the reference items, the inputs being the item priorities P_{ckl} and the outputs being their relative classes. The decision tree uses Gini's diversity index as a splitting criterion. The number of thresholds is equal to the number of classes minus one.

The classification tree is able to work with multiple reference items and is robust to misclassified reference items.

Step 6: Sorting into classes

This is similar to **Step 4** in individual decision-making.

3.10.2.2 Illustrative example

Suppose that two decision-makers (DMs) are sorting 10 items into class A, B, or C according to three criteria c_1, c_2, and c_3.

Step 1: Normalization of item scores

The values of the three criteria (see Table 3.60) were normalized for each item using Eq. (3.211) .

Step 2: Criteria weight evaluation

Two DMs were asked to compare pairwise the importance of the three criteria. The results of this process are given in Table 3.61.

TABLE 3.60 Data on each criterion for all alternatives.

Items	c_1	c_2	c_3
1	25	42	36
2	30	25	43
3	42	46	45
4	78	27	24
5	47	50	60
6	76	42	49
7	45	10	54
8	68	75	72
9	52	57	78
10	79	43	46

TABLE 3.61 Criteria weights estimated by the two DMs.

Criteria	DM_1	DM_2
c_1	0.33	0.4
c_2	0.33	0.2
c_3	0.33	0.4

Step 3: Weight bounding

The range of weights permissible in DEA for each criterion was obtained by setting the lowest Eq. (3.214) and highest Eq. (3.215) values from Table 3.43. The results of this procedure are displayed in Table 3.62.

TABLE 3.62 Range of permissible weights.

Criteria	Lower bound	Upper bound
c_1	0.33	0.4
c_2	0.2	0.33
c_3	0.33	0.4

TABLE 3.63 Priorities of typical items.

Class	DM_1	DM_2
A	$p_8 = 0.6054$	$p_2 = 0.4252$
B	$p_5 = 0.3745$	$p_4 = 0.4470$
C	$p_1 = 0.2356$	$p_7 = 0.5324$

TABLE 3.64 Items assigned to classes A, B, and C.

Items	p_k	Class
1	0.235641	C
2	0.425239	B
3	0.484815	B
4	0.446966	B
5	0.374487	C
6	0.543615	A
7	0.53235	A
8	0.605362	A
9	0.369946	C
10	0.458333	B

Step 4: Calculation of the item priorities

The algorithm in Eq. (3.213) was implemented and the item priority P_k was calculated for each item.

Step 5: Definition of classes

The two DMs selected a typical item for each class; their item priorities are listed in Table 3.63. This training set (Table 3.63) was fed into the classification tree algorithm in MATLAB to train the decision tree described in Fig. 3.39.

Step 6: Assignment to classes

Table 3.64 lists the items assigned to classes A, B, and C. Three items were found to have a score above the limiting profile of class A and were therefore assigned to this class. Four items were assigned to class B, with their scores falling between the limiting profiles of class A and class B. Three items scored below the limiting profile of class C and were therefore assigned to class C.

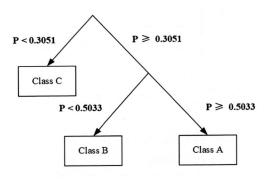

FIGURE 3.39 Trained decision tree.

References

[1] B. Roy, The optimisation problem formulation: criticism and overstepping, Journal of the Operational Research Society 32 (6) (1981) 427–436.

[2] Thomas L. Saaty, A scaling method for priorities in hierarchical structures, Journal of Mathematical Psychology 15 (3) (1977) 234–281.

[3] Alessio Ishizaka, Craig Pearman, Philippe Nemery, AHPSort: an AHP-based method for sorting problems, International Journal of Production Research 50 (17) (2012) 4767–4784.

[4] Francesco Miccoli, Alessio Ishizaka, Sorting municipalities in Umbria according to the risk of wolf attacks with AHPSort II, Ecological Indicators 73 (2017) 741–755.

[5] George A. Miller, The magical number seven plus or minus two: some limits on our capacity for processing information, Psychological Review 101 (2) (1994) 343–352.

[6] Cristina López, Alessio Ishizaka, GAHPSort: a new group multi-criteria decision method for sorting a large number of the cloud-based ERP solutions, Computers in Industry 92 (2017) 12–25.

[7] Álvaro Labella, Alessio Ishizaka, Luis Martínez, Consensual group-AHPSort: applying consensus to GAHPSort in sustainable development and industrial engineering, Computers & Industrial Engineering 152 (2021) 107013.

[8] Thomas L. Saaty, The analytic network process, Iranian Journal of Operations Research 1 (1) (2008) 1–27.

[9] Rozann W. Saaty, Decision Making in Complex Environments: the Analytic Network Process (ANP) for Dependence and Feedback, A manual for the ANP software superdecisions, Creative Decisions Foundation, Pittsburgh, PA, 2002.

[10] Alessio Ishizaka, Vijay Pereira, Utilisation of ANPSort for sorting alternative with interdependent criteria illustrated through a researcher's classification problem in an academic context, Soft Computing 24 (18) (2020) 13639–13650.

[11] J.P. Brans, Ph. Vincke, Note-a preference ranking organisation method: the PROMETHEE method for multiple criteria decision-making, Management Science 31 (6) (1985) 647–656.

[12] J.P. Brans, L'ingénièrie de la décision; Elaboration d'instruments d'aide à la décision. La méthode PROMETHEE, in: Méthode PROMETHEE, 1982, pp. 183–213.

[13] C.A.V. Cavalcante, A.T. de Almeida, A multi-criteria decision-aiding model using PROMETHEE III for preventive maintenance planning under uncertain conditions, Journal of Quality in Maintenance Engineering 13 (4) (2007) 385–397.

[14] Bertrand Mareschal, Jean PierreBrans, Philippe Vincke, PROMETHEE: a new family of outranking methods in multicriteria analysis, ULB Institutional Repository (1984) 477–490.

[15] Jean Pierre Brans, Bertrand Mareschal, PROMETHEE V: MCDM problems with segmentation constraints, Infor 30 (2) (1992) 85–96.

[16] Jean Pierre Brans, Bertrand Mareschal, The PROMETHEE VI procedure: how to differentiate hard from soft multicriteria problems, Journal of Decision Systems 4 (3) (1995) 213–223.

[17] Majid Behzadian, Reza Baradaran Kazemzadeh, Amir Albadvi, Mohammad Aghdasi, PROMETHEE: a comprehensive literature review on methodologies and applications, European Journal of Operational Research 200 (1) (2010) 198–215.

[18] Bertrand Mareschal, Jean Pierre Brans, Geometrical representations for MCDA, European Journal of Operational Research 34 (1) (1988) 69–77.

[19] Cathy Macharis, Johan Springael, Klaas De Brucker, Alain Verbeke, PROMETHEE and AHP: the design of operational synergies in multicriteria analysis: strengthening PROMETHEE with ideas of AHP, European Journal of Operational Research 153 (2) (2004) 307–317.

[20] Philippe Nemery, Claude Lamboray, FlowSort: a flow-based sorting method with limiting or central profiles, Top 16 (1) (2008) 90–113.

[21] Pierre Janssen, Philippe Nemery, An extension of the FlowSort sorting method to deal with imprecision, A Quarterly Journal of Operations Research 11 (2) (2013) 171–193.

[22] Francesco Lolli, Alessio Ishizaka, Rita Gamberini, Bianca Rimini, Michael Messori, FlowSort-GDSS – a novel group multi-criteria decision support system for sorting problems with application to FMEA, Expert Systems with Applications 42 (17) (2015) 6342–6349.

[23] Eric Jacquet-Lagrèze, Yannis Siskos, Preference disaggregation: 20 years of MCDA experience, European Journal of Operational Research 130 (2) (2001) 233–245.

[24] Michael Doumpos, Constantin Zopounidis, Developing sorting models using preference disaggregation analysis: an experimental investigation, European Journal of Operational Research 154 (3) (2004) 585–598.

[25] E. Jacquet-Lagreze, J. Siskos, Assessing a set of additive utility functions for multicriteria decision-making, the UTA method, European Journal of Operational Research 10 (2) (1982) 151–164.

[26] Constantin Zopounidis, Michael Doumpos, PREFDIS: a multicriteria decision support system for sorting decision problems, Computers & Operations Research 27 (7) (2000) 779–797.

[27] Constantin Zopounidis, Michael Doumpos, A preference disaggregation decision support system for financial classification problems, European Journal of Operational Research 130 (2) (2001) 402–413.

[28] Constantin Zopounidis, Michael Doumpos, Multicriteria classification and sorting methods: a literature review, European Journal of Operational Research 138 (2) (2002) 229–246.

[29] Salvatore Greco, Roman Slowinski, José Rui Figueira, Vincent Mousseau, Robust ordinal regression, Trends in Multiple Criteria Decision Analysis (2010) 241–283.

[30] Salvatore Greco, Vincent Mousseau, Roman Słowiński, Ordinal regression revisited: multiple criteria ranking using a set of additive value functions, European Journal of Operational Research 191 (2) (2008) 416–436.

[31] Salvatore Greco, Vincent Mousseau, Roman Słowiński, Multiple criteria sorting with a set of additive value functions, European Journal of Operational Research 207 (3) (2010) 1455–1470.

[32] Salvatore Greco, Miłosz Kadziński, Vincent Mousseau, Roman Słowiński, Robust ordinal regression for multiple criteria group decision: UTAGMS-GROUP and UTADISGMS-GROUP, Decision Support Systems 52 (3) (2012) 549–561.

[33] Salvatore Greco, Miłosz Kadziński, Roman Słowiński, Selection of a representative value function in robust multiple criteria sorting, Computers & Operations Research 38 (11) (2011) 1620–1637.

[34] Miłosz Kadziński, Salvatore Greco, Roman Słowiński, Selection of a representative value function in robust multiple criteria ranking and choice, European Journal of Operational Research 217 (3) (2012) 541–553.

[35] Jose Rui Figueira, Salvatore Greco, Bernard Roy, Roman Słowiński, ELECTRE methods: main features and recent developments, Croatian Operational Research Review 1 (1) (2010) 51–89.

[36] B. Roy, Classement et choix en présence de points de vue multiples, Revue Française d'automatique, d'informatique et de Recherche opérationnelle. Recherche Opérationnelle 2 (8) (1968) 57–75.

[37] José Rui Figueira, Salvatore Greco, Bernard Roy, Roman Słowiński, An overview of ELECTRE methods and their recent extensions, Journal of Multi-Criteria Decision Analysis 20 (2013) 61–85.

[38] B. Roy, Electre III: Un Algorithme de Classements fonde sur une representation floue des Preferences en Presence de Criteres Multiples, Cahiers Du Centre D'études de Recherche Opérationnelle 20 (1978) 3–24.

[39] V. Mousseau, R. Slowinski, Inferring an ELECTRE TRI model from assignment examples, Journal of Global Optimization 12 (2) (1998) 157–174.

[40] J.R. Figueira, J. Almeida-Dias, S. Matias, B. Roy, M.J. Carvalho, C.E. Plancha, Electre Tri-C, a multiple criteria decision aiding sorting model applied to assisted reproduction, International Journal of Medical Informatics 80 (4) (2011) 262–273.

[41] Juscelino Almeida Dias, José Rui Figueira, Bernard Roy, A multiple criteria sorting method where each category is characterized by several reference actions: the Electre Tri-nC method, European Journal of Operational Research 217 (3) (2012) 567–579.

[42] Ching-Lai Hwang, Kwangsun Yoon, Multiple Attribute Decision Making, Lecture Notes in Economics and Mathematical Systems (LNE), vol. 186, Springer, 1981.

[43] Young-Jou Lai, Ting-Yun Liu, Ching-Lai Hwang, TOPSIS for MODM, European Journal of Operational Research 76 (3) (1994) 486–500.

[44] Kwangsun Yoon, Systems selection by multiple attribute decision making, Ph.D. Dissertation, Kansas State University, Manhattan, Kansas, 1980.

[45] Hassanali Faraji Sabokbar, Ali Hosseini, Audrius Banaitis, Nerija Banaitiene, A novel sorting method TOPSIS-sort: an application for Tehran environmental quality evaluation, E & M Ekonomie A Management 19 (2) (2016) 87–104.

[46] Diogo Ferreira de Lima Silva, Adiel Teixeira de Almeida Filho, Sorting with TOPSIS through boundary and characteristic profiles, Computers & Industrial Engineering 141 (2020) 106328.

[47] Serafim Opricovic, Multicriteria optimization of civil engineering systems, Faculty of Civil Engineering, Belgrade 2 (1) (1998) 5–21.

[48] Serafim Opricovic, Gwo-Hshiung Tzeng, Compromise solution by MCDM methods: a comparative analysis of VIKOR and TOPSIS, European Journal of Operational Research 156 (2) (2004) 445–455.

[49] Serafim Opricovic, Gwo-Hshiung Tzeng, Extended VIKOR method in comparison with outranking methods, European Journal of Operational Research 178 (2) (2007) 514–529.

[50] Leyla Demir, Muhammet Enes Akpınar, Ceyhun Araz, Mehmet Ali Ilgın, A green supplier evaluation system based on a new multi-criteria sorting method: VIKORSORT, Expert Systems with Applications 114 (2018) 479–487.

[51] Alessio Ishizaka, Francesco Lolli, Elia Balugani, Rita Cavallieri, Rita Gamberini, DEASort: assigning items with data envelopment analysis in ABC classes, International Journal of Production Economics 199 (2018) 7–15.

[52] C. Bishop, Pattern Recognition and Machine Learning, Statistical Science (2006).

[53] Mehdi Keshavarz Ghorabaee, Edmundas Kazimieras Zavadskas, Zenonas Turskis, Jurgita Antucheviciene, A new combinative distance-based assessment (CODAS) method for multicriteria decision-making, Economic Computation and Economic Cybernetics Studies and Research 50 (3) (2016) 25–44.

[54] A. Ouhibi, H. Frikha, CODAS-SORT: a new CODAS based method for sorting problems, in: 2019 6th International Conference on Control, Decision and Information Technologies (CoDIT), 2019, pp. 855–860.

[55] Carlos A. Bana e Costa, Jean Marie De Corte, Jean Claude Vansnick, MACBETH, International Journal of Information Technology & Decision Making 11 (2) (2012) 359–387.

[56] Marc Roubens, Agnieszka Rusinowska, Harrie C.M. de Swart, Using MACBETH to determine utilities of governments to parties in coalition formation, European Journal of Operational Research 172 (2) (2006) 588–603.

[57] Carlos A. Bana e Costa, Rui Carvalho Oliveira, Assigning priorities for maintenance, repair and refurbishment in managing a municipal housing stock, European Journal of Operational Research 138 (2) (2002) 380–391.

[58] Alessio Ishizaka, Maynard Gordon, MACBETHSort: a multiple criteria decision aid procedure for sorting strategic products, Journal of the Operational Research Society 68 (1) (2017) 53–61.

[59] A.A. Charnes, W.W. Cooper, E. Rhodes, Measuring the efficiency of decision making units, European Journal of Operational Research 2 (6) (1978) 429–444.

Chapter 4

Fuzzy sets and MCDM sorting

4.1 Fuzzy sets: concepts

Multi-criteria decision analysis (MCDM) uses diverse approaches to work with discrete and continuous problems. However, one important theory that has been widely implemented and developed with MCDM is fuzzy sets theory [1–3]. In MCDM there are many situations in which uncertainty is present, because of lack of information, parameter understanding, expert knowledge, or preference expression.

This section aims to explain the basic concepts of fuzzy sets theory to aid understanding of the use of fuzzy numbers in the extended fuzzy MCDM methods. This description will help identify the functions and operations of fuzzy numbers in the fuzzy extension of MCDM methods.

First, it is necessary to understand the difference between classical crisp sets and fuzzy sets. The classical crisp set theory considers a collection of objects as a set of elements. It is a binary relation between an object x and a set A, where $x \in A$ means that the element x is a member of set A. Here, sets are well-determined collections that are characterized entirely by their elements [4].

Let us see how the classical set theory is applied with the teenager concept. This concept would vary from the perception of the society in one culture to another culture. The number of years from a person indicates if she or he is a teenager or not. In one country, a teenager can be from 13 to 19 years old. In a classical set, when the person is 20 years old, she/he is not a teenager anymore. From 13 to 19 years old, it is said, she/he is in full membership. In this classical set, the person belongs to the set teenager until she/he is within the defined threshold (20 years old). In this case, a person belongs to the teenager set if she/he is below the threshold of 20. If the person's age is above the threshold, she/he belongs to the adult set.

Fuzzy set theory provides a more flexible approach about membership that can deal with problems relating to ambiguous, subjective, and imprecise judgments. It can quantify the linguistic facet of available data and preferences for individual or group decision-making [5]. In a fuzzy set, the teenager concept is seen in a different way. The person's age is seen as a membership, indicating that she/he belongs to the set teenager with a grade of membership. The person can be in an age belonging to one class with a grade of membership and other classes with other grades of membership. In other words, we can say this person

Multi-Criteria Decision-Making Sorting Methods. https://doi.org/10.1016/B978-0-32-385231-9.00009-2
161

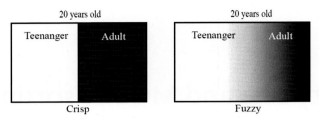

FIGURE 4.1 Membership function of classical and fuzzy sets.

belongs to the teenager set in a grade of membership, and this membership will be reduced as she/he is getting older.

The concept of fuzzy sets can be understood as a way to express the imprecision of objects. Zadeh [6] formulated the concept of fuzzy sets to deal with ill-defined objects. In fuzzy sets, the element is analyzed in the context of set membership. This fuzzy approach allows the identification of the element in various degrees of membership in the set.

The classical set elements can be defined as membership in a binary property {0, 1}. The elements in a fuzzy set present a property where the membership can be defined with various degrees of membership (imprecise property). Fig. 4.1 illustrates the classical (crisp) set and a fuzzy set with the exemplification of the teenager concept.

In fuzzy set theory, X is a collection of object denoted by x. Then a fuzzy set $\tilde{A}$ in the universe X is a set of ordered pairs:

$$\tilde{A} = \{(x, \mu_{\tilde{A}}(x)) \mid x \in X\}$$

where $\mu_{\tilde{A}}(x)$ is the membership function, representing the degree of membership of x in the fuzzy set $\tilde{A}$ with a range from 0 to 1, $\mu_{\tilde{A}}(x) \in [0, 1]$. In other words, it is the degree of truth of x in the fuzzy set $\tilde{A}$. This fuzzy set $\tilde{A}$ is represented as follows:

$$\tilde{A} = \mu_{\tilde{A}}(x_1)/x_1 + \mu_{\tilde{A}}(x_2)/x_2 + \ldots + \mu_{\tilde{A}}(x_n)/x_n$$
$$= \sum_i \mu_{\tilde{A}}(x_i)/x_i, \quad x_i \in X$$

The representation of a membership function is commonly described in some fuzzy numbers as triangular, trapezoidal, and Gaussian. The triangular fuzzy number is represented by three points and two straight lines. The trapezoidal fuzzy number is represented by four points and three straight lines. The Gaussian fuzzy number is represented by a bell shape. Each of them is used in different kinds of problems. An example to represent the membership of a person with a teenager set is presented here.

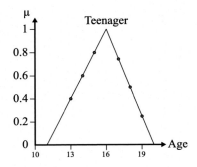

FIGURE 4.2 Membership function of teenager.

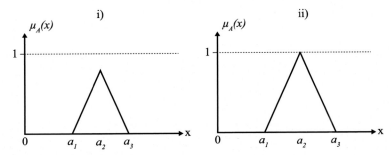

FIGURE 4.3 Nonnormal and normal fuzzy set.

Example 4.1 (Fuzzy set "teenager"). The person considered as a teenager can be in a range of ages. If we analyze the teenager stage with $X = \{13, 14, 15, 16, 17, 18, 19\}$, a member function is defined to calculate it in each x of $X(\mu_{\tilde{A}}(x))$.

$\mu_{\tilde{A}}(13) = 0.4$, $\mu_{\tilde{A}}(14) = 0.6$, ..., $\mu_{\tilde{A}}(19) = 0.25$, then the fuzzy set "teenager" is illustrated in Fig. 4.2 and described as follows:

$$\tilde{A} = \{(13, 0.4), (14, 0.6), (15, 0.8), (16, 1), (17, 0.76), (18, 0.5), (19, 0.25)\}$$

4.1.1 Fuzzy basic definitions

Definition 4.1. [7] [Height] The height is the supremum of the membership grade of elements in fuzzy set A, and it is denoted by $hgt(A)$. When $hgt(A) = 1$, this is accomplished with the normal descriptor.

$$hgt(A) = \sup_{x \in X} \mu_{\tilde{A}}(x_i)$$

Definition 4.2. [7] [Normal] The descriptor normal indicates that there exists, at least in the domain of the membership function, a situation where $\mu_{\tilde{A}}(x) = 1$ (see Fig. 4.3).

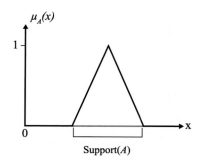

FIGURE 4.4 Support of fuzzy set.

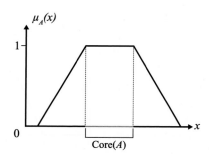

FIGURE 4.5 Core of fuzzy set.

Definition 4.3. [7] [Support] In a fuzzy set, the set $Supp(A)$ contains elements with nonzero membership degree in A (see Fig. 4.4).

$$Supp(A) = \{x \in X \mid \mu_{\tilde{A}} > 0\}$$

For the teenager example, the support is as follows:

$$Supp(teenager) = \{(13, 0.4), (14, 0.6), (15, 0.8), (16, 1), (17, 0.76),$$
$$(18, 0.5), (19, 0.25)\}$$

Definition 4.4. [7] [Core] The $Core(A)$ is a fuzzy set consisting of all elements with the membership grades equal to one (see Fig. 4.5).

$$Core(A) = \{x \in X \mid \mu_{\tilde{A}} = 1\}$$

For the teenager example, the core is as follows:

$$Core(A) = \{(16, 1)\}$$

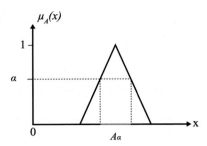

FIGURE 4.6 The α-cut fuzzy set.

Definition 4.5. [7] [$\alpha - cut$] In a fuzzy set A, the $\alpha - cut$ A_α contains elements with their membership degree greater than or equal to α (see Fig. 4.6).

$$A_\alpha = \{x \in X \mid \mu_{\tilde{A}} \geqslant \alpha\}$$

For the teenager example, the $\alpha - cut$ with $\alpha = 0.6$ is as follows:

$$Teenager_{0.6} = \{(14, 0.6), (15, 0.8), (16, 1), (17, 0.76)\}$$

Definition 4.6. [7] [Cardinality] The cardinality of fuzzy set A is denoted by $Card(A)$ and corresponds to the sum of the membership degrees.

$$Card(A) = \sum_{i=1}^{n} \mu_{\tilde{A}}(x_i)$$

For the teenager example, the support is as follows:

$$Card(teenager) = 0.4 + 0.6 + 0.8 + 1 + 0.76 + 0.5 + 0.25$$
$$Card(teenager) = 4.31$$

4.1.2 Operations and properties

There are some basic operations that are necessary to use with fuzzy sets, such as the union (or), intersection (and), and complement (not).

The **union** of the fuzzy set $\tilde{A}$ and $\tilde{B}$ is represented by the fuzzy set $\tilde{C} = \tilde{A} \cup \tilde{B}$ and it is defined by

$$\mu_{\tilde{C}}(x) = max\{\mu_{\tilde{A}}(x), \mu_{\tilde{B}}(x)\}, \quad x \in X$$

The **intersection** of the fuzzy set $\tilde{A}$ and $\tilde{B}$ is represented by the fuzzy set $\tilde{D} = \tilde{A} \cap \tilde{B}$, and it is defined by

$$\mu_{\tilde{D}}(x) = min\{\mu_{\tilde{A}}(x), \mu_{\tilde{B}}(x)\}, \quad x \in X$$

The **complement** of a normalized fuzzy set $\tilde{A}$ is defined by

$$\mu_{\neg\tilde{A}}(x) = 1 - \mu_{\tilde{A}}(x), \quad x \in X$$

The operations with the fuzzy set are defined with their membership functions. Thus, they are essential components of fuzzy sets. For a more detailed description of this concept, see [6].

The fuzzy sets' properties are commutative, associative, distributive, idempotency, identity, transitivity, involution, and Morgan's law. These can be described as follows.

Commutative property
Having two fuzzy sets $\tilde{A}$ and $\tilde{B}$, the property states:

$$\tilde{A} \cup \tilde{B} = \tilde{B} \cup \tilde{A} \tag{4.1}$$

$$\tilde{A} \cap \tilde{B} = \tilde{B} \cap \tilde{A} \tag{4.2}$$

Associative property
Having three fuzzy sets $\tilde{A}$, $\tilde{B}$, and $\tilde{C}$, the property states:

$$\tilde{A} \cup (\tilde{B} \cup \tilde{C}) = (\tilde{A} \cup \tilde{B}) \cup \tilde{C} \tag{4.3}$$

$$\tilde{A} \cap (\tilde{B} \cap \tilde{C}) = (\tilde{A} \cap \tilde{B}) \cap \tilde{C} \tag{4.4}$$

Distributive property
Having three fuzzy sets $\tilde{A}$, $\tilde{B}$, and $\tilde{C}$, the property states:

$$\tilde{A} \cup (\tilde{B} \cap \tilde{C}) = (\tilde{A} \cup \tilde{B}) \cap (\tilde{A} \cup \tilde{C}) \tag{4.5}$$

$$\tilde{A} \cap (\tilde{B} \cup \tilde{C}) = (\tilde{A} \cap \tilde{B}) \cup (\tilde{A} \cap \tilde{C}) \tag{4.6}$$

Idempotency property
For a fuzzy set $\tilde{A}$, the property states:

$$\tilde{A} \cup \tilde{A} = \tilde{A} \tag{4.7}$$

$$\tilde{A} \cap \tilde{A} = \tilde{A} \tag{4.8}$$

Identity property
For the fuzzy set $\tilde{A}$ and the universe X, the property states:

$$\tilde{A} \cup \emptyset = \tilde{A}, \quad \tilde{A} \cap X = \tilde{A} \tag{4.9}$$

$$\tilde{A} \cap \emptyset = \tilde{A}, \quad \tilde{A} \cup X = \tilde{A} \tag{4.10}$$

Transitivity property
Having three fuzzy sets $\tilde{A}$, $\tilde{B}$, and $\tilde{C}$, the property states:

$$if \ \tilde{A} \subseteq \tilde{B} \ and \ \tilde{B} \subseteq \tilde{C}, \ then \ \tilde{A} \subseteq \tilde{C} \tag{4.11}$$

Involution property
For fuzzy set $\tilde{A}$, the property states:

$$\neg(\neg\tilde{A}) = \tilde{A} \tag{4.12}$$

Morgan's law property
For the fuzzy sets $\tilde{A}$ and $\tilde{B}$, the property states:

$$\overline{\tilde{A} \cap \tilde{B}} = \overline{\tilde{A}} \cup \overline{\tilde{B}} \tag{4.13}$$

$$\overline{\tilde{A} \cup \tilde{B}} = \overline{\tilde{A}} \cap \overline{\tilde{B}} \tag{4.14}$$

4.1.2.1 Triangular-norm and triangular-conorm

Two operations that are related to the membership function when working with fuzzy sets are the intersection and union. These are known as t-norm and t-conorm, respectively.

The fuzzy intersection or t-norm

A triangular-norm is the known binary operation t-norm that satisfies the boundary condition, monotonicity, commutativity, and associativity axiom. The binary operation is $T : [0.1] \times [0, 1] \rightarrow [0, 1]$.

(a) Commutativity $T(x, y) = T(y, x)$
(b) Associativity $T(T(x, y), z) = T(x, T(y, z))$
(c) Monotonicity $(x \leqslant x', y \leqslant y') \rightarrow T(x, y) \leqslant T(x', y')$
(d) Boundary condition $T(x, 0) = x$, $T(x,1) = 1$

The fuzzy union or t-conorm

A triangular-conorm is a binary operation t-conorm that satisfies the boundary condition, monotonicity, commutativity, and associativity axiom. The binary operation is $S : [0.1] \times [0, 1] \rightarrow [0, 1]$.

(a) Commutativity $S(x, y) = S(y, x)$
(b) Associativity $S(x, S(y, z)) = S(S(x, y), z)$
(c) Monotonicity $(x \leqslant x', y \leqslant y') \rightarrow S(x, y) \leqslant S(x', y')$
(d) Boundary condition $S(x, 0) = x$, $S(x,1) = 1$

where $x, y, x', y' \in [0, 1]$.

A duality property exists in the t-norm and t-conorm. In T representing the t-norm operator, the corresponding dual t-norm, T', is defined by

$$T'(x, y) = 1 - S(1 - x, 1 - y) \tag{4.15}$$

For the t-conorm operator, the corresponding dual t-conorm, S', is defined by

$$S'(x, y) = 1 - T(1 - x, 1 - y) \tag{4.16}$$

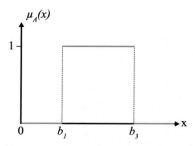

FIGURE 4.7   Membership function $\mu_{\tilde{A}}(x)$ for the interval fuzzy set $I = [b_1, b_3]$.

In this sense, this duality can be redefined by Eqs. (4.17) and (4.18). As we can see, this relationship corresponds with Morgan's law in Eqs. (4.13) and (4.14).

$$T(1 - x, 1 - y) = 1 - S'(x, y) \qquad (4.17)$$

$$S(1 - x, 1 - y) = 1 - T'(x, y) \qquad (4.18)$$

4.1.3   Fuzzy numbers

In this section, some fuzzy numbers are described, such as interval, triangular, trapezoidal, and bell-shaped. However, we first present the definition of fuzzy numbers, which is as follows.

Definition 4.7. [8] [Fuzzy number] If a fuzzy set is convex and normalized, and its membership function is defined in $\Re$ and piecewise continuous, it is called a "fuzzy number."

Interval fuzzy number

An interval is a subset $I \subset \Re$ that contains all real numbers lying between any two numbers of the set. For instance, the interval is denoted as $I = [b_1, b_3]$; $b_1, b_3 \in \Re$, $b_1 < b_3$. This kind of interval set is called a closed interval. Other interval definitions includes open, bounded, and other. However, we will use the closed interval for our description. When we think of a member function to express intervals, it is expressed as in Eq. (4.19) and represented as shown in Fig. 4.7. A more detailed description can be found in [9].

$$\mu_{\tilde{A}}(x) = \begin{cases} 0, & x < b_1 \\ 1, & b_1 \leqslant x \leqslant b_3 \\ 0, & x > b_3 \end{cases} \qquad (4.19)$$

A fuzzy interval is expressed by two end points as stated in Eq. (4.19). However, it is generally expressed by two end points and a peak point b_2 as $[b_1, b_2, b_3]$. It is illustrated in Fig. 4.8.

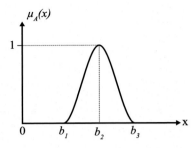

FIGURE 4.8 Membership function $\mu_{\tilde{A}}(x)$ for the interval fuzzy set $[b_1, b_2, b_3]$.

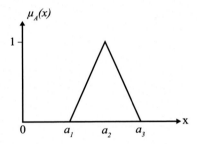

FIGURE 4.9 Triangular fuzzy number with three points $A = (a_1, a_2, a_3)$.

Triangular fuzzy number

The triangular fuzzy number is often applied. This is a fuzzy number represented with three points $A = (a_1, a_2, a_3)$ and its membership function is expressed by Eq. (4.20). Fig. 4.9 illustrates the triangular fuzzy number. As shown, the triangular membership function is formed using straight lines and is piecewise linear. Some examples and descriptions can be found in [9].

$$\mu_{\tilde{A}}(x) = \begin{cases} 0, & x < a_1 \\ \dfrac{x - a_1}{a_2 - a_1}, & a_1 \leqslant x \leqslant a_2 \\ \dfrac{a_3 - x}{a_3 - a_2}, & a_2 \leqslant x \leqslant a_3 \\ 0, & x > a_3 \end{cases} \tag{4.20}$$

Trapezoidal fuzzy number

The trapezoidal fuzzy number is also considered very useful. A fuzzy number A is represented with four points: $A = (a_1, a_2, a_3, a_4)$. The membership function of a trapezoidal fuzzy number is expressed by Eq. (4.21) and illustrated in Fig. 4.10. As shown, the trapezoidal membership function is formed using straight lines and is piecewise linear. Some examples and descriptions can be

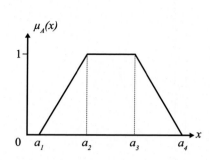

FIGURE 4.10 Trapezoidal fuzzy number with four points $A = (a_1, a_2, a_3, a_4)$.

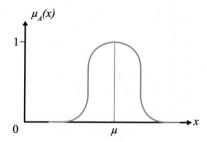

FIGURE 4.11 Gaussian fuzzy number is a bell shape.

found in [9].

$$\mu_{\tilde{A}}(x) = \begin{cases} 0, & x < a_1 \\ \dfrac{x - a_1}{a_2 - a_1}, & a_1 \leqslant x \leqslant a_2 \\ 1, & a_2 \leqslant x \leqslant a_3 \\ \dfrac{a_4 - x}{a_4 - a_3}, & a_3 \leqslant x \leqslant a_4 \\ 0, & x > a_4 \end{cases} \tag{4.21}$$

Bell-shaped fuzzy number

This is a Gaussian fuzzy number with a membership function expressed by

$$\mu_{\tilde{A}}(x) = exp\left(\frac{-x(x - \mu)^2}{2\sigma^2}\right),$$

where μ is a membership function center and σ determines the membership function width. The Gaussian fuzzy number is illustrated in Fig. 4.11. For a more detailed description, see [9–11].

4.1.4 Linguistic variables

A variable can represent the assertion of a logic proposition with values of true or false. These kinds of variables are called "logic variables" and they can be combined by using connectives such as negation, disjunction, and conjunction as logic functions. The value of a logic function can be evaluated according to the values of propositional variables (logic variables) and the truth values of connectives. The algebraic expressions $a \vee b$ and $a \wedge b$ are representation of logic formulas; in this sense, any logic formula defines a logic function.

In logic, a predicate is a group of words that can be applied to individuals. The groups of words "is yellow," "is tall," "is less than," and "belong to" can be applied to the following individual items or people "the sun," "John," "one," and "she" as follows:

The sun is yellow
John is tall
One is less than two
That scarf belongs to me
She is Maria

Definition 4.8. [12] [Predicate logic] is a logic that represents a proposition with the predicate and individual (object).

We can say that some data from judges are expressed in natural language, but this language is very vague and it may be desirable to have a numerical representation with an understood degree of uncertainty for an expression such as "frequently" or "rarely." Then, fuzzy variables provide a means to translate qualitative language into quantitative statements. In this sense, verbal quantifiers can be made precise using fuzzy set theory by creating a fuzzy number [13].

A linguistic variable is defined in terms of a base variable, whose values are real numbers within a specific range [14]. A base variable can be height, darkness, brightness, age, etc. In a linguistic variable, linguistic terms representing approximate values of a base variable, relevant to a particular application, are captured by approximate fuzzy numbers [14]. That is, each linguistic variable consists of the following elements.

Definition 4.9. [12] [Linguistic variable] is a quintuple that can be defined as follows:

$$Linguistic\ variable = (x, T(x), U, G, M) \tag{4.22}$$

where:

- x is the name of the variable;
- $T(x)$ is the set of linguistic terms which can be a value of the variable;
- U is the set of universe of discourse which defines the characteristics of the variable;
- G is the syntactic grammar which produces terms in $T(x)$; and
- M is the semantic rules which map terms in $T(x)$ to fuzzy sets in U.

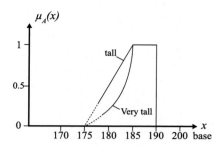

FIGURE 4.12   Linguistic variable for men's heights.

4.1.4.1   Fuzzy predicate

A fuzzy predicate is a predicate whose definition contains ambiguity [12]. Examples are "John is tall" or "Maria is young." In these instances, the terms "tall" and "young" are fuzzy terms and the sets "tall(John)" and "young(Maria)" are fuzzy sets. Given a fuzzy predicate "John is tall," it can be explained as follows [12]:

$tall(x)$ is a fuzzy set. The membership degree of x in the set *tall* is defined by the membership function $\mu_{tall(x)}$.

$\mu_{tall(x)}$ is the satisfactory degree of x for the property *tall*. The membership function is defining the truth value of the fuzzy predicate.

4.1.4.2   Fuzzy modifier

The term "tall" can be seen as a primary term and it can generate new terms adding a modifier (e.g., "very"). Fig. 4.12 illustrates the semantic of the new term and its membership function. The linguistic variable "men's heights" shown in Fig. 4.12 presents the "tall" and "very tall" linguistic terms. The term "tall" is represented by the membership function $\mu_{tall(x)}$. The term "very tall" is represented by the membership function $\mu_{very\,tall(x)}$. The graphs of both membership functions of "tall" and "very tall" are represented in Fig. 4.12 The variable "men's heights" takes a value in the set $T(men's\ heights) = \{tall, very\,tall\}$.

$$U = \{x | x \in [75, 190]\}$$

Fig. 4.13 shows the representation of the linguistic variable "men's heights" presented in [15]. In this case, men's heights is the universe of discourse. It is the range of possible values of the linguistic variable that represents the variable's universe of discourse. In Fig. 4.13, the men's heights consist of five fuzzy sets: very short, short, average, tall, and very tall. It is the exemplification of the linguistic hedge (very). It is an operation that modifies the meaning of a fuzzy set, which can be understood as terms that modify the shapes of fuzzy sets by using the adverb "very" [15].

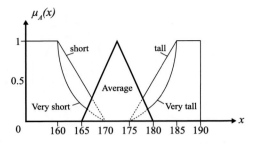

FIGURE 4.13 Linguistic hedge (very) for the linguistic variable men's heights.

4.1.5 Fuzzy relations

4.1.5.1 Product set

The term ordered pair is used when an order exists between elements x and y, and it is denoted by (x, y).

Definition 4.10. [16] [Product set] Let A and B be two nonempty sets. The product set or Cartesian product $A \times B$ is defined as follows:

$$A \times B = \{(a, b) | a \in A, b \in B\}$$

A Cartesian product for a n set, $A_1, A_2, ..., A_n$ the set of all n-tuples $(a_1, a_2, ..., a_n)$ such that $a_1 \in A_1, a_2 \in A_2, ..., a_n \in A_n$ is written as $A_1 \times A_2 \times ... \times A_n$.

$$\prod_{i=1}^{n} A_i$$

In this sense, for the sets $A = \{a_1, a_2\}$, $B = \{b_1, b_2, b_3\}$, the Cartesian product is as follows:

$$A \times B = (a_1, b_1), (a_1, b_2), (a_1, b_3), (a_2, b_1), (a_2, b_2), (a_2, b_3)$$

4.1.5.2 Definition of relation

Definition 4.11. [16] [Binary relation] If A and B are two sets and there is a specific property between elements x of A and y of B, this property can be described using the ordered pairs (x, y) $x \in A$ and $y \in B$, and is called a relation R.

$$R = \{(x, y) | x \in A, y \in B\}$$

where R is a binary relation and a subset of $A \times B$.

The term "x is in relation R with y" is denoted as $(x, y) \in R$ or $x R y$ with $R \subseteq A \times B$. If $(x, y) \notin R$, x is not in relation R with y.

If $A = B$ or R is a relation from A to A, it is written $(x, x) \in R$ or $x R x$ for $R \subseteq A \times A$.

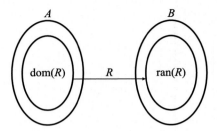

FIGURE 4.14 Domain and range.

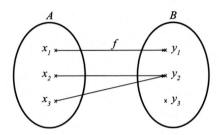

FIGURE 4.15 Mapping $y = f(x)$.

Definition 4.12. [16] [n-ary relation] For sets $A_1, A_2, ..., A_n$, the relation among elements $x_1 \in A_1, x_2 \in A_2, ..., x_n \in A_n$ can be described by n-tuple $(x_1, x_2, ..., x_n)$. A collection of such n-tuples $(x_1, x_2, ..., x_n)$ is a relation R among $A_1, A_2, ..., A_n$. It is defined as follows:

$$(x_1, x_2, ..., x_n) \in R$$
$$R \subseteq A_1 \times A_2 \times ... \times A_n$$

Definition 4.13. [16] [Domain and range] Let R stand for a relation between A and B. The domain and range of this relation are illustrated in Fig. 4.14 and defined as follows:

$$dom(R) = \{x | x \in A, (x, y) \in R \ for \ some \ y \in B\}$$
$$ran(R) = \{y | y \in B, (x, y) \in R \ for \ some \ x \in A\}$$

The set A is defined as support of $dom(R)$ and B as support of $ran(R)$. $dom(R) = A$ is completely specified and $dom(R) \subseteq A$ is incompletely specified [16]. The relation $R \subseteq A \times B$ is a set of ordered pairs (x, y). Thus, if we have a certain element x in A, we can find y of B, i.e., the mapped image of A. We say that "y is the mapping of x," and Fig. 4.15 shows this relation.

If we express this mapping as f, y is called the **image** of x, which is denoted as $f(x)$:

$$R = \{(x, y) | x \in A, y \in B, y = f(x)\} \ or f : A \to B$$

$ran(R)$ is the set gathering of these $f(x)$

$$ran(R) = f(A) = \{f(x)|x \in A\}$$

4.1.6 Defuzzification

Some basic concepts and properties of fuzzy set theory have been explained in previous sections. Another relevant concept related to the fuzzy set process is defuzzification. The fuzzification concept was described with numbers, operations, and relations, transforming a numeric value to a fuzzy set. Defuzzification transforms fuzzy set information into numeric data information [17].

In [17], the defuzzification process is recommended for use as a transformation from an uncertainty-based concept to another uncertainty-based concept, rather than a certainty-based concept. Defuzzification maps from a fuzzy set to a real number. The result is a defuzzified value. A more common description of the defuzzification process is the representation of the crisp number based on the fuzzy set [18,19]. In [19] the structure of a fuzzy logic system is explained where the crisp variables are fuzzified to linguistic variables. A fuzzy inference applies some fuzzy rules, and the defuzzification transforms it into a crisp number.

$$Def(\mathcal{T}) \to \Re$$

The defuzzification process shares some common properties between methodologies. In [20] the 13 features most often observed in these methodologies are described. In [17] the four main properties are summarized, and these are as follows:

1. A defuzzification operator always computes to one numeric value.
2. The membership function determines the defuzzified value.
3. The defuzzified value of two triangular-operated fuzzy sets is always contained within the bounds of individual defuzzified values.
4. In the case of prohibitive information, the defuzzified values should fall in the permitted zone.

Some defuzzification methods are the mean of maxima, the computation by the center of gravity method, the center of means, and the midpoint of an area procedure. These are described briefly here.

4.1.7 Left and right (LR) representation

This section describes briefly the representation of left and right shape functions proposed by Dubois and Prade [21].

Definition 4.14. [21] [Shape function L] A shape function L (or R) is a decreasing function from $\Re^+ \to [0, 1]$. In [22], this is summarized as follows:

1. $L(0) = 1$

2. $L(x) < 1, \forall x > 0$
3. $L(x) > 0, \forall x < 1$
4. $L(1) = 0 [or L(x) > 0, \forall x \, and \, L(+\infty) = 0]$

Definition 4.15. [22,23] [LR type] A fuzzy number ξ is of LR type if there exist shape functions L (for left) and R (for right), and scalers $\alpha > 0$, $\beta > 0$ with membership function:

$$\mu_\xi(x) = \begin{cases} L\left(\dfrac{m-x}{\alpha}\right), & if \, x \leqslant m \\ R\left(\dfrac{x-m}{\beta}\right), & if \, x \geqslant m \end{cases} \tag{4.23}$$

where m is the mean value represented by a real number or a fuzzy interval $[\underline{m}, \overline{m}]$, α is the left spread, and β is the right spread. ξ is denoted by $(m, \alpha, \beta)_{LR}$.

To provide an example, the LR fuzzy number representing a triangular fuzzy number of the triplet (a,b,c) is presented in Eq. (4.24).

$$\mu(x) = \begin{cases} \dfrac{x-a}{b-a}, & if \, a \leqslant x \leqslant b \\ \dfrac{c-x}{c-b}, & if \, b < x \leqslant c \end{cases} \tag{4.24}$$

4.2 Fuzzy MCDM sorting methods

Fuzzy logic is introduced to MCDM methods to overcome the limitation of modeling crisp decisions, to deal with uncertainty associated to evaluations, and to express the judgment of experts.

In this chapter, fuzzy MCDM sorting methods correspond to those methods dealing with fuzzy information as input to the MCDM. However, the categorization process is still crisp. This section describes MCDM sorting methods that apply fuzzy sets in the evaluation of alternatives or definition of models' parameters. The most common implementation of fuzzification for values related with alternative evaluation and parameters is the triangular fuzzy shape.

4.2.1 Fuzzy FlowSort

In Section 3.3, the FlowSort method was presented among other MCDM sorting methods. In this section, Fuzzy FlowSort [24] will be explained as an extension of the FlowSort method [25], but including fuzzy numbers. One significant advantage of Fuzzy FlowSort is the use of triangular fuzzy numbers to deal with imprecise data.

The FlowSort method is based on an outranking approach, the PROMETHEE method [26]. The fuzzy outranking relation $\pi(a, b)$ is computed between each ordered pair of alternatives (a, b) with one of the six preference functions on each criterion in PROMETHEE to define $P_j(a, b)$ based on the decision maker's preferences [26].

$$\pi(a, b) = \sum w_j P_j(a, b) \tag{4.25}$$

4.2.1.1   Sorting procedure

An explanation of the FlowSort method is given in Section 3.3. Here, it is briefly introduced. The FlowSort method, as with other sorting methods, defines the category C_k by the flow value of the upper limiting profile Ir_k and the flow value of the lower profile Ir_{k+1}. Thus, the assignment rules based on the positive and negative flows are as follows:

$$C_{Q+}(a_i) = C_k \; if \; Q_{R_i}^+(Ir_k) > Q_{R_i}^+(a_i) \geqslant Q_{R_i}^+(Ir_{k+1})$$
$$C_{Q-}(a_i) = C_k \; if \; Q_{R_i}^-(Ir_k) \leqslant Q_{R_i}^-(a_i) < Q_{R_i}^-(Ir_{k+1})$$

The assignment of each alternative to exactly one of the categories is based on the net flow rule:

$$C_Q(a_i) = C_k \; if \; Q_{R_i}(Ir_k) > Q_{R_i}(a_i) \geqslant Q_{R_i}(Ir_{k+1})$$

4.2.1.2   Fuzzy approach

The Fuzzy FlowSort method uses the triangular fuzzy membership function. A triangular fuzzy number $\mu(x)$ is represented by a triplet $(m, a, b)_{LR}$, where m is the mean value of the fuzzy number $\mu(x)$ while α and β are its left and right boundary values, respectively. The membership function of the triangular fuzzy numbers is defined as follows:

$$\mu(x) = \begin{cases} 1 - \left| \dfrac{m - x}{\alpha} \right|, & (m - \alpha) < x \leqslant m \\[2mm] 1 - \left| \dfrac{x - m}{\beta} \right|, & m < x \leqslant (m + \beta) \\[2mm] 0, & otherwise \end{cases} \tag{4.26}$$

The parameters of the model, including indifference and preference thresholds (q and p), reference profiles, and criteria weights, are assumed to be crisp numbers. As established in the FlowSort method, the performance of all the alternatives are between the best and worst reference profiles and the categories are ordered [24,25].

The steps involved in the F-FlowSort algorithm are as follows.

Step 1:

Define a weight w_j and a preference function P_j for each criterion g_j. For a complete explanation of the preference functions in the PROMETHEE method, see [27]. The functions of preference V-shape and V-shape with an indifference criterion are the ones most widely used for actual applications.

Step 2:

The outranking degree $p(x, y)$ of each alternative x over an alternative y is computed using arithmetic operations on triangle fuzzy numbers (Section 4.2.4) for all the alternatives x, y of R_i. Thus $R_i = R \cup \{a_i\}$, where $R = \{Ir_1, ..., Ir_{k+1}\}$ is the set of reference profiles and a_i is the alternative to be assigned [25].

$$\pi(x, y) = \sum w_j \otimes P_j(x, y) \tag{4.27}$$

$$\pi(x, y) = \sum w_j \otimes P_j(g_j(x) \ominus g_j(y)) \tag{4.28}$$

Let $f_j(x) = (m, \alpha, \beta)_{LR}$ and $f_j(y) = (n, \gamma, \delta)_{LR}$ and w_j is a scalar number:

$$\pi(x, y) = \sum w_j \otimes P_j((m, \alpha, \beta)_{LR} \ominus (n, \gamma, \delta)_{LR}) \tag{4.29}$$

$$\pi(x, y) = \sum w_j \otimes P_j(m - n, \alpha + \delta, \beta + \gamma)_{LR} \tag{4.30}$$

$$\pi(x, y) = \sum w_j \otimes P_j(m', \alpha', \beta')_{LR} \tag{4.31}$$

$$\pi(x, y) = \sum w_j \otimes P_j(m'^{Pj}, \alpha'^{Pj}, \beta'^{Pj})_{LR} \tag{4.32}$$

$$\pi(x, y) = \sum (w_j m'^{Pj}, w_j \alpha'^{Pj}, w_j \beta'^{Pj})_{LR} \tag{4.33}$$

$$\pi(x, y) = \left(\sum w_j m'^{Pj}, \sum w_j \alpha'^{Pj}, \sum w_j \beta'^{Pj} \right)_{LR} \tag{4.34}$$

$$P_j(m', \alpha', \beta')_{LR} = (P_j(m'); (P_j(m') - P_j(m' - \alpha'));$$
$$(P_j(m' + \beta') - P_j(m')))_{LR} \tag{4.35}$$

Step 3:

The preference degree $p(x, y)$ is defuzzified to transform the fuzzy number into a crisp number. In [24], using Yager's operator is suggested [31]. The defuzzification of a triangular fuzzy number is given as follows:

$$F(m, \alpha, \beta) = \frac{3m - \alpha + \beta}{3} \tag{4.36}$$

Step 4:

The positive, negative, and net flows of each alternative x of R_i are computed using the defuzzified outranking degree $\pi(x, y)$:

$$Q_{R_i}^+(x) = \frac{1}{|R_i| - 1} \sum_{y \in R_i} \pi(x, y)$$

$$Q_{R_i}^-(x) = \frac{1}{|R_i| - 1} \sum_{y \in R_i} \pi(x, y)$$

$$Q_{R_i}(x) = Q_{R_i}^+(x) - Q_{R_i}^-(x)$$

Step 5:

The assignment in FlowSort regards the relative position of an alternative with respect to the reference profiles, in terms of positive, negative, and net flows [25]. It is assumed that category C_k is upper limited by the flow value of Ir_k and lower limited by the flow value of Ir_{k+1}. The procedure shows two different assignment rules based on those flows as follows:

$$C_{Q+}(a_i) = C_k \; if \; Q^+_{R_i}(Ir_k) > Q^+_{R_i}(a_i) \geqslant Q^+_{R_i}(Ir_{k+1})$$
$$C_{Q-}(a_i) = C_k \; if \; Q^-_{R_i}(Ir_k) \leqslant Q^-_{R_i}(a_i) < Q^-_{R_i}(Ir_{k+1})$$

The assignment of each alternative to exactly one of the categories is based on the net flow rule:

$$C_Q(a_i) = C_k \; if \; Q_{R_i}(Ir_k) > Q_{R_i}(a_i) \geqslant Q_{R_i}(Ir_{k+1})$$

In [24] the F-FlowSort and FlowSort methods were compared, showing almost the same result, with just one alternative assigned to a different category by F-FlowSort. In this sense, the methods use almost the same sorting procedure, but F-FlowSort allows fuzzy data evaluation.

4.2.2 SMAA fuzzy-FlowSort

The FlowSort method is a PROMETHEE-based sorting method using limiting profiles or central profiles. A description of FlowSort and its extensions is presented in Section 3.3.2.

The SMAA Fuzzy FlowSort [28] is an extended version of the Fuzzy Flow-Sort [24] method that allows for the use of multiple types of information imperfections (stochastic, ordinal, and interval data, and linguistic variables) to evaluate alternatives and model parameters, along with partial or missing criteria weights [28]. This extended version applies the fuzzy approach for alternative evaluation as the Fuzzy FlowSort [24] and allows the use of linguistic variables of the definition of thresholds category-limiting profiles.

4.2.2.1 Fuzzy approach

In this new version of Fuzzy FlowSort (SMAA Fuzzy FlowSort or SMAA-FFS), the evaluation of alternatives can be done with multiple types of information as interval data, quantitative ordinal, stochastic data, and linguistic variables. The description will be focused on the last type of information.

When the DM is interested in using ordinal linguistic variables to define the alternatives' evaluation (perhaps because the precise information is not available), it is recommended that fuzzy set theory is used. Similar to the Fuzzy FlowSort method, the semantic used in SMAA-FFS to model ordinal linguistic variables is the triangular fuzzy set $\tilde{A} = (b; \alpha; \beta)_{LR}$. No other representations of fuzzy numbers as trapezoidal, rectangular, or Gaussian are defined on the

Fuzzy FlowSort and SMAA-FFS methods. It seems, if another representation is needed, that an adaptation of such a representation is required in those methods.

4.2.2.2 Category limiting profiles

Due to the alternatives being evaluated using linguistic data on specific criteria, in the same way, SMAA-FFS can define the limiting profiles for these criteria by linguistic data.

In a specific situation explained in [28], the case is considered where a car is evaluated by the criterion *comfort* with the linguistic terms "good," "acceptable," and "bad." This is the case when limiting profiles are used to define categories. The method allows the linguistic definition of each criterion of each category. Thus, there is a limiting profile between "bad" and "acceptable" categories and between "acceptable" and "good." In these cases, limiting profiles are represented by triangular fuzzy numbers $\tilde{C} = (c; \gamma; \delta)_{LR})$.

The algebraic operations required to work with the triangular fuzzy number are as follows:

Addition: $\tilde{B} \oplus \tilde{C} = (b; \alpha; \beta)_{LR} \oplus (c; \gamma; \delta)_{LR} = (b + c; \alpha + \gamma; \beta + \delta)$

Subtraction: $\tilde{B} \ominus \tilde{C} = (b; \alpha; \beta)_{LR} \ominus (c; \gamma; \delta)_{LR} = (b - c; \alpha + \gamma; \beta + \delta)$

Multiplication by scalar number: $v \otimes \tilde{C} = (v; 0; 0)_{LR} \otimes (b; \alpha; \beta)_{LR} = (vb; v\alpha; v\beta)_{LR}$

The criteria values $g_j(x)$ and $g_j(y)$ for alternative x and y are represented by the triangular fuzzy expression $g_j(x) = (b; \alpha; \beta)_{LR}$ and $g_j(y) = (c; \gamma; \delta)_{LR}$, respectively. The preference function $\tilde{p}_j(\tilde{g}_j(x) \ominus \tilde{g}_j(y))$ is the type V-shape with indifference criterion (related to the PROMETHEE preference functions [27]). This function uses the q and p thresholds. Section 3.3.1 describes six common preference functions used in PROMETHEE.

$$
\begin{aligned}
&\tilde{P}_j(\tilde{g}_j(x) \otimes \tilde{g}_j(y)) \\
&= \tilde{P}_j((b - c; \alpha + \delta; \beta + \gamma)_{LR}) \\
&= (P_j(b - c); \\
&P_j(b - c) - P_j(b - c - \alpha + \delta); \\
&P_j(b - c + \beta + \gamma) - P_j(b - c))_{LR}
\end{aligned}
\tag{4.37}
$$

Once the preference function is defined, the global fuzzy preference degree function is computed for each pair $(x, y) \in R_i$, where $R_i = R \cup \{a_i\}$ is the union of the reference profiles with the alternative a_i, $i = 1, ..., m$:

$$
\begin{aligned}
\tilde{\pi}(x, y) &= \sum_{j=1}^{n} w_j \ominus \tilde{P}_j(x, y) \\
&= \sum_{j=1}^{n} w_j \ominus \tilde{P}_j(\tilde{g}_j(x) \ominus \tilde{g}_j(y))
\end{aligned}
\tag{4.38}
$$

The global fuzzy preference degree $\tilde{\pi}(x, y)$ is defuzzified to reduces the fuzzy preference degree into a crisp number in the Fuzzy-FlowSort method [24]. Yager's operator is used, denoted by B^{Def} as follows:

$$B^{Def} = b + \frac{\beta + \alpha}{3} \qquad (4.39)$$

Now, with the defuzzified values of the global fuzzy preference degree $\tilde{\pi}(x, y)$, the positive (Eq. (4.40)), negative (Eq. (4.41)), and net fuzzy flows (Eq. (4.42)) can be computed for each $x \in R_i$ as in the traditional FlowSort method.

$$Q_{R_i}^+(x) = \frac{1}{|R_i| - 1} \sum_{y \in R_i} \pi(x, y) \qquad (4.40)$$

$$Q_{R_i}^-(x) = \frac{1}{|R_i| - 1} \sum_{y \in R_i} \pi(x, y) \qquad (4.41)$$

$$Q_{R_i}(x) = Q_{R_i}^+(x) - Q_{R_i}^-(x) \qquad (4.42)$$

4.2.2.3 Sorting procedure

Once the crisp flow values are computed, the assignment rules for the sorting procedure can be performed as in the traditional FlowSort assignment.

$$C_{Q+}(a_i) = C_k \ if \ Q_{R_i}^+(Ir_k) > Q_{R_i}^+(a_i) \geqslant Q_{R_i}^+(Ir_{k+1}) \qquad (4.43)$$

$$C_{Q-}(a_i) = C_k \ if \ Q_{R_i}^-(Ir_k) \leqslant Q_{R_i}^-(a_i) < Q_{R_i}^-(Ir_{k+1}) \qquad (4.44)$$

The assignment of each alternative to exactly one of the categories is based on the net flow rule:

$$C_Q(a_i) = C_k \ if \ Q_{R_i}(Ir_k) > Q_{R_i}(a_i) \geqslant Q_{R_i}(Ir_{k+1}) \qquad (4.45)$$

The main differences of the new method SMAA Fuzzy FlowSort from the previous Fuzzy FlowSort method are the new advantage to use multiple input data, the application of fuzzy linguistic variables in the limiting profile, and the robust results with SMAA [29]. We will summarize these difference as follows.

The SMAA Fuzzy FlowSort method allows the use of triangular fuzzy numbers in the evaluation of alternatives and definition of the categories limiting profiles. Different types of data are used in evaluation of alternatives, criteria weights, thresholds, and categories limiting profiles. The use of SMAA produces robust solutions.

4.2.3 ELECTRE TRI-C and trapezoidal fuzzy numbers

The outranking approach is very popular in MCDM. In this sense, the family of ELECTRE methods have been implemented in many applications. Section 3.5 describes some ELECTRE methods and extensions.

The method that will be described in this section is the fuzzy extended ELECTRE TRI-C method proposed by [30]. The current method allows the definition of imprecision and uncertainty parameters. It also allows information to be provided about reference alternatives in the form of linguistic terms.

The ELECTRE TRI-C method belongs to the outranking approach based on binary relations [31]. A category is defined by a fictitious or a realistic action that is assumed to be "representative" of that category, and this is called the central reference action b_h.

4.2.3.1 Fuzzy approach

Each action of the set $A = \{a_1, a_2, ..., a_n\}$ should be assigned into categories. C_h is the category from a set of ordered categories ($h = 1, ..., H$). A set of fictitious or realistic actions called central reference actions are represented by the set $B = \{b_1, b_2, ..., b_H\}$. The central reference action b_h describes the category C_h. Actions and reference actions are evaluated by the coherent family of criteria $F = \{g_1, g_2, ..., g_m\}$. The performance of an action a on the criterion g_j is defined by $g_j(a)$ and the vector of performances $(g_1(a), g_2(a), ..., g_m(a))$ is the evaluation profile that is used to compare the action against central reference action b_h represented by $(g_1(b_h), g_2(b_h), ..., g_m(b_h))$.

Categories are ordered in terms of preferences and range from the category of actions having the worst profiles C_0 to the best ones C_H.

The family of ELECTRE methods can deal with the imprecise, ill-determined, and uncertain performances through the indifference (q), preference (p), and veto thresholds (v). The ELECTRE methods evaluate the assertion that "a is at least as good as a'." The assertion is evaluated according to the following fundamental preference relations [32]:

The indifference relation ($a I_j a'$)

$$|g(a) - g(a')| \leqslant q_j \Leftrightarrow a I_j a' \tag{4.46}$$

The strict preference relation ($a P_j a'$)

$$|g(a) - g(a')| > p_j \Leftrightarrow a P_j a' \tag{4.47}$$

The weak preference relation ($a Q_j a'$)

$$q_j < |g(a) - g(a')| \leqslant p_j \Leftrightarrow a Q_j a' \tag{4.48}$$

Based on the above relations, the assertion that "a is at least as good as a'" is defined as ($a S_j a'$) $\Leftrightarrow a I_j a' \vee a P_j a' \vee a Q_j a'$.

The partial concordance index

The comparison between a and a' is an outranking degree restricted to g_j and is evaluated by the partial concordance index expressed as $c_j(a, a')$.

The comprehensive concordance index

The partial concordance index $c_j(a, a')$ evaluates the outranking degree for each criterion. The comprehensive concordance index (4.49) regards the coalition of criteria in favor of the assertion "a outranks a'" (aSa'):

$$c(a, a') = \sum_{j=1}^{m} w_j c_j(a, a'), \qquad (4.49)$$

where w_j is the weight of the criterion g_j $(w_j > 0)$.

The partial discordance index

The partial discordance index is measured when the use of the veto effect by the veto threshold v is defined. The index measures the coalition of the criteria against the assertion (aSa').

The partial discordance index helps to identify the unfavorable arguments against aSa' and is expressed as $d_j(a, a')$.

The comprehensive and partial discordance indexes are used to define the credibility index that expresses the favorable and unfavorable arguments of aSa' in Eq. (4.50).

$$\sigma(a, a') = \begin{cases} c(a, a'), & if \; \forall j \; d_j(a, a') \leqslant c_j(a, a') \\ c(a, a') \times \prod_{j \in J(a,a')} \dfrac{1 - d_j(a, a')}{1 - c(a, a')}, & otherwise, \end{cases}$$

$$(4.50)$$

where $J(a, a')$ refers to the set of criteria where $d_j(a, a') > c_j(a, a')$.

In this version, ELECTRE TRI-C models the outranking relation between the alternatives and the reference actions using the four points $(d_{j1}, d_{j2}, d_{j3}, d_{j4})$ to represent the membership function of a trapezoidal fuzzy number $\mu_j(a, b_h)$ [30]:

$$d_{j1} = g_j(b_h) - p'_j; \quad d_{j2} = g_j(b_h) - q'_j;$$
$$d_{j3} = g_j(b_h) + q_j; \quad d_{j4} = g_j(b_h) + p_j;$$

where b_h is a reference action. If $q_j \neq q'_j$, then $\mu_j(a, b_h)$ is a trapezoidal fuzzy number which is expressed by Eq. (4.51).

$$\mu_j(a, b_h) = min\{c_j(b_h, a), cinv_j(a, b_h)\}. \qquad (4.51)$$

Then, if $\mu_j(a, b_h) = 1$, this means that alternative's performance of $gj(a)$ is indifferent with the category's performance $g_j(b_h)$ on the criterion j. Conversely, if $\mu_j(a, b_h) = 0$, this means that $g_j(a)$ is too far from the category $g_j(b_h)$. Consequently, this function can be interpreted as a membership function of C_h, when the category is represented by the central reference alternative b_h [30]. However, other shapes can be considered. We can verify that $q_j = q'_j = 0$ means that $\mu_j(a, b_h)$ becomes a triangular fuzzy number [30].

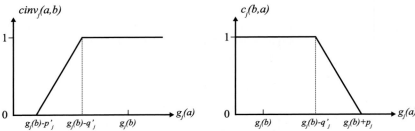

FIGURE 4.16 The inverse concordance index $cinv_j(a, b)$ and the direct concordance index $c_j(b, a)$.

Assuming that the q'_j, p'_j, q_j, p_j thresholds are constants, the inverse concordance index $cinv_j(a, a')$ and the direct concordance index $c_j(b, a)$ are defined in [30] as follows. Fig. 4.16 illustrates both indices.

$$cinv_j(a, b) = \begin{cases} 0 & if \; g_j(b) - g_j(a) > p'_j, \\ 1 & if \; g_j(b) - g_j(a) \leqslant p'_j, \\ \dfrac{g_j(a) - g_j(b) + p'_j}{p'_j - q'_j} & otherwise. \end{cases} \quad (4.52)$$

$$c_j(b, a) = \begin{cases} 0 & if \; g_j(b) - g_j(a) > p_j, \\ 1 & if \; g_j(b) - g_j(a) \leqslant q_j, \\ \dfrac{g_j(a) - g_j(b) + p_j}{p_j - q_j} & otherwise. \end{cases} \quad (4.53)$$

4.2.3.2 Sorting procedure

For all $a \in A$ and $b_h \in B^+$, let us define the following comprehensive concordance indices (the current description is not using the veto threshold):

$$\sigma_D(b_h, a) = \sum_{j=1}^{m} w_j c_j(b_h, a) \quad (4.54)$$

$$\sigma_I(a, b_h) = \sum_{j=1}^{m} w_j cinv_j(a, b_h) \quad (4.55)$$

Therefore, the following assignment rules, based on the ELECTRE TRI-C rules, can be defined:

Trapezoidal descending rule. Let $\lambda \in [0.5, 1]$ be a minimum credibility level. Decrease h from $H + 1$ until the first t such that $\sigma_I(a, b_t) \geqslant \lambda$. Here, t obtains the value of h when $\sigma_I(a, b_t) \geqslant \lambda$ is satisfied:

1. If $t = H + 1$, assign a to C_H.

2. If $t = 0$, assign a to C_1.
3. For $0 < t < H + 1$, if $min\{\sigma_I(a, b_h), \sigma_D(b_t, a)\} > min\{\sigma_I(a, b_{t+1}),$ $\sigma_D(b_{t+1}, a)\}$ then assign a to C_t; otherwise, assign a to C_{t+1}.

Trapezoidal ascending rule. Let $\lambda \in [0.5, 1]$ be a minimum credibility level. Increase h from 0 until the first t such that $\sigma_D(b_t, a) \geqslant \lambda$:

1. If $t = 1$, assign a to C_1.
2. If $t = H + 1$, assign a to C_H.
3. For $0 < t < H + 1$, if $min\{\sigma_I(a, b_t), \sigma_D(b_t, a)\} > min\{\sigma_I(a, b_{t-1}),$ $\sigma_D(b_{t-1}, a)\}$ then assign a to C_t; otherwise, assign a to C_{t-1}.

The ELECTRE-TRI-C method in the current version with trapezoidal membership function models the outranking relation between the alternative a and the reference action b_h. The current version can be used when the DM provides just the membership degree of a verbal value on a qualitative criterion to characterize a category [30].

4.2.4 Continuous cooperation fuzzy sorting

The method is presented as a modified prisoner's dilemma to classify strategies into levels of cooperation [33]. Here, the alternatives are identified as strategies (or individuals); they are classified in relation to their level of cooperation, and the criteria define the cooperative behavior. This is described as a cooperative Game Theory approach for a sorting method.

The method addresses both the definition of classes and the assessment of cooperation (alternatives) from a fuzzy theory perspective. The fuzzy numbers implemented are the triangular membership function. This is justified because of the method's simplicity and applicability to the problem at hand [34].

The model proposed by [33] uses the ELECTRE TRI outranking method to define the classes of cooperation and employs the concepts proposed by [35] to categorize the alternatives into predefined classes of cooperation.

In the current method, the membership function has several classes of cooperation, for each criterion used in assessing cooperation. The triangular membership function applied in this method is defined as follows:

$$f_A(x, a, m, b) = \begin{cases} 0, & if\ x < a \\ \dfrac{(x - a)}{(m - a)}, & if\ a \leqslant x \leqslant m \\ \dfrac{(b - x)}{(b - m)}, & if\ m \leqslant x \leqslant b \\ 0 & if\ x > b \end{cases} \tag{4.56}$$

4.2.4.1 Sorting procedure based on the prisoners' dilemma

The authors in [33] applied the structure for cooperation proposed by [36] with q strategies where each strategy s of a set of strategies S can assume the following values: $\{0, 1/q - 1, 2/q - 1, ..., q - 2/q - 1, 1\}$. The number of q strategies is so large that there is a context of ongoing cooperation.

$$s \in \left\{0, \frac{1}{q-1}, \frac{2}{q-1}, \frac{q-2}{q-1}, 1\right\}. \tag{4.57}$$

$$if \, q = 2 \quad s \in \{0, 1\} \tag{4.58}$$

$$if \, q = 2 \quad s \in \left\{0, \frac{1}{2}, 1\right\}. \tag{4.59}$$

A variable of strategy s is described as a set of cooperation levels with q values between [0, 1], where $q = 0$ means the original dichotomous situation of lack of cooperation and $q = 1$ refers to a situation of total cooperation. The prisoners' dilemma regards some strategic interactions where two players (alternatives) will decide on a level of cooperation q. The method classifies the cooperation on different levels using the ELECTRE TRI multi-criteria method and a fuzzy approach.

The continuous cooperation fuzzy sorting method can be described as follows: let there be a set of strategies S, the generic element of which is s, referring to the cooperation levels to be chosen, for each strategic interaction, by the two players in a prisoners' dilemma; moreover s can assume q different values between 0 and 1 [33].

The strategic interaction G is represented by

$$G = (N, S, P), \tag{4.60}$$

where:

$N = \{n_i | n_i \in A_i \wedge i = 1, 2\}$;
$A = \{a | a \in (player1, player2)\}$;
$S = \{n_i S_j \wedge i = 1, 2 \wedge j = q\}$;
$S_j = \{q | q \in [0, 1]\}$; and
P = framework of payoffs.

As a matter of clarification for the current method explanation, the alternatives are considered as individuals whose cooperation will be classified. The criteria correspond with the cooperative behavior of the individuals.

4.2.4.2 Fuzzy approach

The method requires the evaluation of alternatives (assessments of individuals), definition of classes, and elicitation of the parameters for the profiles, weights, and thresholds. Here the definition of the profiles and thresholds is done jointly, from the fuzzy approach, using the concept of an α-cut and the notion of outranking of the ELECTRE TRI method (see Fig. 4.17). It is assumed that there is some information and mutual knowledge between players, and that information is inaccurate and uncertain, justifying the use of a fuzzy approach.

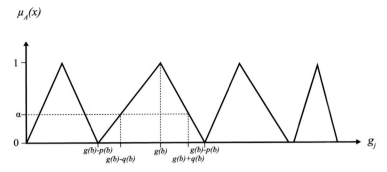

FIGURE 4.17   The ELECTRE TRI parameters in continuous cooperation fuzzy sorting.

Fig. 4.17 shows four classes (C1, C2, C3, C4) based on α-cut, for each criterion g_j. For each of the classes, the indifference threshold $q[g(b)]$, preference threshold, $p[g(b)]$ and profiles $g_j(b_h)$ can be set with the relations presented in Eqs. (4.57), (4.58), and (4.59).

The ELECTRE TRI method considers the evaluations of alternatives for each criterion $\{g_1, g_2, ..., g_j, ..., g_m\}$ and a set of profiles $\{b_1, b_2, ..., b_h, ..., b_p\}$ It defines $(p+1)$ categories, where b_h represents the upper limit of category C_h and the lower limit of category C_{h+1}, where $h = 1, 2, ..., p$ and $p \geqslant 2$.

The fuzzy outranking relation defined in ELECTRE TRI uses the concordance $C = (a, b_h)$ and discordance index $d_j(a, b_h)$ as follows:

$$\sigma(a, b_h) = c(a, b_h) \cdot \prod_{j \in \tilde{F}} \frac{1 - d_j(a, b_h)}{1 - C(a, b_h)} \qquad (4.61)$$

where:

$$\tilde{F} = \{j \in F : d_j(a, b_h) > C(a, b_h)\}$$

The assertion that "a is at least as good as b," expressed by aSb_h, is evaluated and confirmed when $\sigma(a, b_h) \geqslant \lambda$, $\lambda \in [0.5, 1]$.

The outranking relation is constructed based on the concept of α-cuts from the proposal in [35].

The model defines the fuzzy preference relations from fuzzy evaluations. The fuzzy evaluations of alternatives a and b, with respect to a criterion g_j, are represented by the normalized and convex fuzzy numbers A and B, respectively. They are characterized by their membership functions μ_A and μ_B, where the interval $(a_2^{\alpha_i}, a_2^{\alpha_i})$ defines the α_i-cut for A, $(b_1^{\alpha_i}, b_2^{\alpha_i})$ the α_i-cut for B, and $i = 1, N$, where N is the number of α-cuts.

In the case when the criterion is of increasing direction (to be maximized) and the interval a^{α_i} is entirely on the left of the interval b^{α_i}, there is no doubt that a is worse than b and there is a degree of truth in the proposition that "a is not worse than b" is 0. However, as a^{α_i} is translated to the right and the two intervals overlap, this degree of truth increases, and reaches the maximum value 1 at the moment when the lower limit (left) of a^{α_i} is equal to the lower limit (left) of b^{α_i}. The same interpretation could be made for the upper limits (right) of a^{α_i} and b^{α_i}.

For each α-cut level, a left α-cut index $S_l^{\alpha_i}(a^{\alpha_i}, b^{\alpha_i})$ and a right α-cut index $S_r^{\alpha_i}(a^{\alpha_i}, b^{\alpha_i})$ are defined.

$$maximize : S_{l\_max}^{\alpha_i}(a^{\alpha_i}, b^{\alpha_i}) = \begin{cases} 0, & a_2^{\alpha_i} < b_1^{\alpha_i} \\ \dfrac{a_2^{\alpha_i} - b_1^{\alpha_i}}{a_2^{\alpha_i} - a_1^{\alpha_i}}, & a_1^{\alpha_i} < b_1^{\alpha_i} \leqslant a_2^{\alpha_i} \\ 1, & a_1^{\alpha_i} \geqslant b_1^{\alpha_i} \end{cases} \quad (4.62)$$

$$maximize : S_{r\_max}^{\alpha_i}(a^{\alpha_i}, b^{\alpha_i}) = \begin{cases} 0, & a_2^{\alpha_i} < b_1^{\alpha_i} \\ \dfrac{a_2^{\alpha_i} - b_1^{\alpha_i}}{b_2^{\alpha_i} - b_1^{\alpha_i}}, & a_1^{\alpha_i} < a_2^{\alpha_i} \leqslant b_2^{\alpha_i} \\ 1, & a_2^{\alpha_i} \geqslant b_2^{\alpha_i} \end{cases} \quad (4.63)$$

For each pair of alternatives (a, b), the indices $S_l^{\alpha_i}(a^{\alpha_i}, b^{\alpha_i})$ and $S_r^{\alpha_i}(a^{\alpha_i}, b^{\alpha_i})$ are defined as follows:

$$maximize : S_{max}^{\alpha_i}(a^{\alpha_i}, b^{\alpha_i}) = (1 - k) \cdot S_{l\_max}^{\alpha_i}(a^{\alpha_i}, b^{\alpha_i}) + k \cdot S_{r\_max}^{\alpha_i}(a^{\alpha_i}, b^{\alpha_i})$$
$$(4.64)$$

$$minimize : S_{min}^{\alpha_i}(a^{\alpha_i}, b^{\alpha_i}) = (1 - k) \cdot S_{r\_min}^{\alpha_i}(a^{\alpha_i}, b^{\alpha_i}) + k \cdot S_{l\_max}^{\alpha_i}(a^{\alpha_i}, b^{\alpha_i})$$
$$(4.65)$$

The indices $S_{max}^{\alpha_i}(a^{\alpha_i}, b^{\alpha_i})$ and $S_{min}^{\alpha_i}(a^{\alpha_i}, b^{\alpha_i})$ are the outranking relations (S_k) for a criterion g_k. They are aggregated considering the weights of each criterion to obtain the global outranking relation S [35].

4.3 MCDM fuzzy sorting approaches

In this chapter, the MCDM fuzzy sorting approaches correspond to the methodology used to the assignment process that deals with fuzzy numbers defined in the profiles of the categories. This section presents two significant fuzzy sorting approaches that develop a particular fuzzy sorting procedure. The approaches consider the soft boundaries between the classes, intuitionistic fuzzy sets, and fuzzy distance.

4.3.1 AHP-FuzzySort

In Section 4.3.1, AHP was first presented, followed by AHPSort and its extensions. As stated earlier, the first sorting variant was proposed by [37]. A fuzzy variant of AHP (Fuzzy-AHPSort) was proposed by [38], where the fuzzy version is reached in the pairwise comparison to deal with the uncertainty.

The variant of AHP described in this section is AHP-FuzzySort [39], which is focused on the limiting profiles of the categories. This means that the fuzzy numbers are not used in the computation of local priorities. AHP-FuzzySort uses proportional linguistic two-tuples to carry out the sorting process, contributing in two ways. Firstly, it facilitates the soft transition from one class to another by making soft boundaries between the classes. Secondly, it provides additional information about the alternatives' membership to the corresponding classes, and allows the gradation of membership to a class. This last process does not increase the number of pairwise comparisons.

One of AHP-FuzzySort's properties is the facilitation of a soft transition from one class to another. This is achieved with soft boundaries between the classes. The other is additional information about the membership of the alternatives to the corresponding classes.

The AHP-FuzzySortmethod regards the MCDM fuzzy sorting in two ways: fuzzy linguistic representation of the classes and assignment to classes using fuzzy membership degrees. The former builds a fuzzy linguistic scale with its corresponding fuzzy membership functions representing the classes in which the alternatives will be sorted. The letter redefines the assignment to classes based on the two-tuple representation by [40].

Fig. 4.18 shows the extension of AHPSort to the fuzzy representation by the two-tuple. The main differences with AHPSort are the linguistic representation used in the classes definition and the assignment of the alternatives to classes using membership function degrees. These differences are illustrated in Stage 1 and Stage 2 of Fig. 4.18.

Values for parametric membership functions

AHP-FuzzySort [39] deals with parametric (trapezoidal/triangular) membership functions. The parametric functions are defined as either trapezoidal (a, b, d, c) or triangular (a, b, c).

A. Triangular membership function

The explanation for this membership function will be with central profiles cp_i. The least and most preferred classes are defined as left- and right-angled trapezoidal membership functions, but $Clase_2$ to $Clase_{n-1}$ are triangular ones. Based on AHPSort approaches, the central profiles define the function according to the different classes:

For the least preferred class $(Class_n)$, the membership function is a trapezoidal one for the definition to make sense, because values less than cp_n belong to this class. It is therefore defined as follows:

$$(a_n = min, \ b_n = min, \ d_n = cp_n, \ c_n = cp_{n-1}) \qquad (4.66)$$

The most preferred class $(Class_1)$ is a trapezoidal membership function. It is defined as follows:

$$(a_1 = cp_2, \ b_1 = cp_1, \ d_1 = max, \ c_1 = max) \qquad (4.67)$$

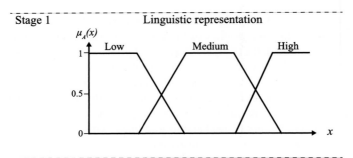

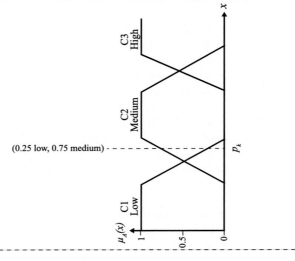

FIGURE 4.18   The AHP-FuzzySort process.

For the remaining classes ($Class_i$, $1 < i < n$), this is a triangular membership function. It is defined as follows:

$$(a_i = cp_{i+1}, \; b_i = cp_i, \; c_i = cp_{i-1}) \qquad (4.68)$$

B. Trapezoidal membership function

The explanation for this membership function will be with limiting profile lp_i. Here lp_i is the equilibrium point in which the degree of membership between $Classes \; i$ and $i+1$ is equal. The definition of the membership functions is ordered from the class least preferred to the one most preferred. Therefore, the parameter a_i for classes ($Class_i$) is fixed from φ_{i+1}.

For the least preferred class ($Class_n$), the membership function will be defined as follows:

$$(a_n = min, \; b_n = min, \; d_n = lp_{n-1} - \varphi_n, \; c_n = lp_{n-1} + \varphi_n) \qquad (4.69)$$

The most preferred class ($Class_1$) in this case is as follows:

$$(a_1 = lp_1 - \varphi_2, \ b_1 = lp_1 + \varphi_2, \ d_1 = max, \ c_1 = max) \qquad (4.70)$$

For the remaining classes ($Class_i$, $1 < i < n$), the parameters are as follows:

$$(a_i = lp_i - \varphi_{i+1}, \ b_i = lp_i + \varphi_{i+1}, \ d_i = lp_{i-1} - \varphi_i, \ c_i = lp_{i-1} + \varphi_i) \qquad (4.71)$$

Fuzzy membership functions

The triangular and trapezoidal definitions for the membership functions outline each class in AHP-FuzzySort.

A. Triangular membership function

The least preferred class ($Class_n$) is defined by a trapezoidal membership function as follows:

$$\mu_{Classs_n}(x) = \begin{cases} 0, & if \quad a_n > x > c_n \\ \dfrac{cp_{n-1} - x}{cp_{n-1} - cp_n}, & if \quad d_n < x \leqslant c_n \\ 1, & if \quad a_n \leqslant x \leqslant c_n \end{cases} \qquad (4.72)$$

The most preferred class ($Class_1$) is defined as follows:

$$\mu_{Classs_1}(x) = \begin{cases} 0, & if \quad a_1 > x > c_1 \\ \dfrac{x - cp_2}{cp_1 - cp_2}, & if \quad a_1 < x \leqslant c_1 \\ 1, & if \quad b_1 \leqslant x \leqslant d_1 \end{cases} \qquad (4.73)$$

Remaining classes ($Class_i$, $1 < i < n$) are defined as follows:

$$\mu_{Classs_i}(x) = \begin{cases} 0, & if \quad a_i > x > c_i \\ \dfrac{x - cp_{i+1}}{cp_i - cp_{i+1}}, & if \quad a_i \leqslant x < b_i \\ \dfrac{cp_{i-1} - x}{cp_{i-1} - cp_i}, & if \quad b_i < x \leqslant c_i \\ 1, & if \quad x = b_i \end{cases} \qquad (4.74)$$

B. Trapezoidal membership function

For the least preferred class ($Class_n$), the membership function is defined as follows:

$$\mu_{Classs_n}(x) = \begin{cases} 0, & if \quad a_n > x > c_n \\ \dfrac{(lp_{n-1} - \varphi_n) - x}{2\varphi_n}, & if \quad d_n < x \leqslant c_n \\ 1, & if \quad a_n \leqslant x \leqslant d_n \end{cases} \qquad (4.75)$$

The most preferred class $(Class_1)$ is defined as follows:

$$\mu_{Classs_1}(x) = \begin{cases} 0, & if \quad a_1 > x > c_1 \\ \dfrac{x - (lp_1 - \varphi_2)}{2\varphi_2}, & if \quad a_1 < x \leqslant b_1 \\ 1, & if \quad b_1 \leqslant x \leqslant c_1 \end{cases} \tag{4.76}$$

Remaining classes $(Class_i, \ 1 < i < n)$ is defined as follows:

$$\mu_{Classs_i}(x) = \begin{cases} 0, & if \quad a_i > x > c_i \\ \dfrac{x - (lp_i - \varphi_{i+1})}{2\varphi_{i+1}}, & if \quad a_i \leqslant x \leqslant b_i \\ \dfrac{(lp_{i-1} + \varphi_i) - x}{2\varphi_i}, & if \quad d_i < x \leqslant c_i \\ 1, & if \quad b_i \leqslant .x \leqslant d_i \end{cases} \tag{4.77}$$

Assignment to classes

The assignment process of an alternative a_k, to a class based on fuzzy proportional two-tuples consists of the following steps:

1. computation of the global priorities p_k, lp_i, or cp_i;
2. obtaining a proportional two-tuple for p_k; and
3. applying an assignment process based on the proportional two-tuple.

The first step is described extensively by Ishizaka et al. (2012) and Miccoli and Ishizaka (2017).

Proportional two-tuple

Once the limiting (lp_i) or central (cp_i) profiles are obtained, the membership functions are defined and represent the classes with their respective semantics and syntax that shows an order as follows.

After computing the global priority p_k, for each alternative a_k, the comparison process for AHP-FuzzySort is carried out with the computation of a proportional two-tuple global priority, $\overline{p_k} = h(p_k) = (\alpha \cdot s_i, (1 - \alpha) \, s_{i+1})$, in the ordinal proportional two-tuple set generated by the fuzzy linguistic class scale:

$$\begin{aligned} h &: [min, max] \longrightarrow \overline{S} \\ \gamma &= max \ \mu_{S_j}(P_k)/S_j \in S \ and \ s_l = arg \ max_{s_j}(\mu_{S_j}(P_k)) \\ &\quad if \ \mu_{S_{l+1}}(P_k) > 0 \Rightarrow s_i = s_l \ and \ \alpha = \gamma \\ &\quad Otherwise \ s_i = s_{l-1} \ and \ \alpha = 1 - \gamma \end{aligned} \tag{4.78}$$

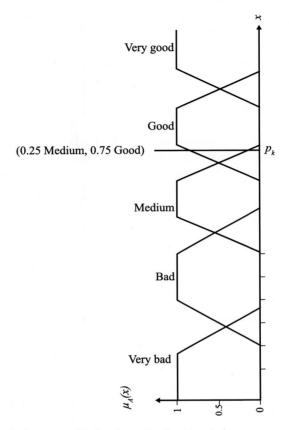

FIGURE 4.19 Assignment to class based on proportional two-tuple.

Therefore:

$$\overline{p_k} = h(p_k) = (\alpha S_i, (1-\alpha)s_{i+1})_k$$

$\overline{p_k}$ is the proportional two-tuple linguistic value that represents the global priority of the alternative a_k. $\overline{p_k}(0.25\,Bad, 0.75\,Good)$ is shown in Fig. 4.19.

Assignment process

The input value for the assignment of alternative a_k to a class is the proportional two-tuple, $\overline{p_k} = (\alpha \cdot S_i, (1-\alpha)s_{i+1})_k$, obtained from Eq. (4.78). The process is implemented as follows:

1. If $\alpha > (1-\alpha)$, then alternative a_k is assigned to class s_i.
2. If $\alpha < (1-\alpha)$, then alternative a_k is assigned to class s_{i+1}.
3. If $\alpha = (1-\alpha)$, then there are two options to assign a_k to a class:
   a. optimistic view: a_k is assigned to s_i; or
   b. pessimistic view: a_k is assigned to s_{i+1}.

4.3.2 Intuitionistic fuzzy outranking sorting for group decision making

This is an outranking sorting method for group decision making (GDM) using intuitionistic fuzzy sets (IFS). The method combines the outranking relation and the characteristics of the IFS to develop an intuitionistic fuzzy outranking relation. The construction of an outranking relation is based on two major concepts, the concordance test and nondiscordance test, presented in [41].

The concordance test validates the outranking relation $A_i S A_k$. It states that there is a sufficient majority of the criteria or argument in favor of the assertion. The nondiscordance test is validated when the concordance condition holds; none of the criteria or arguments in the minority should oppose assertion $A_i S A_k$ too strongly. The method includes an intuitionistic fuzzy support function to perform the concordance test.

4.3.2.1 MCDM fuzzy sorting

Let A be a set of alternatives $\forall A_i, A_k \in A$. and let G be a set of criteria $\forall g_j \in G$. The intuitionistic fuzzy support function $\psi(A_i, A_k)$ indicates the support degree to which the jth criterion agrees with the assertion that A_i outranks A_k. It corresponds to the concordance index in the ELECTRE family:

$$\psi_j(A_i, A_k) = \begin{cases} 1, & if & S_{ij} + q_j > S_{kj} \\ 0, & if & S_{ij} + p_j < S_{kj} \\ \dfrac{p_j - (S_{kj} - S_{ij})}{p_j - q_j}, & otherwise \end{cases} \qquad (4.79)$$

where q_j and p_j are the indifference and preference thresholds, respectively. S_{ij} is the score function (performance) for alternative A_i on the criterion g_j. For a detailed description of the thresholds and the outranking index, see [42].

The nondiscordance test is a function that is developed as a intuitionistic fuzzy risk function based on the hesitancy degree. This test is computed by taking into account the performance differences for the criterion considered, as well as for the two thresholds: indifference u_j and veto v_j ($0 \leqslant uj \leqslant vj \leqslant 1$):

$$\tau_j(A_i, A_k) = \begin{cases} 1, & if & \pi_{ij} - u_j < \pi_{kj} \\ 0, & if & \pi_{ij} - v_j > \pi_{kj} \\ \dfrac{v_j - (\pi_{ij} - \pi_{kj})}{v_j - u_j}, & otherwise \end{cases} \qquad (4.80)$$

where π_{ij} is the hesitancy degree of alternative A_i on criterion g_j.

The intuitionistic fuzzy credibility function $\rho(A_i, A_k)$ is computed for the set of alternatives $A, \forall A_i, A_k \in A$. $\rho(A_i, A_k)$ indicates the credibility degree of the conclusion that A_i outranks A_k and is defined as follows:

$$\rho(A_i, A_k) = \sum_{j=1}^{n} w_j \left(\psi_j(A_i, A_k) \times \tau_j(A_i, A_k)\right) \tag{4.81}$$

where:

w_j is the degree of importance for criterion g_j; and

$w_j \in [0, 1]$ and $\sum_{j=1}^{n} w_j = 1.$

The intuitionistic fuzzy credibility function defined in the current method combines the intuitionistic fuzzy support $\psi_j(A_i, A_k)$ and risk functions $\tau_j(A_i, A_k)$ to indicate the degree to which A_i outranks A_k.

The next phase uses the intuitionistic fuzzy outranking index $\rho(A_i, A_k)$ to provide a recommendation. It is necessary to calculate the outranking flows to generate a total preorder, it is similar to PROMETHEE. Here, the net intuitionistic fuzzy outranking flow index $\Phi(A_i)$ is used to calculate the entering and leaving flows for each alternative. The net outranking flow index $\Phi(A_i)$ represents the net outranking character of A_i over all remaining alternatives, and is defined as follows:

$$\Phi(A_i) = \sum_{k=1, k \neq i}^{m} \rho(A_i, A_k) - \rho(A_k, A_i) \tag{4.82}$$

4.3.2.2 Group decision-making technique

The method assigns an alternative A_i to the unique category C_k. It uses the assertion "at least as good as" from the S definition. At the assignment process, it is evaluated if A_i is "at least as good as" its lower limiting profile b_{k-1} and is not "at least as good as" its upper limit profile b_k (the relation "at least as good as" being S).

The alternatives need to be compared against the set of profile indices $\{b_i, b_2, ..., b_{h-1}\}$ from the h categories. Here, b_p represents the upper C_p category and the lower C_{p+1}.

The intuitionistic fuzzy credibility function $\rho(A_i, b_p)$ is then compared with a cutting level θ, to decide whether the intuitionistic fuzzy outranking holds $\rho(A_i, b_p) \geqslant \theta \Leftrightarrow A_i S b_k$. For the assignment of the alternatives, an exploitation phase is necessary. The alternative A_i is assigned to the highest category C_{p+1} such that $A_i S b_p$.

The assignment procedure requires the following actions. A_i is compared successively to b_p, for $p = h - 1, ..., 2, 1, 0$. When the relation $A_i S b_p$ is found, A_i is assigned to category $C_{p+1}(A_i \rightarrow C_{p+1})$.

In the group decision-making process, each DM uses the intuitionistic fuzzy outranking sorting method to assign alternatives and obtain individual results. Then the aggregation phase of individual decision results determines the group consensus throughout the group intuitionistic fuzzy credibility index $\rho_G(A_i, b_p)$:

$$
\begin{aligned}
\rho_G(A_i, b_p) \\
= \sum_{l=1}^{y} \lambda_{(l)} \cdot \rho_{(1)}(A_i, b_p) \\
= \sum_{l=1}^{y} \sum_{j=1}^{n} \lambda_{(l)} \cdot w_j \cdot (\psi_j(A_i, A_k) \times \tau_j(A_i, A_k))
\end{aligned}
\tag{4.83}
$$

where $\lambda_{(l)} \in [0, 1] (l = 1, 2, ..., y)$ are the DMs' weights, and $\sum_{l=1}^{y} \lambda_{(l)} = 1$.

Eq. (4.83) reflects the weighted sum of the group members' individual intuitionistic fuzzy credibility degrees. Following the exploitation phase, the θ-cut is used to determine the crisp relation between A_i and b_i as $A_i S b_p$ $(\rho(A_i, b_p) \geqslant \theta \Leftrightarrow A_i S b_k)$.

As part of the group decision-making stage, it is necessary to carry out some actions. The consensus checking process uses a personal satisfaction degree, a group satisfaction degree, and an alternative sorting satisfaction degree. The detailed procedure about group consensus checking is presented in [41].

The personal satisfaction degree $\varphi_{(l)}$ represents the personal level of satisfaction for the group's sorting result.

$$
\varphi_{(l)} = \frac{\sum_{i=1}^{m} \phi_{(l)}(A_i)}{m}
\tag{4.84}
$$

where:

$$
\phi_{(l)}(A_i) = \begin{cases} 1, & if \ u_{(l)}(A_i) = U(A_i) \\ 0, & otherwise \end{cases}
$$

where $u_{(l)}(A_i)$ is the alternative A_i sorting result of the lth person, $U(A_i)$ is its group sorting result, and m is the number of alternatives. A $\phi_{(l)}$ value closer to 1 means the highest agreement between the individual sorting result and group sorting result. A value closer to 0 means the lowest agreement.

The group satisfaction degree φ_G is the weighted sum of the personal satisfaction indices, which provides an index for group satisfaction.

$$
\varphi_G = \sum_{l=1}^{y} \lambda_{(l)} \cdot \varphi_{(l)} = \sum_{l=1}^{y} \sum_{i=1}^{m} \frac{\lambda_{(l)} \cdot \phi_{(l)}(A_i)}{m}
\tag{4.85}
$$

In a group decision-making process, the analyst is supported by this kind of measure (Eq. (4.85)) to identify the group consensus or satisfaction level.

In this method, the γ threshold is defined to accept a certain satisfaction degree, $\varphi_G \geqslant \gamma$. The current method does not suggest any value for the consensus threshold. However, [43] suggests a value between [0.75, 0.85] to reach an acceptable consensus level.

Finally, to determine the alternative sorting satisfaction degree, $\mathcal{X}(A_i)(i = 1, 2, ..., m)$ measures the group satisfaction level for alternative A_i (Eq. (4.86)). The satisfaction degree is used in interactive procedures to reach a consensus assignment, since it assists in identifying the group deviation degree from the alternative [41]. It can be useful in case the group is interested in one or a subgroup of alternatives.

$$\mathcal{X}(A_i) = \sum_{l=1}^{y} \lambda_{(l)} \cdot \phi_{(l)}(A_i)$$ (4.86)

where:

$$\phi_{(l)}(A_i) = \begin{cases} 1, & if \ u_{(l)}(A_i) = U(A_i) \\ 0, & otherwise \end{cases}$$

4.4   Conclusion

This chapter introduced fuzzy set concepts and explained fuzzy sorting methods and fuzzy sorting approaches. The first section allowed readers to understand how fuzzy logic represents, manages, and operates fuzzy numbers. The second section described the method that uses fuzzy input information related to the alternatives to be assigned in ordered categories. The third section described fuzzy sorting approaches, corresponding to the fuzzy strategy implemented to deal with fuzzy numbers defining the profiles of the categories.

This chapter will help in general to apply MCDM sorting methods to assign alternatives in predefined categories. Moreover, it will aid understanding of how the methods use fuzzy logic in the input information and the assignment of alternatives in fuzzy profiles.

There is a lack of MCDM sorting methods implementing fuzzification in the input information. This would support DMs in the definition of values of alternatives regarding own preferences. It is necessary to develop MCDM fuzzy sorting approaches for representative fuzzy profiles to the assignment of alternatives into categories.

References

[1] C. Kahraman, Multicriteria decision making methods and fuzzy sets, in: C. Kahraman (Ed.), Fuzzy Multi-Criteria Decision Making, Springer, Boston, MA, 2008.

[2] Krzysztof Palczewski, Wojciech Salabun, The fuzzy TOPSIS applications in the last decade, Procedia Computer Science 159 (2019) 2294–2303, Knowledge-Based and Intelligent Information & Engineering Systems: Proceedings of the 23rd International Conference KES2019.

[3] Ihsan Kaya, Murat Colak, Fulya Terzi, A comprehensive review of fuzzy multi criteria decision making methodologies for energy policy making, Energy Strategy Reviews 24 (2019) 207–228.

[4] Joan Bagaria, Set theory, in: Edward N. Zalta (Ed.), The Stanford Encyclopedia of Philosophy. Metaphysics Research Lab, spring 2020 edition, Stanford University, 2020.

[5] Hwang Bon-Gang, Methodology, in: Hwang Bon-Gang (Ed.), Performance and Improvement of Green Construction Projects, Butterworth-Heinemann, 2018, pp. 15–22, Chapter 3.

[6] L.A. Zadeh, Fuzzy sets, Information and Control 8 (3) (1965) 338–353.

[7] Robert Babuska, Fuzzy Modeling for Control, Springer, Dordrecht, 1998.

[8] Kwang Hyung Lee, Fuzzy sets, in: Janusz Kacprzyk (Ed.), First Course on Fuzzy Theory and Applications, Springer, Berlin Heidelberg, 1995, Chapter 1.

[9] Kwang Hyung Lee, Fuzzy number, in: Janusz Kacprzyk (Ed.), First Course on Fuzzy Theory and Applications, Springer, Berlin Heidelberg, 1995, Chapter 5.

[10] Palash Dutta, Bulendra Limboo, Bell-shaped fuzzy soft sets and their application in medical diagnosis, Fuzzy Information and Engineering 9 (1) (2017) 67–91.

[11] A. Virgin Raj, G. SathiyaPriya, Intuitionistic bell shape fuzzy number, International Journal of Applied Engineering Research 14 (2019) 79–82.

[12] Kwang Hyung Lee, Fuzzy logic, in: Janusz Kacprzyk (Ed.), First Course on Fuzzy Theory and Applications, Springer, Berlin Heidelberg, 1995, Chapter 8.

[13] M. Smithson, J. Verkuilen, An overview of fuzzy set mathematics, in: Fuzzy Set Theory, SAGE Publications, Inc., 1995.

[14] George J. Klir, 2 – from classical mathematics to fuzzy mathematics: emergence of a new paradigm for theoretical science, in: Dennis H. Rouvray (Ed.), Fuzzy Logic in Chemistry, Academic Press, San Diego, 1997, pp. 31–63.

[15] Z.X. Guo, W.K. Wong, 2 – fundamentals of artificial intelligence techniques for apparel management applications, in: W.K. Wong, Z.X. Guo, S.Y.S. Leung (Eds.), Optimizing Decision Making in the Apparel Supply Chain Using Artificial Intelligence (AI), in: Woodhead Publishing Series in Textiles, Woodhead Publishing, 2013, pp. 13–40.

[16] Kwang Hyung Lee, Fuzzy relation and composition, in: Janusz Kacprzyk (Ed.), First Course on Fuzzy Theory and Applications, Springer, Berlin Heidelberg, 1995, Chapter 3.

[17] Shounak Roychowdhury, Witold Pedrycz, A survey of defuzzification strategies, International Journal of Intelligent Systems 16 (6) (2001) 679–695.

[18] A. Mohammad, S. Masoum, Ewald F. Fuchs, Optimal placement and sizing of shunt capacitor banks in the presence of harmonics, in: A. Mohammad, S. Masoum, Ewald F. Fuchs (Eds.), Power Quality in Power Systems and Electrical Machines, second edition, Academic Press, Boston, 2015, pp. 887–959, Chapter 10.

[19] Kesheng Wang, Computational intelligence in agile manufacturing engineering, in: A. Gunasekaran (Ed.), Agile Manufacturing: The 21st Century Competitive Strategy, Elsevier Science Ltd, Oxford, 2001, pp. 297–315.

[20] T.A. Runkler, M. Glesner, A set of axioms for defuzzification strategies towards a theory of rational defuzzification operators, in: [Proceedings 1993] Second IEEE International Conference on Fuzzy Systems, vol. 2, 1993, pp. 1161–1166.

[21] Didier Dubois, Henri Prade, Operations on fuzzy numbers, International Journal of Systems Science 9 (6) (1978) 613–626.

[22] Zhou Jian, Yang Fan, Wang Ke, Fuzzy arithmetic on LR fuzzy numbers with applications to fuzzy programming, Journal of Intelligent & Fuzzy Systems 30 (1) (2016) 71–87.

[23] D. Dubois, P. Prade, Possibility Theory, Plenum Press, 1988.

[24] Ana Carolina Scanavachi Moreira Campos, Bertrand Mareschal, Adiel Teixeira de Almeida, Fuzzy FlowSort: an integration of the FlowSort method and fuzzy set theory for decision making on the basis of inaccurate quantitative data, Information Sciences 293 (2015) 115–124.

[25] P. Nemery, C. Lamboray, FlowSort: a flow-based sorting method with limiting or central profiles, Top 16 (2008) 90–113.

[26] J.P. Brans, Ph. Vincke, A preference ranking organisation method: the PROMETHEE method for multiple criteria decision-making, Management Science 31 (6) (1985).

[27] J. Pierre Brans, Bertrand Mareschal, PROMETHEE v: MCDM problems with segmentation constraints, INFOR. Information Systems and Operational Research 30 (2) (1992) 85–96.

[28] Renata Pelissari, Maria Célia Oliveira, Sarah Ben Amor, Alvaro José Abackerli, A new FlowSort-based method to deal with information imperfections in sorting decision-making problems, European Journal of Operational Research 276 (1) (2019) 235–246.

[29] Risto Lahdelma, Joonas Hokkanen, Pekka Salminen, SMAA – stochastic multiobjective acceptability analysis, European Journal of Operational Research 106 (1) (1998) 137–143.

[30] Javier Pereira, Elaine C.B. de Oliveira Luiz, F.A.M. Gomes, Renato M. Araújo, Sorting retail locations in a large urban city by using ELECTRE TRI-C and trapezoidal fuzzy numbers, Soft Computing 23 (2019) 4193–4206.

[31] J. Almeida, J. Figueira, B. Roy, ELECTRE TRI-C: a multiple criteria sorting method based on central reference actions, in: Cahier du Lamsade, Université Paris Dauphine, 2008.

[32] B. Roy, Multicriteria Methodology for Decision Aiding, Kluwer, Dordrecht, 1996.

[33] Maisa Mendonça Silva, Ana Paula Cabral Seixas Costa, Ana Paula Henriques de Gusmão, Continuous cooperation: a proposal using a fuzzy multicriteria sorting method, International Journal of Production Economics 151 (2014) 67–75.

[34] Witold Pedrycz, Why triangular membership functions?, Fuzzy Sets and Systems 64 (1) (1994) 21–30.

[35] Razvan Gheorghe, Ahmed Bufardi, Paul Xirouchakis, Construction of a two-parameters fuzzy outranking relation from fuzzy evaluations, Fuzzy Sets and Systems 143 (3) (2004) 391–412.

[36] Zhi-Hua Li, Hong-Yi Fan, Wen-Long Xu, Han-Xin Yang, q-strategy spatial prisoner's dilemma game, Physics Letters A 375 (41) (2011) 3557–3561.

[37] Alessio Ishizaka, Craig Pearman, Philippe Nemery, AHPSort: an AHP-based method for sorting problems, International Journal of Production Research 50 (17) (2012) 4767–4784.

[38] Jana Krejčí, Alessio Ishizaka Fahpsort, A fuzzy extension of the AHPSort method, International Journal of Information Technology & Decision Making 17 (04) (2018) 1119–1145.

[39] Alessio Ishizaka, Menelaos Tasiou, Luis Martínez, Analytic hierarchy process-fuzzy sorting: an analytic hierarchy process-based method for fuzzy classification in sorting problems, Journal of the Operational Research Society 71 (6) (2020) 928–947.

[40] Jin-Hsien Wang, Jongyun Hao, A new version of 2-tuple fuzzy linguistic representation model for computing with words, IEEE Transactions on Fuzzy Systems 14 (3) (2006) 435–445.

[41] Feng Shen, Jiuping Xu, Zeshui Xu, An outranking sorting method for multi-criteria group decision making using intuitionistic fuzzy sets, Information Sciences 334–335 (2016) 338–353.

[42] J. Figueira, V. Mousseau, B. Roy, Electre Methods: Multiple Criteria Decision Analysis: State of the Art Surveys, Springer, New York, NY, 2005.

[43] P.A. Álvarez, D. Morais, J. López, A.T. Almeida, An ELECTRE III based consensus-reaching process to improve a collective solution, International Transactions in Operational Research (2020).

Chapter 5

Analysis of MCDM sorting methods

5.1 Suitability and necessity

5.1.1 AHPSort II

AHPSort [1] or AHPSort II [2] are sorting methods based on the analytical hierarchy process (AHP). The sorting problem is mostly addressed with AHPSort or AHPSort II as the supplier selection. Due to the comparison of alternatives and profiles in each criterion, it is possible to derive weights and priorities used for assigning the alternatives into classes.

For the supplier selection problem, if there is a large number of suppliers, sorting MCDM methods can provide a better view of the performance of suppliers than rankings can [3]. For example, in a ranking problem, the first position is the best supplier; however, its performance can be low, and the rest of the suppliers will keep the worst performance. In a sorting problem, a supplier assigned to a specific category presents a performance that meets the category's characteristics.

In the presence of a large number of suppliers, AHPSort II is a suitable method for this large-scale problem considering that it requires far fewer comparisons. Implementing this method will make the comparison process easier [3].

The AHPSort II method reduces the number of comparisons by selecting representative points and the limiting or central profiles for each criterion. The representative points are the main focus of the method, and they must be selected carefully and in the most representative way. Similarly, the definition of limiting profiles is a sensitive step. These definitions must be done carefully because the entire sorting process depends on them [2].

5.1.2 UTADIS

The UTADIS method and its extension are methods from the full aggregation approach most used in multiple-criteria decision-making. The UTADIS method is most commonly applied in education. Second is maintenance management, and financial management and risk assessment are other application areas of the full aggregation approach [4].

Multi-Criteria Decision-Making Sorting Methods. https://doi.org/10.1016/B978-0-32-385231-9.00010-9

UTADIS is a method where the decision-maker must define a set of imprecise assignment examples from actions to one or several contiguous classes. The assignments are considered reference actions that represent the DM's preference information, which is used to build the preference model of the DM represented by a set of general additive value functions that are compatible with the assignment examples.

The classical UTADIS method deals with a subset of the entire set of compatible additive value functions. Based on the set of all compatible value functions, two binary relations can be defined in the set of all actions A:

- a necessary weak preference relation $\gtrsim^N$, in case $U(a) \geq U(a)$ for **all** compatible value functions; and
- a possible weak preference relation $\gtrsim^P$, in case $U(a) \geq U(a)$ for **at least one** compatible value functions.

Due to the support of the UTADIS method to assist the decision-maker (DM) in defining parameters, it can be applied with less cognitive complexity for the DM in problems with a large number of criteria. In this sense, if the problem includes several criteria, it does not generates more effort for the DM. However, the DM needs to define a reference set manually, assigning alternatives in the categories that will help derive a method's parameters. A problem arises if there are several categories, as the DM will be required to assign some alternatives in any category.

5.1.3   ELECTRE TRI

The ELECTRE TRI method and its extension are methods from the outranking approach. The ELECTRE TRI method is applied most often in risk assessment. Other significant applications are resource management, policy analysis, human resources, and health [4].

The ELECTRE TRI method and different extensions are applied in real-life problems. Those methods are considered flexible as they present some of the following characteristics. The method allows the evaluation of alternatives directly by each criterion. It means that normalization is not required. The method includes the possibility of dealing with the qualitative as well as the quantitative scales of criteria [5]. However, the ELECTRE family requires threshold parameters: the indifference, preference, and veto thresholds (q, p, and v), and the degree of importance (w).

5.1.4   FlowSort

As we explained in Section 3.3, FlowSort [6] is a PROMETHEE-based sorting method for assigning alternatives to predefined classes with either limiting profiles or central profiles. FlowSort method is an outranking method as PROMETHEE and it does not use a veto threshold. The first version of FlowSort [6] does not deal with uncertainties in the parameters such as thresholds, weights, and evaluation of profiles or actions. However, some extensions have been developed that model other real situations.

In the work presented in [8], FlowSort was applied for innovation performances of small and medium enterprises from the French Lorraine region. On the other hand, the Fuzzy FlowSort (F-FlowSort) method proposed by [9] extended the FlowSort with fuzzy logic properties. Its potential relates to the possibility of processing imprecise data when they are defined by intervals. It is suitable to deal with imprecise data and as the method avoids the loss of the input information, it is considered to improve the decision-making process.

The extension of FlowSort has allowed applicability in other contexts as uncertainty or imprecise data. Interval-FlowSort [7] deals with data where the parameters of the model are not precisely defined. Fuzzy-FlowSort and Interval-FlowSort have the limitation of not allowing stochastic input data. On the other hand, SMAA-FFS (SMAA and FlowSort) [10] deals with information inaccuracies (stochastic input data). SMAA-FFS presents the ability to deal with the criteria weights elicitation process, and SMAA permits stochastic and interval input data and the elicitation of criteria weights.

The properties presented by the different extensions of FlowSort allow the problem to be addressed via different characteristics such as imprecise or uncertain data, and robust results. Some areas where FlowSort has been applied are project evaluation, financial management, risk assessment, and supplier selection.

5.1.5 DEASort

DEA was previously used to rank projects, but the DEASort proposal in [11] was developed for sorting. In this study, the DEA-based sorting method was used for sorting items instead of ranking.

DEASort is suitable for private organizations and even for entities such as regions or countries [12]. It is a measure that estimates the performance of decision-making units (DMUs) that are evaluated by common inputs and outputs. It is estimated that an efficiency frontier has a score of 1 (or 100%). In that sense, DMUs operating beneath the frontier have an efficiency score equal to or less than 1, and thus have the capacity to improve future performance if this is the case [12].

The DEASort model [11] can be combined with AHP, the output of which is used to take into account the expertise of decision-makers in calculating the weights. DEASort provides screening of alternatives, mainly when a DM is not able to express preferences at the beginning of system design or planning. It is easy for practitioners to apply and understand the methodology and the results. DEA-based sorting methods have been developed recently, and they have been applied in financial management, inventory management, materials management, and project evaluation [4].

5.1.6 TOPSIS-SORT

In [13] it is stated that the TOPSIS methodology for ranking problems has been successfully applied to a wide range of application areas and industrial sectors with varying terms and subjects. It requires a broader emphasis on interdisciplinary and social decision problems.

In sorting problemas, four methods have been developed: AHP–TOPSIS-2 N [14], TOPSIS-SORT [15], TOPSIS-Sort-C [16], and PDTOPSIS-Sort [17]. These methods have been applied in environmental assessment, financial management, and project evaluation.

The TOPSIS method for sorting needs a small amount of input from users, and its output is easy to understand. The only parameters that require human participation are the weights of the criteria. A TOPSIS-based sorting method will help in financial management or risk management. For example, the assessments of companies include financial ratios related to credit risk and the likelihood of bankruptcy. The method can sort a set of alternatives (companies, assets, stocks) into different classes of risk, where the first class represents investment alternatives with the lowest associated risk. In contrast, the last class represents the alternatives with the highest risk.

5.1.7 Preference disaggregation analysis (PDA)

Preference disaggregation analysis (PDA) is a common technique used to support the decision-maker (DM) in the decision process to find parameters that fill its preferences. In this sense, some methods implement recognition of preference information from the information expressed in a reference set of assigned alternatives from the DM. PDA is a technique that uses indirect elicitation that corresponds to the DM's preferences expressed by holistic judgments on representative case sets. It is important to note that using PDA in the MCDM context provides extra support to the DM to assist in the elicitation stage.

In multiple-criteria sorting problems, the parameter elicitation can be carried out with PDA regarding the holistic decisions given by the DM. In another stage, an MCDM sorting method compares alternatives against limiting profiles (or centroids) and assigns alternatives in classes.

Eliciting preferential information from the DMs and formalizing it through preferential parameters is hence a crucial phase in a multiple-criteria decision aid model [18]. The definition of parameters is considered a complex task and requires great effort from DMs. In [18] some problems concerning preference elicitation are identified, as follows:

- the data considered in the decision problem might be imprecise or uncertain;
- DMs may have a vague understanding of what the parameters represent and their point of view can evolve during the elicitation process; and
- in group decisions, lack of consensus among DMs can also be a critical issue.

The PDA technique can support the parameter elicitation stage. This is significant when the DM is not familiar with the sorting method, the multi-criteria problem, a redefinition of parameters in a feedback process, and a large number of criteria. In the literature, different sorting methods have been proposed with PDA support. Methods of each approach that implement a PDA technique are as follows.

In the full aggregation approach, we can see interactive UTADIS [19] and different extensions, Multimoora Sort [20], DIS-CARD [21], nonmonotonic sorting [22], PDA sorting with partial monotonicity constraints [23], and nonmonotonic sorting with regularization framework [24], among others. The methods applying PDA techniques on the outranking approach are ELECTRE TRI-C [25], SMAA-TRI [26], SMAA-FFS [10], PDA-THESEUS [27], and I-MCSGA [28], among others. The goal, aspiration, or reference-level approach includes some known methods that apply PDA techniques, DEA-based sorting [29], AHP–TOPSIS-2N [14], and probabilistic sorting [30]. On the other hand, the nonclassical MCDM approach does not require additional PDA techniques. The methods belonging to the current approach support DMs to avoid parameter definition; examples of these methods include Rough-set [31], STEPCLASS [32], and TRINOMFC [33].

5.1.8 Group decision-making for sorting

In multiple-criteria group decision-making, the sorting problem is to assign alternatives to predefined classes by a group of decision-makers. The classes are defined in an ordinal way based on DMs' preferences. In this sense, the two or several DMs cooperate to make a collective decision. In group decision-making, two schemes are common. The group members define the parameters and the alternatives are assigned regarding the agreed defined parameters. In the second schema, each member obtains individual sorting results. This can be carried out by using a sorting method, and defining the parameter values to assign the alternatives regarding each individual preference. Later, additional procedures or techniques are needed to propose a collective or consensus solution that satisfies each group's members.

The group decision-making (GDM) support for sorting methods is still an open area to work on, as described in the most recent survey carried out in [4]. In the full aggregation approach, the following have been developed: Interactive GDM sort with RINCON algorithm [34], UTADIS$^{GMS-GROUP}$ [35], GDM sort with evidential reasoning [36], MHDIS [37], and GAHPSort [38]. In the outranking approach, the following have been developed: SMAA-TRI for GDM [26], GDM ELECTRE sort [39], Relation H sort [40], Delphi ELECTRE TRI [41], FlowSort-GDSS [42], ELECTRE TRI for GDM [43], and intuitionistic GDM outranking sort [44]. Finally, the most recent work in the goal, aspiration, or reference-level approach is AHP–TOPSIS-2N [14].

5.2 Characterization

In multiple-criteria decision-making (MCDM) problems, it seems more common to use ranking and sorting methods. Both offer an interesting way to analyze MCDM problems. When the alternatives are ranked in a complete or partial order, understandably, the decision-maker is looking for the more promising or best alternative. However, in some cases, nothing assures the DM that the best-ranked action is well-suited for this particular problem. It seems that in some cases, the best alternative may not be adopted as the best solution for the specific problem. When alternatives are assigned into categories, it seems that the grouped alternatives match some characteristics that accomplish the DM's needs. Thus, a good a priori definition of the categories is necessary for the good assignment of alternatives and confidence in the final sorting solution.

In our daily life, in multi-criteria decision-making problems it is natural to think in classes (categories) to identify or distinguish alternatives. Thus, the decision-maker defines the classes relative to the consequences that will be given to the actions belonging to the same class [45].

In literature, we sometimes find the same problem is addressed as a ranking or sorting problem. In [19], the authors believe that many problems that are treated as ranking problems are in fact sorting problems.

In sorting methods, there are many applications for decision-making problems. The most addressed implementations are focused on risk assessment, education, project evaluation, financial management, and supplier selection [4]. We will describe the characteristics of these problems and how they are solved by MCDM sorting methods.

5.2.1 Risk assessment

The risk assessment presents several variants related to finance, safety, environment, failure control, construction, and more. In this section, the main problems are briefly described, including country risk, business and bankruptcy risk, and environmental risk.

Country risk

Country risk refers broadly to the likelihood that a sovereign state or borrower from a particular country may be unable and/or unwilling to fulfill their obligations toward one or more foreign lenders and/or investors [46].

In [37], the authors characterize the economic performance and the creditworthiness of a country. They analyzed the data from World Bank indicators from 1995 of 143 countries. They involve a significantly large number of indicators and variables relative to country risk assessment including inflation and exchange rates, the balance of payments, tax policies, macroeconomic indicators, indicators upon structural transformation, as well as trade indicators and external debt indicators. For this study, the authors used the 12 most relevant criteria that best describe the economic performance and the creditworthiness of countries (see Table 5.1).

TABLE 5.1 Criteria to characterize the economic performance and the creditworthiness of a country.

Description

Current account balance/gross domestic product (GDP)

Export volume growth

Gross domestic investment/GDP

Import volume growth

Inflation (GDP deflator)

Net trade in goods and services

Present value of debt/exports of goods and services

Present value of debt/gross national product (GNP)

Total debt service/GNP

Income velocity of money (GDP/M2)

GNP growth

Gross international reserves in months of imports

This classification constitutes the basis for the development of the appropriate country risk assessment model [37]. According to the World Bank, the countries under consideration are categorized into four classes according to their income level (see Fig. 5.1):

- high-income economies (Class 1);
- upper-middle economies (Class 2);
- lower-middle income economies (Class 3); and
- low-income economies (Class 4).

In [47], the country ratings of two international credit rating agencies were used, namely Standard & Poor's (S&P) and Moody's, as classification criteria for the countries that are taken as alternatives; see Table 5.2. S&P and Moody's rating system includes more than 20 classification groups. In [47] the groups of classification were reduced by combining them into three subgroups for simplification purposes. Fig. 5.2 illustrates the classes.

Business and bankruptcy risk

Business failure prediction is a scientific field in which many academic and professional people have been working for at least the last three decades [48]. Business failure prediction is one of the most essential problems in the field of financial management. Research into developing quantitative business failure prediction models has been focused on building discriminative models to distinguish between failed and nonfailed firms [48].

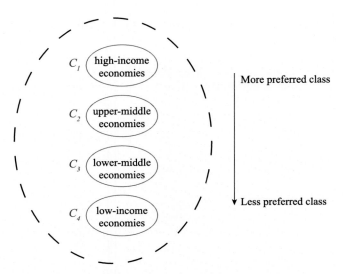

FIGURE 5.1 Classes to categorize countries according to their income level.

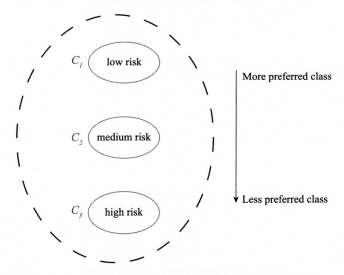

FIGURE 5.2 Classes to categorize country ratings regarding their level of risk.

Knowing about business failure can be of interest for financial organizations, investors, and clients. Business failure prediction offers managers of financial institutions significant aid in the evaluation and selection of viable firms for financing [49].

In [48], the failure risk of Greek industrial firms was predicted. The data used were first analyzed in [49]. The financial statements of these firms were col-

TABLE 5.2 Criteria to characterize the country risk rating evaluation.

Description
GDP growth (annual %)
Inflation, GDP deflator (annual %)
External debt per GDP
Current account balance/GDP
Export growth
Import growth
Gross domestic investment/GDP
Net trade in goods and services (balance of payments, current US$)
Total reserves in months of imports
Money and quasimoney (M2) as % of GDP

lected for a period of 5 years, starting from year −5 (5 years before bankruptcy) and ending with the year −1 (1 year before the year of bankruptcy, the last year that the firm had been in business).

The evaluation criteria used for the business failure risk are listed in Table 5.3 and correspond to 12 financial ratios. The authors [48] explained that the selection of these ratios was based upon the following three points: the availability of the financial data of the firms, the relevance for business failure prediction in literature, and the experience of an expert credit analyst.

TABLE 5.3 Financial ratios for the business failure risk.

Description
Net income/gross profit
Gross profit/total assets
Net income/total assets
Net income/net worth
Current assets/current liabilities
Quick assets/current liabilities
(Long-term debt current liabilities)/total assets
Net worth/(net worth + long-term debt)
Net worth/net fixed assets
Inventories/working capital
Current liabilities/total assets
Working capital/net worth

In [50], financial industrial and commercial firms were categorized on predefined risk classes. The authors solved a real-world problem first presented in [51]. This corresponds to the Greek industrial development bank called ETEVA.

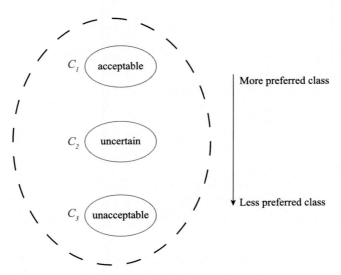

FIGURE 5.3 Classes in which to categorize firms based on the bankruptcy risk.

To decide in which firm to invest, firms were evaluated according to their risk level. A sample of 39 firms was chosen for analyzing the bankruptcy risk. With the cooperation of the bank's financial manager, the selected firms were classified into three predefined classes of risk for the year 1988. Table 5.4 shows the criteria used to analyze the firms; the first six criteria are financial ratios. Criteria seven to twelve are related to general information about the firm other than the financial ratios but are relevant to managers. These criteria provide qualitative information about the risk prediction. Fig. 5.3 shows the classes used to categorize firms based on the bankruptcy risk.

Environmental risk assessment

In [52], a risk assessment problem of zoning the watershed in France is analyzed. The authors considered a set of 40 land zones evaluated on five criteria with decreasing direction of preference (see Table 5.5).

The objective of the study is to indicate the most appropriate intervention for protecting the reproduction habitat of Salmonidae fish in these watersheds. The interventions are designed based on the risk classes illustrated in Fig. 5.4.

5.2.2 Education

The decision-making problems in education have been studied by MCDM researchers in different situations. The main elements studied in the education topic are universities or academic programs, faculty, and students.

TABLE 5.4 Criteria to the assignment of risk for firms to invest.

Description
Earnings before interest and taxes as a fraction of total assets
Net income as a fraction of net worth
Total liabilities divided by total assets
Total liabilities divided by annual cash flow
Interest expenses divided by sales
General and administrative expenses as a percentage of sales
Managers' work experience
Subjective measure of market niche or position
Subjective measure of technical structure and facilities
Organization and personnel
Assessment of special competitive advantage
Market flexibility

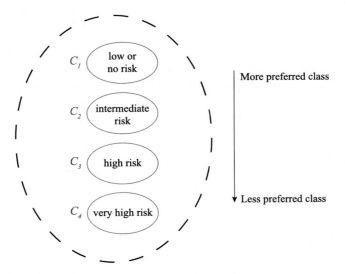

FIGURE 5.4 Classes to categorize land zones based on their risk.

Universities or academic programs

In [53], the authors state that higher education is becoming more and more competitive, with many academic players in the market, vying for the best faculty and students. It seems that universities are not in the same situation as when they were fully government-funded, and now the universities need to be nimble and smart and to be capable of more self-auditing and accountability [53]. In [19], it is stated that ranking of universities or academic programs produced by

TABLE 5.5 Criteria for environmental risk assessment.

Description
Overall slope of the land zone
Quality of the connectivity between the land zone and the stream
Type of embankment in the lower part of the land zone
Nature of crops in the land zone
Bank alteration by the cows when they drink water directly from the stream

many publishers are typical examples where a sorting approach would be more suitable.

For the evaluation of academic programs or units, it is important to define each class of the program clearly, as well as the purpose of the evaluation [54]. In evaluating academic programs, an arguably important step is defining clearly the type of academic programs or units that are intended to be evaluated. It seems easy to evaluate universities and business schools, because they are clearly identified and contain organizational units. In [54], it is stated that it is much more difficult to evaluate interdisciplinary academic programs that do not fall neatly into specific departments or units. Considering the purpose of evaluation, some different purposes can be stated, such as academic excellence of the programs or the impact of a program on society [54].

Different studies had been carried out about MBA programs. In [19], 81 MBA programs were considered in sorting problems using the model implemented in the UTADIS method. The data were obtained from the global MBA programs ranked by the Financial Times (https://rankings.ft.com), considering three main decision criteria: alumni career progress, diversity, and idea generation. The complete set of criteria is listed in Table 5.6. The programs were assigned into categories: 1, 2, and 3.

Faculty

The academic members of an institution are another element of evaluation in the education area.

The necessity of universities to prove good indicators in different areas generates new environments, where faculty members or academics are expected to produce more within the core tripartite areas of research, teaching, and administration [53]. The evaluation of academics has been carried out based on their research performance [53]. It is focused on research outputs, income generations, supervision and mentoring, and academic leadership. Table 5.7 show the list of criteria used.

The analytic network process for sorting problematic (ANPSort) is applied for the classification of academics according to their research performance [53]. The research time was allocated (i.e. 0%; 10%; 20%; 40%) according to the classification. The decision-maker decided to classify the academic staff into four classes, as illustrated in Fig. 5.5.

TABLE 5.6 Criteria for MBA.

Description
Weighted salary (US$)
Salary percentage increase
Faculty with doctorates (%)
International faculty (%)
International students (%)
Aims achieved (%)
Employment at 3 months (%)
Women faculty (%)
FT research rank
International mobility rank
FT doctoral rating rank
Value for money rank
Career progress rank
Placement success rank
Alumni recommend rank
International experience rank

TABLE 5.7 Criteria for faculty.

Description
Research outputs
Articles in journal on the Association of the Business School (ABS) or Australian Business Deans Council (ABDC) list.
Monographs
Book chapters
Conference papers with peer-reviewed proceedings
Income generation
Research grants covers any funding for scientific research
Innovation service/knowledge transfer.
Supervision and mentoring
PhD supervision as first, second, or third supervisor
Mentoring younger or inexperienced colleagues
Academic leadership and citizenship
Member of an editorial board
Member of a conference committee
Holding a keynote and tutorial at conferences
Press appearance to propagate scientific results or to comment on specialized topics

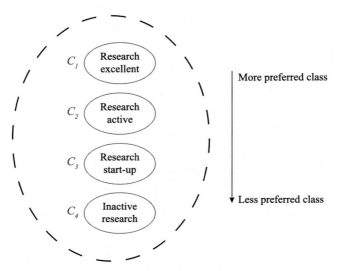

FIGURE 5.5 Classes to categorize academic staff based on their research level.

Research excellent: they are the leaders in the field, they publish in top journals, attract research and innovation service income, supervise PhD students, and have external activities.

Research active: they have publications, income generation, PhD supervision, and some external activities.

Research start-up: they are not yet fully involved in research but have the potential to become research active.

Inactive research: they are not involved in research.

Students

The evaluation of students for a specific postgraduate program is mostly addressed by considering the student qualification from the subjects studied (see [55,56]).

In [57], the evaluation of students was investigated in the MCDM regarding three courses: mathematics, physics, and literature. The students were assigned to three classes: bad $\prec$ medium $\prec$ good.

A set of students from the computer science faculty was evaluated to the Intelligent Decision Support Systems specialization [55]. The students were sorted into three classes: desirable, acceptable, and nonacceptable (see Fig. 5.6). Table 5.8 shows the list of decision criteria; the first two are attributes, and the last five are criteria with different domains to the attributes.

The applications commonly addressed in MCDM sorting are risk assessment, education, project evaluation, financial management, supplier selection, materials management, resource management, and others. A recent survey [4] showed that risk assessment is addressed more often by outranking approach.

TABLE 5.8 Criteria for students.
Description
Additional project
Training
examination in statistics
examination in computer networks
project in computer networks
examination in databases
project in databases

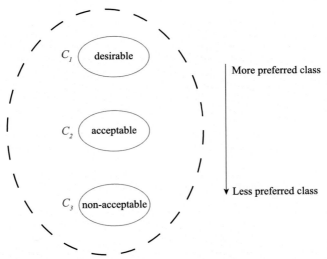

FIGURE 5.6 Classes in which to categorize students based on their qualification from subjects studied.

The education problematic is addressed mainly by a full aggregation approach. The goal, aspiration, or reference-level approach does not seem to be focused on a specific approach; instead, it is applied equally in environmental assessment, financial management, inventory management, materials management, project evaluation, and resource management. The nonclassical MCDM approach presents few applications; however, the majority are focused on risk assessment and education.

References

[1] A. Ishizaka, C. Pearman, P. Nemery, Ahpsort: an AHP-based method for sorting problems, International Journal of Production Research 50 (17) (2012) 4767–4784.
[2] F. Miccoli, A. Ishizaka, Sorting municipalities in Umbria according to the risk of wolf attacks with AHPSort II, Ecological Indicators 73 (2017) 741–755.

[3] Zhou Xu, Jindong Qin, Jun Liu, Luis Martínez, Sustainable supplier selection based on AHP-Sort II in interval type-2 fuzzy environment, Information Sciences 483 (2019) 273–293.

[4] Pavel Anselmo Alvarez, Alessio Ishizaka, Luis Martínez, Multiple-criteria decision-making sorting methods: a survey, Expert Systems with Applications 183 (2021) 115368.

[5] José Rui Figueira, Salvatore Greco, Bernard Roy, Roman Slowinski, An overview of Electre methods and their recent extensions, Journal of Multi-Criteria Decision Analysis 20 (1–2) (2013) 61–85.

[6] Philippe Nemery, Claude Lamboray, FlowSort: a flow-based sorting method with limiting or central profiles, Top 16 (1) (2008) 90–113.

[7] Pierre Janssen, Philippe Nemery, An extension of the FlowSort sorting method to deal with imprecision, 4OR 11 (2) (2013) 171–193.

[8] P. Nemery, A. Ishizaka, M. Camargo, L. Morel, Enriching descriptive information in ranking and sorting problems with visualizations techniques, Journal of Modelling in Management 7 (2) (2012) 130–147.

[9] Ana Carolina Scanavachi Moreira Campos, Bertrand Mareschal, Adiel Teixeira de Almeida, Fuzzy FlowSort: an integration of the FlowSort method and fuzzy set theory for decision making on the basis of inaccurate quantitative data, Information Sciences 293 (2015) 115–124.

[10] Renata Pelissari, Maria Célia Oliveira, Sarah Ben Amor, Alvaro José Abackerli, A new FlowSort-based method to deal with information imperfections in sorting decision-making problems, European Journal of Operational Research 276 (1) (2019) 235–246.

[11] Alessio Ishizaka, Francesco Lolli, Elia Balugani, Rita Cavallieri, Rita Gamberini Deasort, Assigning items with data envelopment analysis in ABC classes, International Journal of Production Economics 199 (2018) 7–15.

[12] Jean-Marc Hugueni, Data envelopment analysis, in: Alessio Ishizaka, Philippe Nemery (Eds.), Multi-Criteria Decision Analysis: Methods and Software, Wiley, United Kingdom, 2013, Book section 10.

[13] Majid Behzadian, S. Khanmohammadi Otaghsara, Morteza Yazdani, Joshua Ignatius, A state-of the-art survey of TOPSIS applications, Expert Systems with Applications 39 (17) (2012) 13051–13069.

[14] L.P. De Souza, C.F.S. Gomes, A.P. De Barros, Implementation of new hybrid AHP-TOPSIS-2n method in sorting and prioritizing 6 of an it CAPEX project portfolio, International Journal of Information Technology & Decision Making 17 (4) (2018) 977–1005.

[15] H.F. Sabokbar, A. Hosseini, A. Banaitis, N. Banaitiene, A novel sorting method TOPSIS-sort: an application for Tehran environmental quality evaluation, E & M Ekonomie a Management 19 (2) (2016) 87–104.

[16] Diogo Ferreira de Lima Silva, Adiel Teixeira de Almeida Filho, Sorting with TOPSIS through boundary and characteristic profiles, Computers & Industrial Engineering 141 (2020) 106328.

[17] Diogo Ferreira de Lima Silva, Luciano Ferreira, Adiel Teixeira de Almeida-Filho, A new preference disaggregation TOPSIS approach applied to sort corporate bonds based on financial statements and expert's assessment, Expert Systems with Applications 152 (2020) 113369.

[18] Luís Dias, Vincent Mousseau, José Figueira, Joao Clímaco, An aggregation/disaggregation approach to obtain robust conclusions with Electre Tri, European Journal of Operational Research 138 (2) (2002) 332–348, MCDA Methodologies for Classification and Sorting.

[19] M. Koksalan, S.B. Ozpeynirci, An interactive sorting method for additive utility functions, Computers & Operations Research 36 (9) (2009) 2565–2572.

[20] Füsun Küçükbay, Ebru Surucu-Balci, Corporate sustainability performance measurement based on a new multicriteria sorting method, Corporate Social-Responsibility and Environmental Management 26 (3) (2019) 664–680.

[21] M. Kadzinski, R. Slowinski, Dis-card: a new method of multiple criteria sorting to classes with desired cardinality, Journal of Global Optimization 56 (3) (2013) 1143–1166.

[22] Mengzhuo Guo, Xiuwu Liao, Jiapeng Liu, A progressive sorting approach for multiple criteria decision aiding in the presence of non-monotonic preferences, Expert Systems with Applications 123 (2019) 1–17.

[23] Milosz Kadzinski, Krzysztof Martyn, Marco Cinelli, Roman Slowinski, Salvatore Corrente, Salvatore Greco, Preference disaggregation for multiple criteria sorting with partial monotonicity constraints: application to exposure management of nanomaterials, International Journal of Approximate Reasoning 117 (2020) 60–80.

[24] Jiapeng Liu, Xiuwu Liao, Milosz Kadzinski, Roman Slowinski, Preference disaggregation within the regularization framework for sorting problems with multiple potentially non-monotonic criteria, European Journal of Operational Research 276 (3) (2019) 1071–1089.

[25] J.R. Figueira, J. Almeida-Dias, S. Matias, B. Roy, M.J. Carvalho, C.E. Plancha, Electre Tri-c, a multiple criteria decision aiding sorting model applied to assisted reproduction, International Journal of Medical Informatics 80 (4) (2011) 262–273.

[26] D.C. Morais, A.T. de Almeida, J.R. Figueira, A sorting model for group decision making: a case study of water losses in Brazil, Group Decision and Negotiation 23 (5) (2014) 937–960.

[27] E. Fernandez, J. Navarro, A new approach to multi-criteria sorting based on fuzzy outranking relations: the THESEUS method, European Journal of Operational Research 213 (2) (2011) 405–413.

[28] L. Cruz-Reyes, E. Fernandez, P. Sanchez, C. Gomez, Incorporation of decision-maker preferences in an interactive evolutionary multi-objective algorithm using a multi-criteria sorting, International Journal of Combinatorial Optimization Problems and Informatics 7 (3) (2016) 28–43.

[29] E. Karasakal, P. Aker, A multicriteria sorting approach based on data envelopment analysis for R&D project selection problem, Omega-International Journal of Management Science 73 (2017) 79–92.

[30] B. Celik, E. Karasakal, C. Iyigun, A probabilistic multiple criteria sorting approach based on distance functions, Expert Systems with Applications 42 (7) (2015) 3610–3618.

[31] S. Greco, B. Matarazzo, R. Slowinski, Rough sets methodology for sorting problems in presence of multiple attributes and criteria, European Journal of Operational Research 138 (2) (2002) 247–259.

[32] E.M. Furems, Stepclass-based approach to multicriteria sorting, Scientific and Technical Information Processing 42 (6) (2015) 481–489.

[33] J. Leger, J.M. Martel, A multicriteria assignment procedure for a nominal sorting problematic, European Journal of Operational Research 138 (2) (2002) 349–364.

[34] F.L. Cai, X.W. Liao, K.L. Wang, An interactive sorting approach based on the assignment examples of multiple decision makers with different priorities, Annals of Operations Research 197 (1) (2012) 87–108.

[35] Salvatore Greco, Milosz Kadzinski, Vincent Mousseau, Roman Slowinski, Robust ordinal regression for multiple criteria group decision: UTAGMS-GROUP and UTADISGMS-GROUP, Decision Support Systems 52 (3) (2012) 549–561.

[36] J.P. Liu, X.W. Liao, J.B. Yang, A group decision-making approach based on evidential reasoning for multiple criteria sorting problem with uncertainty, European Journal of Operational Research 246 (3) (2015) 858–873.

[37] M. Doumpos, C. Zopounidis, Assessing financial risks using a multicriteria sorting procedure: the case of country risk assessment, Omega-International Journal of Management Science 29 (1) (2001) 97–109.

[38] C. Lopez, A. Ishizaka Gahpsort, A new group multi-criteria decision method for sorting a large number of the cloud-based ERP solutions, Computers in Industry 92–93 (2017) 12.

[39] A. Bregar, J. Gyorkos, M.B. Juric, Interactive aggregation/disaggregation dichotomic sorting procedure for group decision analysis based on the threshold model, Informatica 19 (2) (2008) 161–190.

[40] K. Jabeur, J.M. Martel, An ordinal sorting method for group decision-making, European Journal of Operational Research 180 (3) (2007) 1272–1289.

[41] L.C. Dias, C.H. Antunes, G. Dantas, N. de Castro, L. Zamboni, A multi-criteria approach to sort and rank policies based on Delphi qualitative assessments and Electre Tri: the case of smart grids in Brazil, Omega-International Journal of Management Science 76 (2018) 100–111.

[42] F. Lolli, A. Ishizaka, R. Gamberini, B. Rimini, M. Messori, FlowSort-GDSS – a novel group multi-criteria decision support system for sorting problems with application to FMEA, Expert Systems with Applications 42 (17–18) (2015) 6342–6349.

[43] S. Damart, L.C. Dias, V. Mousseau, Supporting groups in sorting decisions: methodology and use of a multi-criteria aggregation/disaggregation DSS, Decision Support Systems 43 (4) (2007) 1464–1475.

[44] Feng Shen, Jiuping Xu, Zeshui Xu, An outranking sorting method for multi-criteria group decision making using intuitionistic fuzzy sets, Information Sciences 334–335 (2016) 338–353.

[45] P. Nemery, On the use of multicriteria ranking methods in sorting problems, l'Université Libre de Bruxelles, France, 2008.

[46] T.E. Krayenbuehl, Country risk: assessment and monitoring, Lexington, Massachusetts, 1985.

[47] A. Ulucan, K.B. Atici, A multiple criteria sorting methodology with multiple classification criteria and an application to country risk evaluation, Technological and Economic Development of Economy 19 (1) (2013) 93–124.

[48] Constantin Zopounidis, Michael Doumpos, Business failure prediction using the UTADIS multicriteria analysis method, Journal of the Operational Research Society 50 (11) (1999) 1138–1148.

[49] A.I. Dimitras, R. Slowinski, R. Susmaga, C. Zopounidis, Business failure prediction using rough sets, European Journal of Operational Research 114 (2) (1999) 263–280.

[50] Y. Chen, D.M. Kilgour, K.W. Hipel, A decision rule aggregation approach to multiple criteria-multiple participant sorting, Group Decision and Negotiation 21 (5) (2012) 727–745.

[51] R. Slowinski, C. Zopounidis, Application of the rough set approach to evaluation of bankruptcy risk, Intelligent Systems in Accounting, Finance and Management 4 (1) (1995) 27–41.

[52] M. Kadzinski, T. Tervonen, J.R. Figueira, Robust multi-criteria sorting with the outranking preference model and characteristic profiles, Omega-International Journal of Management Science 55 (2015) 126–140.

[53] Alessio Ishizaka, Vijay Pereira, Utilisation of ANPSort for sorting alternative with interdependent criteria illustrated through a researcher's classification problem in an academic context, Soft Computing (2019).

[54] Ralph L. Keeney, Kelly E. See, Detlof von Winterfeldt, Evaluating academic programs: with applications to U.S. graduate decision science programs, Operations Research 54 (5) (2006) 813–828.

[55] K. Dembczynski, S. Greco, R. Slowinski, Methodology of rough-set-based classification and sorting with hierarchical structure of attributes and criteria, Control and Cybernetics 31 (4) (2002) 891–920.

[56] L.P. An, Z.Q. Chen, L.Y. Tong, Generation and application of decision rules within dominance-based rough set approach to multicriteria sorting, International Journal of Innovative Computing Information and Control 7 (3) (2011) 1145–1155.

[57] J.L. Marichal, P. Meyer, M. Roubens, Sorting multi-attribute alternatives: the Tomaso method, Computers & Operations Research 32 (4) (2005) 861–877.

Chapter 6

Applications of MCDM sorting

6.1 GIS aware decisions

In many real-world decision-making problems, the use of the Geographic Information System (GIS) is an essential tool to improve the visualization and understanding of the decision results, because of its techniques and procedures. A GIS is often recognized as a decision support system (DSS) involving the integration of spatially referred data in a problem-solving environment [1]. In Chapter 1 the importance of MCDM problems in our society was described and the different types of MCDM methods were identified that have been widely used in real-world decision problems. As stated, MCDM provides diverse methods that support the decision-maker at different stages of the decision-making process. This chapter makes a brief but comprehensive review of the application of MCDM sorting methods in significant decision problems that include the use of GIS to take advantage of its high visualization properties in spatial dimensions.

In [2] it was stated that GIS presents some difficulties in becoming the general tool for solving all types of spatial problems, because "they arise from the deficiencies in the analytical methods usually integrated into a GIS, and the tools that usually constitute a GIS are too generic and unspecialized" [2,3, p.546]. However, despite this, GIS and MCDM have been used to transform data visually to support decision-making. Therefore, "GIS and MCDM can be thought of as a process that transforms and combines geographical data and value judgments (the decision-maker's preferences) to obtain information for decision-making" [4, p.703]. The commonly reported GIS-based computational tools used for integration with MCDM are gvSIG (http://www.gvsig.com), ArcGIS (https://www.arcgis.com), and QuantumGIS (https://qgis.org).

In [4], a survey was performed of GIS-based multi-criteria decision analysis focused on two approaches: one is the GIS components of the GIS-MCDM methods, and the other is the generic elements of the MCDM methods.

- The GIS components of the GIS-MCDM methods
  - The approach includes the geographical data models, the spatial dimension of the evaluation criteria, and the spatial definition of decision alternatives.
- The generic elements of the MCDM methods

Multi-Criteria Decision-Making Sorting Methods. https://doi.org/10.1016/B978-0-32-385231-9.00011-0

– The approach includes the nature of evaluation criteria, the number of individuals involved in the decision-making process, and the nature of uncertainties.

Fig. 6.1 presents a general schematic procedure for decision problems integrating GIS and MCDM methodologies. The steps are as follows.

Step 1: the problem is defined as an MCDM problem regarding decision criteria and alternatives.

Step 2: data collection is performed regarding the spatial dimension of the data. The spatial criteria can be explicit or implicit (see Section 6.1.2).

Step 3: the GIS and MCDM methodologies are integrated in some substeps.

Step 3.1: the preference information is defined by the expert (or decision-maker). Commonly, the preference information relates to the definition and relative importance of criteria and the categories' profiles.

Step 3.2: the MCDM sorting method selected is applied to assign the alternatives in the predefined categories.

Step 3.3: the GIS tool is applied with the outcomes of the sorting method.

Step 4: the results are validated by the expert. If the expert is not satisfied with the resulting recommendation, she/he would be able to adjust her/his preferences to generate new geographical data visualization.

Sections 6.1.1 and 6.1.2 aim to introduce the GIS tool and the spatial criteria. Section 6.1.1 explains the relevance of using GIS in the analysis and visualization of data and data models used. Section 6.1.2 describes the spatial characteristic that is inherent to spatial criteria. These sections help us to understand how GIS and spatial criteria are integrated into MCDM and the solution to real multi-criteria decision-making problems addressed in Section 6.2.

6.1.1   Geographic Information System (GIS)

GIS can be defined as tools for querying, analyzing, and editing data, maps, and spatial information in general [3]. GISs are computational tools that work with information related to spatial data to manage geographic information. The linkage between GIS and data allows the geographical map representation and data analysis.

GISs are used for the storage, management, analysis, and visualization of geographically referred data, being valuable tools for assisting planning and decision-making in multiple contexts in which georeferred information plays a relevant role [5].

It should be noted that some works reported in GIS-MCDM publications have been based on a combination of the raster and vector data models [4]. "Raster models are represented by a mesh or grid of rectangles, all of the same size. Each element is called a pixel or cell and has its information and geographic location assigned to it" [3, p.546]. "In a vector model, the geographic features in GIS are expressed as vectors, maintaining the geometric features of the figures.

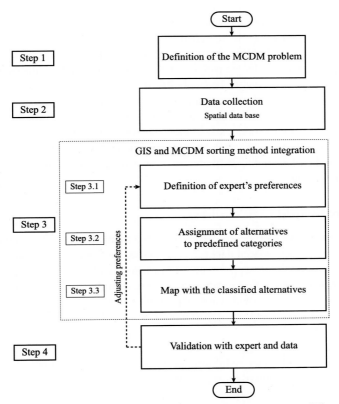

FIGURE 6.1 General schematic procedure for decision problem integrating GIS and MCDM methodologies.

They are used to define boundaries and, therefore, spatial geometries" [3, p.546]. The vector elements have associated information in the database. The vector geometric elements used are usually dots, lines, and polygons.

6.1.2 The spatial criteria

The decision problems may involve spatial characteristics as criteria. We first introduce the spatial data concept to explain it. Spatial data are "the sum of our interpretations of geographic phenomena. In digital form, the data are the primary information needed by geographic information systems, the software tools used for spatial-data analysis" [6]. It seems that spatial data are used to describe phenomena on or near the earth's surface. These data can be referred to as geospatial data [6].

On the other hand, in some cases, decision criteria include spatial characteristics. We can say that these criteria are spatial criteria. When spatial criteria have been evaluated, they may be described as explicit or implicit. "For example, in the context of a site search problem, such site characteristics as size, shape, contiguity, and compactness are explicitly spatial criteria" [7,8].

Many decision problems involve criteria (objectives) that are implicitly spatial [9]. A criterion is said to be implicitly spatial, if spatial data are needed to compute the level of achievement of the criterion [4]. For example, in the context of marginalization problems [10], such marginality characteristics are: quality of homes, elementary services at homes, income, and educational level. These help to visualize the social phenomenon in some regions of any country. Those criteria can involve spatial attributes such as distance, proximity, accessibility, elevation, and slope.

6.2 Real-world case studies

GIS is an attractive methodology to model land management. The main characteristic is integrating spatial data for visualization in a geographic environment. The GIS methodology supports decision-makers with the data visualization. Moreover, it is known that increasing the accessibility of GIS integrated with MCDM methodology provides new opportunities for researchers and practitioners, including web-based participation and advanced visualization of decision processes [11].

In the following subsections some key applications will be reviewed and described that show the successful joint performance of GISs and MCDM sorting models. Table 6.1 summarizes these applications.

6.2.1 Environmental management

6.2.1.1 Environmental risk assessments in farming parcels

An environmental risk problem was addressed in [12]. Here, farming parcels in the Coteaux de Gascogne area, France are analyzed. These involve pesticide use and its possible contamination of water for human consumption.

The pesticide molecules can be transferred: "It depends initially on their chemical properties, namely whether they are soluble or insoluble in water" [12, 13]. This kind of study can support stakeholders involved with water resources, agriculture, and the environment.

In the pesticide transfer context, a criterion is a tool representing a physical process for evaluating and comparing farming parcels according to the surface water contamination risk [12]. The study uses the following decision criteria.

- slope/area (g1): effect of combination of slopes and areas of the parcels;
- soil type (g2): nature of soils;
- connectivity (g3): connectivity of each agricultural parcel to the stream;
- VFS (g4): vegetative filter strips (VFS) between the parcels and the stream;
- RZ (g5): riparian zone (RZ) beside the stream; and

TABLE 6.1 Application with GIS integrated with MCDM.

Application	Authors	MCDM method
Environmental management		
Farming parcels	Macary et al. [12]	ELECTRE TRI-C
Ideal landfills for waste disposal	Biluca et al. [14]	ELECTRE TRI, AHP
Risk of wolf attacks	Miccoli and Ishizaka [15]	AHPSort II
Security level of cities		
Security level of city units	Gurgel and Mota [16]	DRSA
Safety of London boroughs	Ishizaka et al. [17]	AHPSort, AHP-FuzzySort
Solar energy		
Absorption capacity of solar farms	Sánchez Lozano et al. [5]	ELECTRE TRI
Suitability roofs for photovoltaic systems	Thebault et al. [18]	ELECTRE TRI
Others		
Economic attractiveness of the landscape	Assumma et al. [19]	AHPSort, GAHPSort I
Geographical marginality	Alvarez [10]	MR-sort

- pesticide Treatment Frequency Index (TFI) (g6): agricultural pressure caused by pesticides application.

The study evaluated 87 parcels. The criteria represent the vulnerability of surface water and anthropogenic pressure exerted by agricultural pesticides. A short version of the valuation matrix of the parcels is shown in Table 6.2. The complete evaluation matrix of parcels is listed in [12].

The ELECTRE TRI-C sorting method was applied with GIS to assign farming parcels on risk categories regarding water pesticide contamination. Expert agronomists defined five categories, and these are shown in Fig. 6.2. The categories are very high (C1), high (C2), intermediate (C3), low (C4), and very low (C5). Each category is characterized by a virtual benchmark parcel as reference action (b_h), as shown in Table 6.3.

The evaluation of 87 parcels in Auradé watershed is presented in a spatial visualization of the ELECTRE TRI-C assignment in Fig. 6.3. The resulting visualization is due to the interaction between MCDM modeling and the GIS spatial structure. Fig. 6.3 shows results with the effect of best environmental practices in decreasing pesticides transfer to streams.

The agricultural land was classified, and the assignment of parcels in the risk categories shows 8.9% of parcels in the very high class of risk, 33% in high, 40.1% in intermediate, 12.4% in low, and 5.7% in very low.

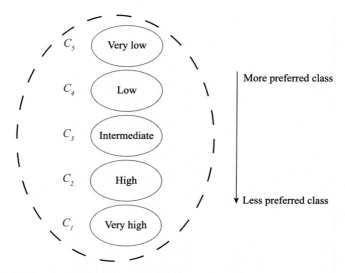

FIGURE 6.2 Categories of contamination risk in the Auradé watershed.

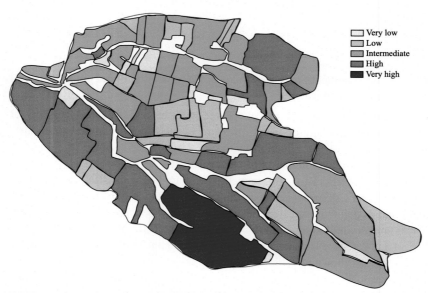

FIGURE 6.3 Surface water contamination risk in the Auradé watershed for pesticides with the effect of best environmental practices (based on [12]).

6.2.1.2 Ideal landfills for waste disposal

Managing waste disposal is a crucial problem in reducing the environmental impacts. When recycling is an available option to reduce the impact, an appro-

TABLE 6.2 Performances of the agricultural parcels (based on [12]).

	Slope/area	Soil type	Connectivity	VFS	RZ	Pesticides TFI
a1	796 710	4.1	9	15	3	2.43
a2	93 010	5.67	8	14	3	1.76
a3	311 645	7.87	5	0	0	1.76
a4	124 073	4.38	1	0	0	1.73
a5	337 654	5.73	9	6	5	1.73
a6	64 302	4	8	9	3	5
a7	207 925	4.68	1	0	0	1.61
a8	8336	8	1	0	2	0
a9	170 622	4.56	3	6	2	1.61
a10	1 002 812	6.03	9	2	2	1.61
...						
a87	29 300	5.83	1	0	0	10

TABLE 6.3 Reference actions of categories (based on [12]).

C_h	Slope/area	Soil type	Connectivity	VFS	RZ	Pesticides TFI
C1	1 000 000	7	9	14	9	4.5
C2	500 000	5	8	11	7	3
C3	300 000	3	5	8	5	1.75
C4	200 000	2	3	5	3	0.75
C5	100 000	1	1	2	2	0.25

priate destination can be recycling plants or landfills. In this sense, the problem is choosing suitable landfills or recycling plants in cities.

Regarding the current topic, [14] mapped suitable sites to receive inert waste from small and medium cities. They evaluated and selected landfills for urban solid waste disposal by applying GIS and multis suitable to receive inert waste from different cities. The experimental study was carried out using GIS and multi-criteria analysis in Francisco Beltrão, a city in southwestern Parana, Brazil.

The decision criteria used for the selection of landfills are:

- distance to population centers;
- distance to roads and highways;
- distance to educational establishments;
- distance to health facilities;
- distances to water bodies;
- slope;
- type of soil;
- use of the soil; and
- required area size.

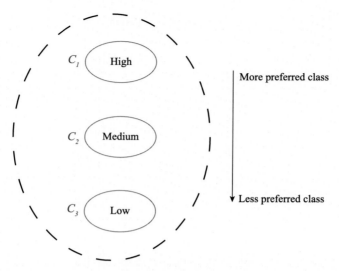

FIGURE 6.4   The aptitude classes of landfills for urban solid waste disposal.

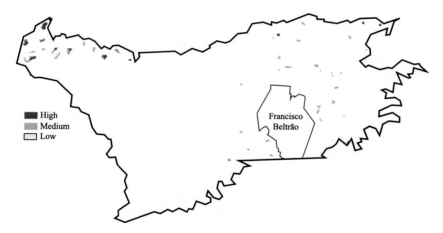

FIGURE 6.5   Classification of suitable areas for waste disposal (based on [14]).

The multi-criteria decision analysis method applied is ELECTRE TRI. The integration of both methodologies allows the classification of landfills or recycling plants in cities. The weights definition was carried out using the analytic hierarchy process method.

The study combined the information of the decision criteria in a multi-criteria analysis and the ArcGIS software to classify the landfill areas with 5 km² in low, medium, and high aptitude classes. The aptitude mapping is sorted in aptitude classes, as illustrated in Fig. 6.4.

An area of approximately 4000 m^2 is required for installing the project, landfill area, and power plant. The study excluded areas smaller than 4 km^2. In total, 95 landfill areas were identified [14]. In the first classification with GIS, the Jenks natural breaks algorithm was used [14]. The classification of the 95 areas to a level of aptitude is shown in Fig. 6.5.

In [14], the GIS and ELECTRE TRI methods were compared to analyze and discuss the compensatory and noncompensatory characteristics in the ideal landfills for the waste disposal problem. The results of ELECTRE TRI were not presented in an illustrated way, but the authors compared some variations of the results that can be revised in [14].

The study used "CBERS satellite images and the Geographic Service of the Brazilian Army Directorate to provide the topographic maps of the Francisco Beltrão city" [14, p.319]. Identifying suitable areas for installing an inert waste plant can help public managers in diverse decision-making situations. Projects related to inert waste plant may impact cities' structures and the governance decision process [14].

6.2.1.3   Risk of wolf attacks

In a region of Italy an environmental management problem is addressed [15]. It is related to the wolf species and the conflicts with livestock farmers.

In [15], authors evaluated the risk of Umbria's municipalities due to wolf attacks on livestock farms to facilitate and pacify the debate. The attacks are on cattle, sheep, goats, and horses. Therefore, the study analyzes the risk of wolf predation on the zones.

The problem is defined as a hierarchy. The goal of the problem is defined at the top level as the risk of wolf attacks. The second level contains the criteria that are used to quantify this risk. The decision criteria are number of predated animals, presence of wolves, number of live animals, protected areas, and population density. In the third level, the subcriteria (circle items) are defined. The complete decision criteria are as follows:

■ Number of predated animals

   – Cattle predated
   – Sheep/goats predated
   – Horses predated

■ Presence of wolves

   – Presence of wolves

■ Number of live animals

   – Living cattle
   – Living sheep/goats
   – Living horses

■ Protected areas

   – Protected areas

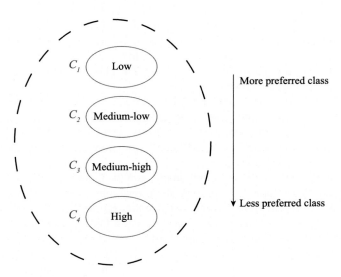

FIGURE 6.6   Risk classification.

■ Population density

– Population density

For the risk of the wolf attacks problem, 92 municipalities are analyzed. The partial information of the municipalities and criteria values are listed in Table 6.4.

For the classification process, four risk classes are defined: low risk (C1), medium-low risk (C2), medium-high risk (C3), and high risk (C4) concerning the risk of wolf attack (see Fig. 6.6). The classes are delimited by the three limiting profiles shown in Table 6.5.

The problem is addressed by AHPSort II [15]; the multi-criteria sorting method is designed to address a large number of alternatives. "AHPSort II requires only 1.4% of the comparisons that would have been required by AHPSort" [20]. Moreover, when applied with clustering, it requires only 0.54% of comparisons.

AHPSort II [15] was applied to assess the risk of wolf attacks in municipalities of Umbria, Italy. The 92 municipalities were sorted into their respective class. "The municipalities with a score below 0.007 have a low risk, between 0.007 and 0.045 a medium-low risk, between 0.045 and 0.122 a medium-high risk, and 0.122 or above high risk" [15, p.751].

The visualization of a risk wolf attack in a geographical representation is shown in Fig. 6.7, obtained with QuantumGIS software. The results show that Bastia Umbra and Terni municipalities are classified as low risk. The medium-low risk class includes the highest number of municipalities. Here, it seems that attacks and the presence of wolves are low. Municipalities near protected

TABLE 6.4 Municipalities values of each criterion (based on [15]).

Municipality	Cattle predated	Sheep/goats predated	Horses predated	Presence of wolves	Living cattle	Living sheep/goats	Living horses	Protected areas	Population density
Acquasparta	1	4	0	1	334	1172	155	0.0	60.3
Allerona	2	422	2	10	148	3086	47	39.5	22.1
Alviano	0	2	0	0	114	211	36	11.3	61.5
Amelia	7	113	0	0	1145	2164	312	0.0	90.5
....									
Valtopina	0	11	0	0	120	307	98	6.1	36.0

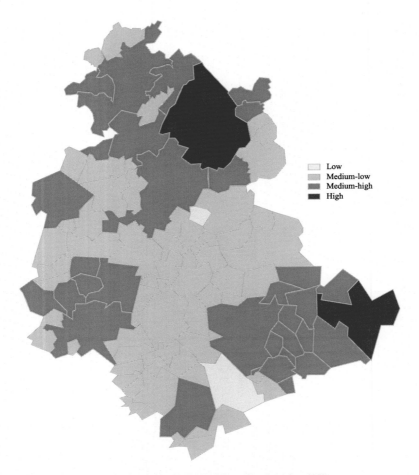

FIGURE 6.7   Risk map of wolf attacks in the Umbria region (based on [15]).

areas create a "shelter zone" for wolves, supporting the sorting outcome [15]. "These municipalities are situated in the region's mountainous areas, where the availability of wild game is high, and the population density is low. All these factors favor the presence of wolves" [15, p.745].

The study helps us to understand the risk of a wolf attack in municipalities of Umbria, which can help adequately manage any potential human–wolf conflict. The developed geographic information system shows the hotspots at risk, which can help the local government in planning conflict mitigation strategies. The situation of wolf attack is analyzed in [15], and the results can support the implementation of methods to control the wolves. This can be supported with a decision support system using the MCDM and GIS methodologies to design effective conservation and management plans.

TABLE 6.5 Limiting profiles for levels of risk of wolf attacks (based on [15]).

Municipality	Lp1	Lp2	Lp3
Cattle predated	20	40	60
Sheep/goats predated	200	400	700
Horses predated	12	24	42
Presence of wolves	10	30	40
Living cattle	1000	2000	3000
Living sheep/goats	1000	2000	3000
Living horses	200	500	700
Protected areas	10	30	50
Population density	500	300	200

6.2.2 The security level of cities

6.2.2.1 The security level of city units

The studies regard security are essential for decision-making in the social and political context. However, studies applying MCDM and GIS to evaluate security regarding criminality activities are not very common. In [16], a GIS-MCDM model is presented to prioritize regions for allocation resources considering several criteria. In [21], a multi-criteria approach is proposed that is aimed at setting police patrol sectors.

A study to evaluate security level with an MCDM sorting method and GIS is presented in [22]. The authors mapped the most favorable locations for the occurrence of robberies in Recife, Brazil. The study combined the MCDM and GIS within the context of crime. The aim was to explore several factors that can help us to understand Recife's violence regarding the spatial environment.

Five decision criteria were used in the study and related to the robbery. The criteria considered influence the occurrence of the type of robbery. They are as follows:

- Income (by person): the lower the income of the person, the greater the chances of the person committing a crime (the currency is the Brazilian real).
- Gini index: measuring the distribution of the income; the smaller this is, the closer people are to having equal distribution.
- Infrastructure: the precarious conditions make the place prone to crime. These conditions include elements such as bathrooms and piped water.
- Education (years): better education conditions decrease the chances of people getting involved in crime.
- Demographic density per km^2: the population increase makes the environment more propitious for the crime.

Recife city has a spatial division called human development units (HDUs). These HDUs are equivalent to sectors with specific administrative or political

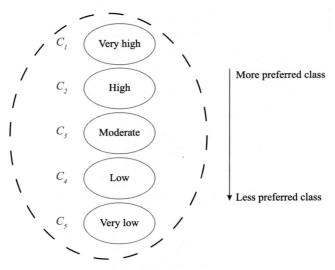

FIGURE 6.8   The security categories of city units for Recife city.

divisions. There are 62 HDUs evaluated as decision alternatives based on their security level.

The Dominance-Based Rough Set (DRSA) method uses preference information from experts. The expert expresses her/his previous knowledge as preference information to build the preference mode. The expert assigns specific units (from the set of HDU) to a certain level of risk. The method uses the information to induce some decision rules related to the alternatives and the decision criteria from the spatial environment context. The decision rules can be seen as conditional and decision parts. The generated rules allow the classification of the remaining alternatives according to the ordered security category previously defined. The study in [22] applied the DRSA method with the free software called jMAF. The visualization is presented with the ArcGIS environment.

In the study, five ordered classes were determined (C_l) according to the preferences of the DM to the security level: C_1 very high, C_2 high, C_3 moderate, C_4 low, and C_5 very low. Thus, C_1 very high is a place with a low incidence of robberies and a very high level of security, while C_5 very low is a place with a high incidence of robberies and a very low level of security. It is schematically represented in Fig. 6.8.

The Dominance-Based Rough Set (DRSA) method uses expert knowledge to induce decision rules. For the classification problem of security of Recife units, the expert defined 13 reference actions. This means that the expert assigned 13 HDUs to a specific security category. Table 6.6 shows the values of the criteria of the selected units as reference action and the security category which are assigned. The DRSA method induces 17 rules to be used in the assignment of the remaining units (see [22] for more details).

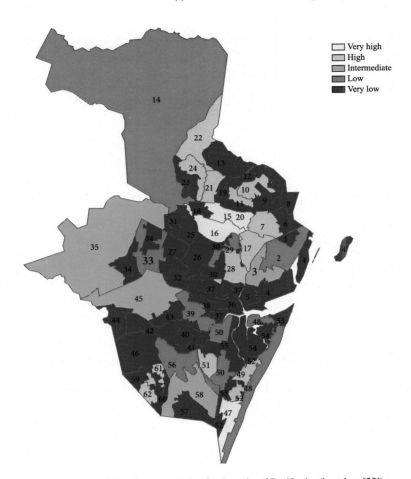

FIGURE 6.9 The security level representation for the units of Recife city (based on [22]).

The classification of the HDUs from Recife is illustrated in Fig. 6.9. It shows the security level of each unit represented in colors regarding the categorization resulting from the DRSA method. These results are helpful for decision-making and planning to solve public security problems through proper implementation of the results obtained, which can give a final recommendation for the current decision problem [22].

6.2.2.2 Safety of London boroughs

This case study [17] regards the safety of London boroughs. It considers the criminality situation of the boroughs due to the affection of the community. In the 1990s, London experienced increased levels of street crime, and this continued into the mid-2000s [23].

TABLE 6.6 Reference actions: units of Recife assigned to a security category by the expert (based on [22]).

Reference action	HDU code	Gini	Income	Infrastructure	Demographic density per km^2	Education	Security category
R1	16	0.5	1353.42	94.74	6436	11.73	C1
R2	19	0.47	126	75	23956	5.51	C1
R3	21	0.45	141.47	78.81	18506	5.97	C1
R4	15	0.52	902.38	97.31	10888	10.58	C2
R5	20	0.47	158	78	28220	6.12	C2
R6	7	0.5	893.13	94.45	8796	11.09	C3
R7	35	0.55	187.1	78.24	1516	6.55	C3
R8	45	0.5	143	89	1930	5.52	C3
R9	2	0.5	616	98	3927	10.27	C4
R10	3	0.5	686.6	99	6577	11.2	C4
R11	48	0.61	1864	96	9887	11.77	C4
R12	4	0.6	169	67	1893	5.64	C5
R13	50	0.47	571	95	6739	10.09	C5

In the current study [17], some safety categories are considered. The boroughs are evaluated regarding the number of different crime types. The boroughs are in London, UK and are evaluated according to their safety levels.

The boroughs are classified in a safety level regarding seven decision criteria. The criteria correspond to different types of recorded crime [17]. They are as follows:

- Robbery (g1): includes offenses where a person uses force or threat to steal from another person, either outside of or within one's premises.

- Vehicle-related (g2): includes theft from, or of a vehicle, or interference with a vehicle.

- Misbehavior (g3): includes personal, environmental, and nuisance antisocial behavior, offenses that cause deliberate damage to buildings and vehicles, or any other offenses causing fear, alarm, or distress, or possession of a weapon such as a firearm.

- Violent (g4): includes offenses against a person, such as common assaults, grievous bodily harm, and sexual offenses.

- Crimes without the use of force (g5): include crimes that involve theft directly from the victim (including handbag, wallet, cash, cell phones, or bicycles) but without the use or threat of physical force.

- Drug-related (g6): includes offenses related to possession, supply, and production of drugs.

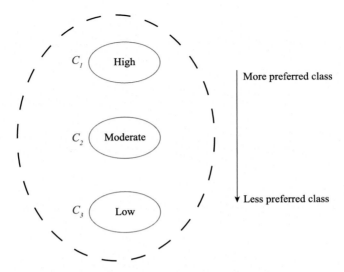

FIGURE 6.10   Classification of London boroughs according to safety levels.

- Weapon-related (g7): includes offenses related to the possession of a weapon, such as a firearm or a knife [17, p.12].

The study considers the 33 boroughs of London. The analytic hierarchy process-fuzzy sorting (AHPSort) method [20] and the AHP-FuzzySort method [17] are applied and integrated with GIS to classify London's boroughs. The partial information about boroughs' local and global priorities is listed in Table 6.7.

The authors classified the boroughs into three categories to show the safety level. The categories low, moderate, and high are illustrated in Fig. 6.10.

The preference information was obtained by an expert related to the crime topic. Table 6.8 shows the central profiles of safety levels for boroughs in London.

The classification was performed with both methods in [17], using the classic AHPSort and the new AHP-FuzzySort. Figs. 6.11 and 6.12 show the heatmaps of the classification generated by AHPSort and the new AHP-FuzzySort, respectively, in categories low safety, moderate safety, and high safety.

On the one hand, Fig. 6.11 shows the classification of boroughs in safety levels. In the evaluation, the City of London is a less safe borough. Some boroughs around the City of London are classified as moderately safe and others are classified as highly safe. On the other hand, Fig. 6.12 maps the results of AHP-FuzzySort regarding the borough membership. RGB gradients are used for the visualization of safety levels of categories. It is helpful to map some differences in boroughs of the same category. The visualization allows the identification of safety areas. Boroughs in the west are safer overall. However, boroughs in the

TABLE 6.7 Local and global priorities of boroughs (based on [17]).

Borough	g1	g2	g3	g4	g5	g6	g7	Global
Barking and Dagenham	0.152	0.065	0.162	0.143	0.285	0.187	0.203	1.196
Barnet	0.124	0.069	0.219	0.168	0.287	0.226	0.236	1.328
Bexley	0.177	0.080	0.203	0.147	0.289	0.214	0.223	1.333
Brent	0.132	0.079	0.202	0.147	0.283	0.171	0.209	1.224
Bromley	0.129	0.076	0.201	0.162	0.290	0.227	0.238	1.324
...								
Westminster City Council	0.068	0.037	0.113	0.069	0.168	0.115	0.151	0.720

TABLE 6.8 Central profiles of safety levels for boroughs (based on [17]).

Safety class	g1 Robbery	g2 Vehicle-related	g3 Misbehavior	g4 Violent	g5 Crimes without the use of force	g6 Drug-related	g7 Weapon-related	Global
High (CP1)	0.261	0.138	0.277	0.259	0.292	0.262	0.265	1.754
Moderate (CP2)	0.075	0.063	0.086	0.066	0.0752	0.070	0.081	0.516
Low (CP3)	0.032	0.040	0.032	0.034	0.043	0.035	0.045	0.261

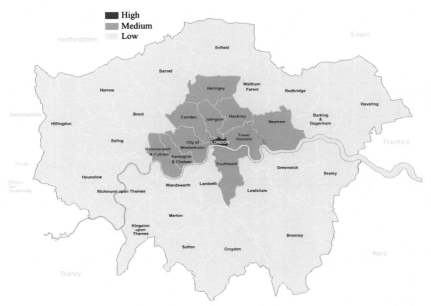

FIGURE 6.11 Classification of boroughs related to the safety levels with the AHPSort method (based on [17]).

north are riskier than the rest. The visualization of the classic AHPSort [20] does not allow the differences of boroughs in the same class [17].

6.2.3 Solar energy

6.2.3.1 Absorption capacity of solar farms

In [5], the photovoltaic solar farms site selection is studied. Solar farms use electricity generation plants through photovoltaic solar systems. The study aimed to identify the best plots suitable for installing photovoltaic solar farms in the municipality of Torre Pacheco, in the southeast of Spain. This municipality covers an area of 189.60 km^2, where the territory is divided into different types of land according to its Urban Municipal General Plan.

The GIS-MCDM methodologies are applied in the photovoltaic solar farms site selection. The GIS provides a cartographic and alphanumeric database, including two factors of distinct nature: restrictions and criteria. The restrictions are entered into the GIS using layers defined from the current legislation (urban land, undeveloped land, special protection areas for birds, community sites, infrastructures), which reduce the study area by eliminating those areas in which photovoltaic solar farms cannot be implemented [5].

The data are introduced into the GIS, taking into account as decision criteria weather, environmental, location, and terrain evaluation aspects. The criteria

FIGURE 6.12 Classification of boroughs related to the safety levels with the AHP-FuzzySort method (based on [17]).

considered are taken from the literature and considered by experts in the field of renewable energy sources. The criteria are then used to assess the merit of each plot for implanting a photovoltaic plant therein [5], and include:

- agrological capacity (g1);
- slope (g2);
- field orientation (g3);
- plot area (g4);
- distance to main roads (g5);
- distance to power lines (g6);
- distance to town or villages (g7);
- distance to electricity transformer substations (g8);
- solar radiation (g9); and
- average temperature (g10)

There are 20 alternatives as plots for evaluation. A partial evaluation matrix is provided in Table 6.9.

The gvSIG is the system used in two stages. In the first one, restrictions that prevent a solar plant from being implanted in a particular area are represented. These areas unsuitable for implantation are removed, leaving only the areas that are feasible for this purpose. In the second stage, all the information about all retained alternative locations for all evaluation criteria is supplied to the decision support system called Interactive Robustness analysis and parameters' Inference

TABLE 6.9 Evaluation matrix of plots in the municipality of Torre Pacheco (based on [5]).

Plot	g1	g2	g3	g4	g5	g6	g7	g8	g9	g10
a1	1	17.7	7.26	13 559.32	68.82	126.21	1846.93.	4265.78	2047.04	17.60
a2	4	10.50	7.10	37 855.87	562.86	1.25	1668.60	4869.39	2049.17	17.69
a3	4	16.02	7.45	8691.09	1154.72	106.17	1738.34	5782.16	2048.65	17.60
a4	5	11.76	7.89	49 659.87	1473.29	59.99	1977.82	6025.01	2050.18	17.60
...										
a20	2	19.35	6.09	11 984.62	741.60	236.24	813.25	6414.66	2050.60	17.60

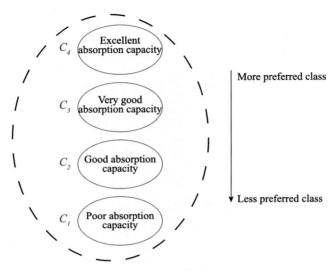

FIGURE 6.13 Categories of absorption capacity for installing photovoltaic solar farms.

for multi-criteria Sorting problems (IRIS). The plots are classified according to multiple evaluation aspects, by developing a multi-criteria model and applying the ELECTRE TRI method using the decision support system IRIS [24].

For the identification of the best plots suitable for installing photovoltaic solar farms in the municipality of Torre Pacheco, four classes were defined: poor absorption capacity (C1), good absorption capacity (C2), very good absorption capacity (C3), and excellent absorption capacity (C4) (see Fig. 6.13). The values for the bounds of the categories have been provided by the DM according to his personal knowledge and experience (see Table 6.10).

TABLE 6.10 Limiting profiles for absorption capacity of solar farms (based on [5]).

Criterion	Lp1	Lp2	Lp3
Agrological capacity (g1)	2	4	7
Slope (g2)	−30	−20	−10
Field orientation (g3)	5	8	10
Plot area (g4)	25 000	50 000	10 0000
Distance to main roads (g5)	−1000	−500	−25
Distance to power lines (g6)	−10 000	−1000	−100
Distance to town or villages (g7)	100	500	750
Distance to electricity transformer substations (g8)	−6250	−2500	−500
Solar radiation (g9)	1200	1700	2000
Average temperature (g10)	16	18	20

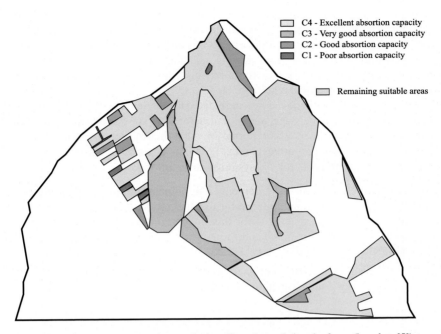

C4 - Excellent absorption capacity
C3 - Very good absorption capacity
C2 - Good absorption capacity
C1 - Poor absorption capacity

Remaining suitable areas

FIGURE 6.14 Absorption capacity map for installing photovoltaic solar farms (based on [5]).

About 35% of the total area of the municipality (189.60 km^2) was then found to be suitable to implant solar farms. This corresponds to 65.36 km^2. The cartographic visualization of absorption capacity of solar farms is shown in Fig. 6.14. From the total suitable area of the municipality available to implant solar farms, only 20 plots were evaluated in the study from [5].

It was observed that one plot had excellent capability (C4) to host the implementation of a photovoltaic solar farm; four plots had very good capability (C3); 10 plots had good capability (C2); and five plots had poor capability. The remaining plots were suitable plots but were not classified in the study, in order for the DM to view the results more clearly and concisely.

6.2.3.2 Suitability of roofs for photovoltaic systems

A study developed in [18] aimed to sort the suitability of roofs for photovoltaic systems. The photovoltaic panel (PV) is part of the technologies included in solar energy. Related technologies are solar thermal energy and concentrated solar power. The authors stated that solar energy is abundant and widely available.

The land-property registers are known as cadastres. A cadastre gives information about the buildings of a given region. In this regard, GIS is focused on the cadastres for the availability of PV panels. In [18], the authors analyzed the degree of suitability of a roof to be equipped with PV systems.

Concerning the suitability of roof categories, roofs having a high degree of suitability can be considered a priority to install PV because the generation of energy would be beneficial. Roofs having moderate suitability need further studies to confirm the benefits. For roofs having a low degree of suitability, PV integration is considered less suitable [18].

In the study, different decision criteria were used related to energy, economy, historic buildings and heritage, and roof structure and superstructure states. The participation of an expert was reported in validating the representativeness of the decision criteria in an urban context [18]. The decision criteria used in [18] for the suitability of roofs for PV systems are as follows:

- Superstructure elements: "elements like chimneys and vertical windows reduce the available space for the integration of PV systems but also increase the constraints for this integration as the shadows cast by these elements, which need to be estimated, lessen the degree of suitability of the roof" [18, p.15].

- Solar irradiation: "It is expressed per square meter. It quantifies how much energy a square meter of PV system would produce each year" [18, p.16].

- Economic feasibility: "the Payback Period (PP) corresponds to the amount of time (in years) for the benefits (including subsidies) to equal the investment. The PP is used to display economic feasibility" [18, p.16].

- The structural robustness of the roof [25,26]: elements related to the type of roof and the additional load are considered for successful integration of PV system [18].

- The heritage and aesthetic qualities of buildings: "It is considered because that may induce additional financial costs and be more time-consuming" [18, p.18].

There are 190 roof sections as decision alternatives to evaluate the suitability of roofs for PV systems. In the study, the case of the Jonction district was analyzed with data concerning the buildings, along with the solar cadastre. This is a district in the heart of Geneva, with different types of buildings and architecture.

When evaluating the available space, all the superstructure elements and their projected shadows should be identified. For the evaluation of available space for PV integration, some elements were removed from the total surface area of the roof [27]. The considered surfaces had at least $1000\,kWh/m^2$ and the presence of the large superstructure elements. This available surface was used to calculate solar irradiation and economic feasibility.

The study applied the ELECTRE TRI method. The authors considered it a relevant sorting method, and the sustainable energy with PV farms was studied with the ELECTRE TRI method. The software ArcGIS was integrated with the ELECTRE TRI method.

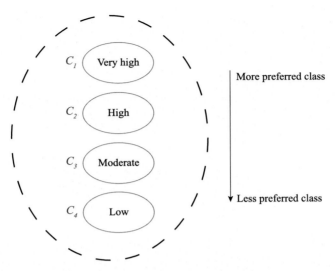

FIGURE 6.15   Categories of suitability roofs for photovoltaic systems.

The roof categories to be assigned were low, moderate, high, and very high (see Fig. 6.15). The sorting results of the 190 roof sections were imported into ArcGIS to display the sorting as a GIS layer. The results were visualized in the map shown in Fig. 6.16. Fig. 6.16(a) shows the area of analysis in an urban district, where the white shapes are the available surface area of the roofs. Fig. 6.16(b) shows the section of roofs classified in the described categories.

The most extensive roofs are mainly assigned to high and very high degrees of suitability. The most extensive roofs are expected to have better economic feasibility. Smaller roofs were assigned to the low degree of suitability category [18].

The result of the study is accessible even to a general audience. The study is based on the roofs' degrees of suitability to be equipped with PV systems. The sorting results can be helpful for the actors interested in that technology in "urban contexts, real-estate owners, associations or entrepreneurs interested in the deployment of solar energy and willing to invest in it" [18, p.29].

The deployment of this energy source in cities can be accelerated by studying the roof areas for assignment to a certain degree of suitability [18]. Local authorities may use the suitability of roof sorting for PV deployment, to meet goals that have been set for 2050 [28].

6.2.4   Economic attractiveness of the landscape

In [19], the economic attractiveness of a wine region landscape was studied. Wine regions are landscapes that can be considered strong and fragile. The study aimed to sort municipalities according to the economic attractiveness of

a)

b)

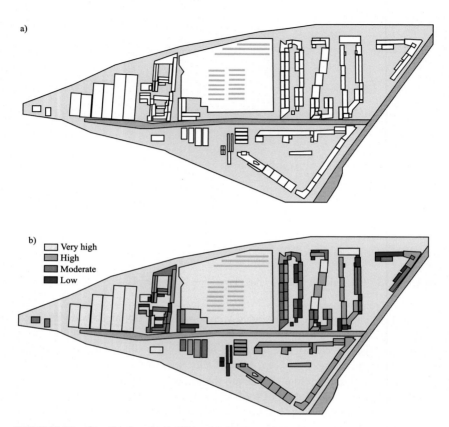

- Very high
- High
- Moderate
- Low

FIGURE 6.16 Classification of suitability roofs for photovoltaic systems (based on [18]).

the landscape. The municipalities were included as cultural landscapes in the World Heritage List by the United Nations Educational, Scientific and Cultural Organization (UNESCO). They comprise Italy's "Vineyard Landscape of Piedmont: Langhe-Roero, and Monferrato."

Four dimensions were considered in the evaluation of economic attractiveness: agriculture, tourism, real estate, and forestry. The four dimensions and respective subcriteria are as follows:

■ Agriculture dimension
- Agriculture workers (no.)
- Bio farms (no.)
- Product designation of origin – protected geographical indication farms (no.)
- Utilized agriculture surface (ha)

■ Tourism dimension

- Tourist presences
- Beds in farmhouses

■ Real estate dimension
  - Real estate market value (E/m^2)
  - Average agriculture value (E/ha)

■ Forestry dimension
  - Forestry agents (no.)
  - Forest surface (ha)

In [19], the four dimensions are described.

  ■ Agriculture dimension: considers rural employment and local investment [29].

  ■ Tourism dimension: analyzes the capability of landscape to attract tourism flows [30]

  ■ Real estate dimension: this is the contribution of landscape to real estate markets [31].

  ■ Forestry dimension: benefits generated by forest management [19].

The vineyard landscape considered in the study is a surface of 80 000 ha included in the UNESCO World Heritage List. The landscape consists of six core zones and two buffer zones, and its boundaries were defined according to the Landscape Units by the Regional Landscape Plan of Piedmont [25]. The assessment of the economic attractiveness related to 101 municipalities in the wine region.

The study of the economic attractiveness of the landscape applied the GIS and MCDM methodologies. Analyzing economic indicators for landscape may support the policies and strategies for planning and management of landscape [19]. The Group Analytic Hierarchy Process Sorting II method (GAHPSort II) was applied in the assessment of the economic attractiveness of a wine region landscape. For methodological reference of the method, see the AHPSort methodology [20].

Four classes of performance were defined to assess the economic attractiveness of a wine region landscape: poor, medium, good, and excellent landscape economic value (see Fig. 6.17).

A group of experts was involved in collecting relevant information. They were supported to define four categories of economic attractiveness, the limiting profile for decision criteria, and the importance of each criterion with the fundamental scale of Saaty [32]. In addition, representative points were defined to reduce the number of comparisons and revise the categorization of the economic attractiveness of municipalities.

The data regarding limiting profiles and evaluation matrix of municipalities were not shown in [19]. However, the geographical visualization of the result

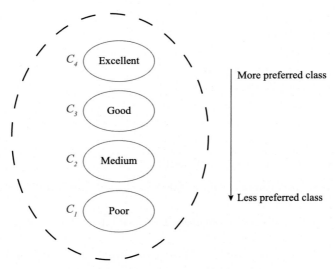

FIGURE 6.17 Categories of economic value for vineyard landscape.

was reported and is depicted in Fig. 6.18. This shows the results of the individual evaluations of the DMs (AHPSort) into a final map.

The municipalities were assigned to the economic value category. Poor, medium, good, and excellent categories include municipalities with priorities less than 0.337, 1.049, and 4.811, and higher than 4.811, respectively. The GIS and MCDM allow decision-makers to visualize the municipalities assigned to respective categories of economic attractiveness.

Only two municipalities were sorted as having excellent economic attractiveness. The municipalities in this category showed some important characteristics as product designation of origin-protected geographical indication (PDO-PGI) products, cultural heritage, and protected areas related to territorial resources [19]. The municipalities belonging to the core zones of UNESCO were sorted as good, confirming their added value. The authors stated that municipalities assigned to the medium category were affected by depopulation and an increasingly sectorial local economy based on agriculture, while the municipalities categorized as poor were strongly unpopulated [19].

6.2.5 Geographical marginality

In [10], the spatial dimensions of the marginality in a region of Mexico were studied. The study of inequality in marginalized regions is essential for identifying the lack of services and poverty. In [33], marginalization is defined as "an involuntary position and condition of an individual or group on the margins of the social, political, economic, ecological, and physical system that prevents them from accessing resources, goods, and services." The locational characteristics of marginality are described by the geometrical or spatial dimension of

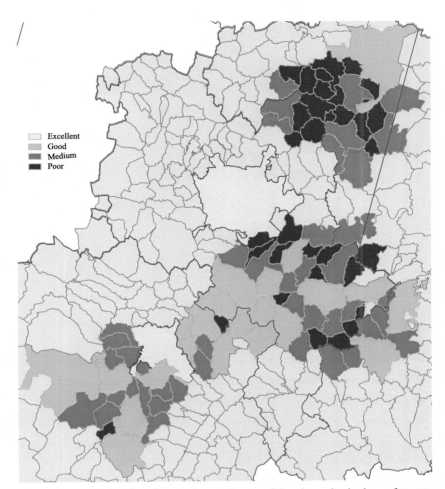

FIGURE 6.18 Classification of economic attractiveness of the wine region landscape from municipalities of Piedmont (based on [19]).

marginality [34], and a study with a geographic information system seems pertinent for identifying marginalized regions.

In Mexico, the marginality was studied by the National Council of Population (CONAPO). The CONAPO generates socioeconomic information about the population. It analyzes the education, housing, monetary income, and an affectation dimension regarding the spatial location. The marginalization problem was characterized and analyzed with the following criteria [35]:

- g1: percentage of the illiterate population aged 15 years or over;
- g2: percentage of the population without complete primary education aged 15 years or over;

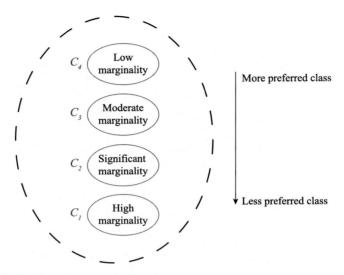

FIGURE 6.19 Categories of marginality.

- g3: percentage of occupants in private homes without drainage or sanitary service;
- g4: percentage of occupants in private homes without electricity;
- g5: percentage of occupants in private homes without piped water;
- g6: percentage of private homes with some level of overcrowding;
- g7: percentage of occupants in private dwellings with dirt floors;
- g8: percentage of the population residing in towns with fewer than 5000 inhabitants; and
- g9: percentage of the employed population with incomes of up to two times the minimum wage.

In [10], the marginalities of 18 municipalities of Sinaloa, Mexico were analyzed in order for them to be assigned to a category of marginality. The evaluation matrix is provided in Table 6.12.

The MCDM sorting method used in the application is the majority rule (MR-sort). It is a noncompensatory sorting method studied by Bouyssou and Marchant [37,38].

The defined categories of marginality are low, moderate, significant, and high. They are represented in the schema of Fig. 6.19. The class C_4 considers the lowest level of marginality. C_3 is a category with a moderate characteristic of marginality. C_2 includes municipalities with a significant level of marginality. C_1 is the category with the highest level of marginality. In [10], three limiting profiles shown in Table 6.11 are defined.

TABLE 6.11 Evaluation matrix of municipalities of Sinaloa, retrieved from [36].

Municipality	g1	g2	g3	g4	g5	g6	g7	g8	g9
A1	2.75	12.99	1.36	0.44	1.8	29.88	2.02	30.36	36.55
A2	4.39	23.67	1.98	0.32	1.93	28.94	1.63	73.71	40.72
A3	10.87	32.47	23.84	6.32	12.11	37.29	16.63	100	45.18
A4	6.85	22.03	6.34	1.57	2.67	34.47	6.96	70.77	35.33
A5	10.23	28.88	8.32	0.44	8.7	35.95	6.34	60.61	37.09
A6	3.13	12.89	1.16	0.21	1.4	26.22	1.78	14.73	21.59
A7	11.12	36.09	8.86	3.82	18.18	36.21	10.08	71.8	52.1
A8	8.49	27.7	2.21	0.16	2.86	47.13	3.47	63.51	34.82
A9	6.81	19.64	2.46	1.38	8.8	39.19	3.88	32.37	32.62
A10	6.03	23.5	3.34	1.05	5.45	35.75	6.91	63.31	59.04
A11	5.69	22.25	2.6	0.23	5.38	32.42	3.47	51.25	46.92
A12	1.95	10.61	0.45	0.1	0.83	27.24	1.18	8.48	29.48
A13	8.69	31.81	6.87	0.91	13.54	34.91	6.3	74.33	48.86
A14	5.53	19.32	4.08	1.31	4.71	34.81	5.28	67.6	37.58
A15	3.33	14.59	0.88	0.09	0.86	29.91	1.46	12.47	30.71
A16	7.09	27.62	7.34	2.16	4.67	34.44	6.08	100	43.77
A17	10.07	33.5	5.33	2.8	7.55	36.16	7.75	86.92	58.58
A18	6.73	26.32	10.93	0.21	3.76	42.48	3.07	53.43	39.65

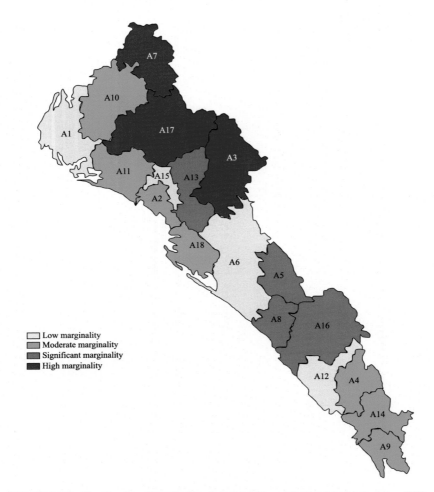

FIGURE 6.20 Classification of marginality of municipalities of Sinaloa, Mexico (based on [10]).

The classification of municipalities based on their level of marginalization confirmed in [10] is depicted in Fig. 6.20. The classification shows in category C_4 four municipalities, corresponding to the lowest degree of marginalization. C_3 includes seven municipalities, representing the moderate level. In category C_2, four municipalities were assigned with a significant level of marginality. Finally, C_1 contains the three municipalities with the highest level. The geographical visualization shows the municipalities with the most critical marginality situation.

The analysis with the MR-sort sorting method shows the geographical marginality of the municipalities of Sinaloa. It seems that the "geographical marginality of Sinaloa region is very high in those municipalities with a ge-

TABLE 6.12 Limiting profiles for marginality of municipalities [10].

Criterion	Lp1	Lp2	Lp3
g1	3.5	7	9
g2	13	24	29
g3	1.5	5	7.5
g4	0.5	1.7	2.5
g5	2	6	10
g6	30	34	35
g7	2.5	5	7
g8	30	60	75
g9	30	40	49

ographical location in the Mountain range (A7, A17, A3)" [10, p.56]. On the other hand, "the municipalities with lowest marginality level is in municipalities far away from this Mountain range (A1, A15, A6, A12)" [10, p.56].

References

[1] D. Cowen, GIS versus CAD versus DBMS: what are the differences?, Photogrammetric Engineering and Remote Sensing 54 (11) (1988) 1551–1555.

[2] Joaquin Bosque Sendra, Montserrat Gómez Delgado, Antonio Moreno Jimímez, Francesco Dal Pozzo, Hacia un sistema de ayuda a la decision espacial para la localización de equipamientos, Estudios Geográficos 61 (241) (2000) 567–598.

[3] Juan M. Sánchez-Lozano, Jerónimo Teruel-Solano, Pedro L. Soto-Elvira, M. Socorro García-Cascales, Geographical information systems (GIS) and multi-criteria decision making (MCDM) methods for the evaluation of solar farms locations: case study in South-eastern Spain, Renewable and Sustainable Energy Reviews 24 (2013) 544–556.

[4] Jacek Malczewski, GIS-based multicriteria decision analysis: a survey of the literature, International Journal of Geographical Information Science 20 (7) (2006) 703–726.

[5] Juan M. Sánchez-Lozano, Carlos Henggeler Antunes, M. Socorro García-Cascales, Luis C. Dias, GIS-based photovoltaic solar farms site selection using ELECTRE-TRI: evaluating the case for Torre Pacheco, Murcia, southeast of Spain, Renewable Energy 66 (2014) 478–494.

[6] S.C. Guptill, Spatial data, in: Neil J. Smelser, Paul B. Baltes (Eds.), International Encyclopedia of the Social & Behavioral Sciences, Pergamon, Oxford, 2001, pp. 14775–14778.

[7] Christopher J. Brookes, A parameterized region-growing programme for site allocation on raster suitability maps, International Journal of Geographical Information Science 11 (4) (1997) 375–396.

[8] Richard L. Church, Ross A. Gerrard, Michael Gilpin, Peter Stine, Constructing cell-based habitat patches useful in conservation planning, Annals of the Association of American Geographers 93 (4) (2003) 814–827.

[9] M. Herwijnen, P. Van Rietveld, Spatial dimensions in multicriteria analysis, in: J.-C. Thill (Ed.), Multicriteria Decision-Making and Analysis: A Geographic Information Sciences Approach, Routledge, London, 1999, pp. 77–99.

[10] Pavel Anselmo Alvarez, Study of the geographical marginality in a Mexican region using the MR-sort method, in: Ernesto León-Castro, Fabio Blanco-Mesa, Victor Alfaro-García, Anna Maria Gil-Lafuente, José M.M. Merigó, Janusz Kacprzyk (Eds.), Soft Computing and Fuzzy

Methodologies in Innovation Management and Sustainability, Springer International Publishing, Cham, 2022, pp. 49–59.

[11] Randal Greene, Rodolphe Devillers, Joan E. Luther, Brian G. Eddy, GIS-based multiple-criteria decision analysis, Geography Compass 5 (6) (2011) 412–432.

[12] Francis Macary, J. Almeida Dias, Daniel Uny, Anne Probst, Assessment of the effects of best environmental practices on reducing pesticide contamination in surface water, using multi-criteria modelling combined with a GIS, International Journal of Multicriteria Decision Making 3 (2/3) (2013) 178–211.

[13] E. Barriuso, Estimation des Risques Environnementaux des Pesticides, INRA, Paris, 2004.

[14] Juliana Biluca, Claudinei Rodrigues de Aguiar, Flavio Trojan, Sorting of suitable areas for disposal of construction and demolition waste using GIS and ELECTRE TRI, Waste Management 114 (2020) 307–320.

[15] F. Miccoli, A. Ishizaka, Sorting municipalities in Umbria according to the risk of wolf attacks with AHPSort II, Ecological Indicators 73 (2017) 741–755.

[16] André Morais Gurgel, Caroline M.M. Mota, A multicriteria prioritization model to support public safety planning, Pesquisa Operacional 33 (2013) 251–267.

[17] Alessio Ishizaka, Menelaos Tasiou, Luis Martínez, Analytic hierarchy process-fuzzy sorting: an analytic hierarchy process-based method for fuzzy classification in sorting problems, Journal of the Operational Research Society 71 (6) (2020) 928–947.

[18] Martin Thebault, Vincent Clivillé, Lamia Berrah, Gilles Desthieux, Multicriteria roof sorting for the integration of photovoltaic systems in urban environments, Sustainable Cities and Society 60 (2020) 102259.

[19] V. Assumma, M. Bottero, A. Ishizaka, M. Tasiou, Group analytic hierarchy process sorting II method: an application to evaluate the economic value of a wine region landscape, Environmental Modeling & Assessment 26 (2021) 355.

[20] A. Ishizaka, C. Pearman, P. Nemery, Ahpsort: an AHP-based method for sorting problems, International Journal of Production Research 50 (17) (2012) 4767–4784.

[21] M. Camacho-Collados, F. Liberatore, J.M. Angulo, A multi-criteria police districting problem for the efficient and effective design of patrol sector, European Journal of Operational Research 246 (2) (2015) 674–684.

[22] Ciro José Jardim de Figueiredo, Caroline Maria de Miranda Mota, Classification model to evaluate the security level in a city based on GIS-MCDA, Mathematical Problems in Engineering 2016 (2016) 1–10.

[23] K. Curran, M. Dale, M. Edmunds, M. Hough, A. Millie, M. Wagstaff, Street Crime in London: Deterrence, Disruption and Displacement, Government Office for London, London, 2005.

[24] Luis C. Dias, Vincent Mousseau, IRIS: a DSS for multiple criteria sorting problems, Journal of Multi-Criteria Decision Analysis 12 (4–5) (2005) 285–298.

[25] Piemonte Regione, Schede degli ambiti di paesaggio – piano paesaggistico regionale, 2015.

[26] Rosalie Wills, James A. Milke, Sara Royle, Kristin Steranka, Best Practices for Commercial Roof-Mounted Photovoltaic System Installation, Springer New York, New York, 2015.

[27] Gilles Desthieux, Claudio Carneiro, Reto Camponovo, Pierre Ineichen, Eugenio Morello, Anthony Boulmier, Nabil Abdennadher, Sébastien Dervey, Christoph Ellert, Solar energy potential assessment on rooftops and facades in large built environments based on lidar data, image processing, and cloud computing. Methodological background, application, and validation in Geneva (solar cadaster), Frontiers in Built Environment 4 (2018).

[28] X. Cipriano, G. Gamboa, S. Danov, G. Mor, J. Cipriano, Developing indicators to improve energy action plans in municipalities: an accounting framework based on the fund-flow model, Sustainable Cities and Society 32 (2017) 263–276.

[29] Enrico Gottero, Claudia Cassatella, Landscape indicators for rural development policies. Application of a core set in the case study of Piedmont region, Environmental Impact Assessment Review 65 (2017) 75–85.

[30] Theano S. Terkenli, Landscapes of Tourism, John Wiley & Sons, Ltd, 2014, pp. 282–293, chapter 22.

[31] Liisa Tyrvainen, Antti Miettinen, Property prices and urban forest amenities, Journal of Environmental Economics and Management 39 (2) (2000) 205–223.

[32] T. Saaty, The Analytic Hierarchy Process, McGraw-Hill, New York, 1980.

[33] F.W. Gatzweiler, H. Baumuller, C. Husmann, J. Von Braun, Marginality: addressing the root causes of extreme poverty, SSRN Electronic Journal (2011) 1–19.

[34] Stanko Pelc, Etienne Nel, Social Innovation and Geographical Marginality, Springer International Publishing, Cham, 2020, pp. 11–21.

[35] CONAPO, Índice de marginación por entidad federativa y municipio 2010. Colección: Índices Sociodemográficos, México, 2012.

[36] INEGI, Encuesta intercensal 2015, 2015.

[37] Denis Bouyssou, Thierry Marchant, An axiomatic approach to noncompensatory sorting methods in MCDM, I: the case of two categories, European Journal of Operational Research 178 (1) (2007) 217–245.

[38] Denis Bouyssou, Thierry Marchant, An axiomatic approach to noncompensatory sorting methods in MCDM, II: more than two categories, European Journal of Operational Research 178 (1) (2007) 246–276.

Chapter 7

Future research and remarks on MCDM sorting

7.1 MCDM sorting: trends and new avenues

The MCDM paradigm has been the fastest-growing operational research and management science area during the last 35 years [1]. It is known that the MCDM paradigm addresses different decision-making problematics. However, part of this growth corresponds to developed methods on MCDM sorting problems. This is indicated by the fact that many publications on operations research management science and management relate to MCDM sorting problems.

The main objective of this chapter is to highlight the revision about past and current trends in MCDM sorting done in previous chapters. Additionally, it points out the novel trends on the topic that need to be developed in order to overcome current limitations and discuss related research topics. We must keep in mind that new approaches and methodologies have been developed, which contribute to changing the paradigm of MCDM. The identification of the approach allows an understanding of how the MCDM sorting methods have been developed.

Across the different chapters of this book, the main trends and results of MCDM sorting methods over the last 20 years have been reviewed. The development of related methods of aggregation approach such as AHPSORT [2], ANPSORT [3], UTADIS [4], UTADIS GMS-GROUP [5], MACBETHSORT [6], and CODAS-SORT [7] is remarkable. On the reference-level approach, the developed methods have been TOPSIS-SORT [8], VIKORSORT [9], and DEA-SORT [10]. In terms of outranking approach, FlowSort [11], FlowSort-GDSS [12], ORESTE-SORT [13], and ELECTRE TRI [14] and its extensions have been widely used. The developments on MCDM sorting have covered a wide variety of topics, of which several, such as risk assessment, education, project evaluation, financial management, port group competitiveness, and supplier selection [15], have attracted the attention of many researchers.

In spite of the number of new sorting-based models and applications pointed out previously, the reviews provided in Chapters 2 and 3 help us to understand different weaknesses related to the MCDM sorting methods, such as the lack of developed software, the lack of support for selecting the utility function and for defining the information required by methods, and the lack of solved real problems. Although the revised MCDM sorting methods show real applications,

Multi-Criteria Decision-Making Sorting Methods. https://doi.org/10.1016/B978-0-32-385231-9.00012-2

further exploration of the structuring of new real-world sorting problems is still required.

The need to manage uncertainty in MCDM and consequently in MCDM sorting indicates the importance of fuzzy sets and fuzzy logic in MCDM under uncertainty. By describing methods of MCDM based on fuzzy set theory, readers have been enabled to understand the significance of real-world applications of sorting problems. Interesting developments have occurred regarding methods such as Fuzzy FlowSort, SMAA Fuzzy FlowSort, ELECTRE TRI-C, and continuous cooperation fuzzy sorting.

In spite of the efforts made for fuzzy-based MCDM sorting methods, it is still desirable to develop techniques for criteria evaluation using fuzzy-based techniques to capture the true meanings of linguistic assessments in human perceptions. Therefore, a key trend on MCDM sorting for the near future should be the fuzzification of two processes:

1. the values of decision criteria; and
2. the computation of the alternatives' membership for assigning them to fuzzified categories.

The fuzzy-based process will provide additional information about the alternatives' membership to the corresponding classes, and allows the gradation of membership to a class.

Previously, it has been mentioned that during last two decades, within MCDM sorting different methods have been developed in each category of the four described in Chapter 1. It is remarkable that several distinctive methods have been applied more often to specific real-world problems. A summary of applications is provided here in order to indicate some future trends in MCDM sorting.

- AHPSort or AHPSort II mostly address the supplier selection problem.
- The UTADIS method is most commonly applied in education, followed by maintenance management, financial management, and risk assessment, which are other application areas of the full aggregation approach.
- The ELECTRE TRI method is applied the most often in risk assessment.
- Some areas where FlowSort has been applied are project evaluation, financial management, risk assessment, and supplier selection.
- DEA-based sorting methods have been developed recently, and they have been applied in financial management, inventory management, materials management, and project evaluation.
- The extensions of TOPSIS-SORT have been developed in AHP–TOPSIS-2 N [16], TOPSIS-SORT [8], TOPSIS-Sort-C [17], and PDTOPSIS-Sort [18], and applied in environmental assessment, financial management, and project evaluation.

Considering the above applied MCDM sorting methods, some related trends must be highlighted that would be relevant to develop in the near future.

- In spite of the increasing development of methods in the full aggregation approach, more applied works are needed to validate the methods by solving real problems. The most used method is UTADIS, and its extensions [15]. New research has been developed beyond UTADIS, such as the non-monotonic problem [19,20], partial monotonicity [21], interactivity with the decision-maker (DM) with a specific case [22], and the inverse problem to perform actions that have an impact on object evaluations [23]. However, further efforts are still necessary.
- The outranking approach is attractive and quite often used in MCDM sorting problems. However, this approach lacks support to solve group decision-making problems. Only 13% of papers deal with group decision-making problems. Some missing applications on outranking are democracy, environmental assessment, and inventory management. The outranking approach seems an excellent opportunity to exploit applied methods in new problems and develop methods within the group decision-making context.
- New MCDM sorting developments should focus on the nonclassical approach as decision rules-based methods in applied studies. A relevant strength of the nonclassical MCDM is how it aggregates DMs' preferences regarding the adjacent knowledge-constructing decision rules to assign alternatives in the classes. The replication of this knowledge with new alternatives or similar problems seems to be true to a DM's preferences [15].
- Preference disaggregation analysis (PDA) infers parameters based on the DM's preferences. The PDA technique can support the parameter elicitation stage. The PDA in the MCDM context is a real support to the DM to assist the elicitation stage. Additional research efforts are necessary in order to exploit further the potential of the preference disaggregation philosophy within the context of MCDM sorting. It will be necessary to develop more sophisticated aggregation models, exploit the provided results further, or adopt the aggregation-disaggregation philosophy used in other decision-making approaches [24]. The new research developments of aggregation-disaggregation approaches may be focused on robustness analysis and group decision-making [15]. It is additionally stated that postoptimality analysis should be covered [24].

Throughout the book, the most important MCDM sorting approaches applied to real-world problems have also been described. The most-addressed decision situations have been focused on risk assessment, education, project evaluation, financial management, and supplier selection [15].

- *Risk assessment*: two types of problems have been addressed. First, problems describing the economic performance, creditworthiness of a country's business, and bankruptcy risk. Second, problems addressing the environmental risk assessment.
- *Education*: different topics have been evaluated by faculty and students. First, the academic members of an institution are an element of evaluation in the education area. Second, the evaluation of students for a specific postgraduate

program is mostly addressed by considering the student qualification from the subjects studied.

- *Project evaluation*: R&D projects are evaluated commonly for a grant program. Another topic is the prioritization of a project portfolio. Here many aims can be considered such as strategy, environmental, and technological aspects, and the usual strictly financial criteria.
- *Financial management*: the bank performance rating can be evaluated by Capital-CA, Assets-AS, Management-MC, Earnings-ER, Liquidity-LQ, and Sensitivity to market risks-SM dimension. On the other hand, a firm's evaluation is essential in financial management. Firms can be evaluated by financial ratios, e.g., cash to total assets, debt, stockholders' equity, and total liabilities.

Other topics within MCDM sorting have been addressed, albeit to a lesser extent, together with the use of GISs providing GIS-MCDM-based problems that have been described in this book. Chapter 5 focused on a review of Geographic Information System-based Multi-criteria Decision-Making (GIS-MCDM), in which GIS techniques and procedures support the analyzing spatial decision problems and MCDM provides a rich collection of decision techniques. The most commonly addressed real-world GIS-MCDM-based problems are environmental management, the security level of cities, solar energy, the economic attractiveness of the landscape, and geographical marginality.

Thus, based on the previous description of addressed problems and some trends, the following key directions should be considered for further research in multi-criteria decision sorting problems:

- New MCDM sorting methods should be capable of representing knowledge. Newly developed methods need to find adjacent knowledge from decision inductions. Some strategies would be based on the dominance relation, machine learning, or other optimization methods for knowledge discovery.
- MCDM sorting methods need to venture into problems with a large number of criteria. Two possible paths are in the fields of MCDM and nonclassical MCDM. New methods based on preference disaggregation analysis in MCDM to deal with preference information with a large number of criteria should be developed. On the other hand, machine learning or unsupervised learning can be implemented to develop new sorting methods that include DMs' preferences.
- More studies are needed to provide DMs with the assignment of alternatives in the appropriate classes that are not significantly affected by value variations of parameters, to ensure a robust solution.
- Defining actions for real-world problems is an open area. In inverse multi-criteria classification problems, actions are not predefined and need to be designed throughout new techniques.
- More computational tools are necessary. This will help more practitioners to adopt the current and new multi-criteria sorting models. At present, only a tiny number of computational tools are available.

7.2   Concluding remarks

Regarding MCDM sorting methods, the full aggregation and outranking approaches are the most used ones. The UTADIS- and ELECTRE-based methods are the most developed and implemented among the MCDM sorting methods.

We can identify the increasing development of novel sorting methods, the challenge of addressing more real-life applied studies, and the need for more hybrid methods with machine learning or other fields to deal with large volumes of data.

The MCDM sorting methodology supports different ways of making decisions, not only in terms of assigning alternatives in predefined categories but also as regards identifying the particular situations of each problem. In the geographical analysis of regions, identifying the best alternatives may help solving specific problems like available loans, adequate academy programs, investment portfolios, suppliers categorization, and others. The sorting techniques are adequate for this type of problem by avoiding arbitrary criteria to determine the best subgroup of actions.

The MCDM sorting methodology also considers DMs' preferences. Here, the active interaction between the expert/DM and analyst would be a pivotal factor in tackling the multiple-criteria decision-making problem properly. They participate in selecting decision criteria and determining the profiles of the categories of desirable assets. The incorporation of DMs' preferences allows relevant results to be obtained for them.

To solve MCDM sorting problems, further fuzzy-based methods should be considered in future work. Fuzzy FlowSort [25], SMAA Fuzzy-FlowSort (SMAA-FFS) [26], ELECTRE TRI-C, and trapezoidal fuzzy numbers [27], continuous cooperation fuzzy sorting [28], AHP-FuzzySort [29], and intuitionistic fuzzy outranking sorting GDM [30] show different ways to integrate the fuzzy approaches for the data, the fuzzification of the profiles, or the process assignment that should be researched further in the future.

This book comprised seven chapters. The book covered current trends and exposed new ones in MCDM sorting. The book's benefits are due to research on conceptual and operational validation of the use of MCDM sorting in solving real-world spatial problems.

Other, more general concerns surrounding the use of sorting MCDM require careful consideration. More attention should be paid to the theoretical foundations and operational validation of the MCDM sorting methods.

Reformulating some real-world problems, which are currently addressed with other methodologies, is one of the likely future trends in MCDM sorting. Thus, research efforts should be focused not only on the development of new methods but also on the adaptation of existing methods to new applications.

References

[1] C. Romero, T. Rehman, Multiple Criteria Analysis for Agricultural Decisions, Elsevier, 2003.

[2] Alessio Ishizaka, Craig Pearman, Philippe Nemery, AHPSort: an AHP-based method for sorting problems, International Journal of Production Research 50 (17) (2012) 4767–4784.

[3] Alessio Ishizaka, Vijay Pereira, Utilisation of ANPSort for sorting alternative with interdependent criteria illustrated through a researcher's classification problem in an academic context, Soft Computing 24 (18) (2020) 13639–13650.

[4] Michael Doumpos, Constantin Zopounidis, Developing sorting models using preference disaggregation analysis: an experimental investigation, European Journal of Operational Research 154 (3) (2004) 585–598.

[5] Salvatore Greco, Miłosz Kadziński, Roman Słowiński, Robust ordinal regression for multiple criteria group decision: UTAGMS-group and UTADISGMS-group, Decision Support Systems 52 (3) (2012) 549–561.

[6] Alessio Ishizaka, Maynard Gordon, MACBETHSort: a multiple criteria decision aid procedure for sorting strategic products, Journal of the Operational Research Society 68 (1) (2017) 53–61.

[7] Mehdi Keshavarz Ghorabaee, Edmundas Kazimieras Zavadskas, Zenonas Turskis, Jurgita Antucheviciene, A new combinative distance-based assessment (CODAS) method for multi-criteria decision-making, Economic Computation and Economic Cybernetics Studies and Research 50 (3) (2016) 25–44.

[8] H.F. Sabokbar, A. Hosseini, A. Banaitis, N. Banaitiene, A novel sorting method TOPSIS-sort: an application for Tehran environmental quality evaluation, E & M Ekonomie a Management 19 (2) (2016) 87–104.

[9] Leyla Demir, Muhammet Enes Akpınar, Ceyhun Araz, Mehmet Ali Ilgın, A green supplier evaluation system based on a new multi-criteria sorting method: VIKORSort, Expert Systems with Applications 114 (2018) 479–487.

[10] Alessio Ishizaka, Francesco Lolli, Elia Balugani, Rita Cavallieri, Rita Gamberini, DEASort: assigning items with data envelopment analysis in ABC classes, International Journal of Production Economics 199 (2018) 7–15.

[11] Philippe Nemery, Claude Lamboray, FlowSort: a flow-based sorting method with limiting or central profiles, Top 16 (1) (2008) 90–113.

[12] Francesco Lolli, Alessio Ishizaka, Rita Gamberini, Bianca Rimini, Michael Messori, FlowSort-GDSS – a novel group multi-criteria decision support system for sorting problems with application to FMEA, Expert Systems with Applications 42 (17) (2015) 6342–6349.

[13] J. Qin, Y. Liang, L. Martinez, A. Ishizaka, W. Pedrycz, Oreste-sort: a novel multiple criteria sorting method for sorting port group competitiveness, Annals of Operations Research (2022).

[14] V. Mousseau, R. Slowinski, Inferring an Electre Tri model from assignment examples, Journal of Global Optimization 12 (2) (1998) 157–174.

[15] Pavel Anselmo Alvarez, Alessio Ishizaka, Luis Martínez, Multiple-criteria decision-making sorting methods: a survey, Expert Systems with Applications 183 (2021) 115368.

[16] L.P. De Souza, C.F.S. Gomes, A.P. De Barros, Implementation of new hybrid AHP-TOPSIS-2n method in sorting and prioritizing 6 of an it CAPEX project portfolio, International Journal of Information Technology & Decision Making 17 (4) (2018) 977–1005.

[17] Diogo Ferreira de Lima Silva, Adiel Teixeira de Almeida Filho, Sorting with TOPSIS through boundary and characteristic profiles, Computers & Industrial Engineering 141 (2020) 106328.

[18] Diogo Ferreira de Lima Silva, Luciano Ferreira, Adiel Teixeira de Almeida-Filho, A new preference disaggregation TOPSIS approach applied to sort corporate bonds based on financial statements and expert's assessment, Expert Systems with Applications 152 (2020) 113369.

[19] Mengzhuo Guo, Xiuwu Liao, Jiapeng Liu, A progressive sorting approach for multiple criteria decision aiding in the presence of non-monotonic preferences, Expert Systems with Applications 123 (2019) 1–17.

[20] Jiapeng Liu, Xiuwu Liao, Milosz Kadzinski, Roman Slowinski, Preference disaggregation within the regularization framework for sorting problems with multiple potentially non-monotonic criteria, European Journal of Operational Research 276 (3) (2019) 1071–1089.

[21] Milosz Kadzinski, Krzysztof Martyn, Marco Cinelli, Roman Slowinski, Salvatore Corrente, Salvatore Greco, Preference disaggregation for multiple criteria sorting with partial monotonicity constraints: application to exposure management of nanomaterials, International Journal of Approximate Reasoning 117 (2020) 60–80.

[22] C. Ulu, M. Koksalan, An interactive approach to multicriteria sorting for quasiconcave value functions, Naval Research Logistics 61 (6) (2014) 447–457.

[23] V. Mousseau, O. Ozpeynirci, S. Ozpeynirci, Inverse multiple criteria sorting problem, Annals of Operations Research 267 (1–2) (2018) 379–412.

[24] Yannis Siskos, Evangelos Grigoroudis, New trends in aggregation-disaggregation approaches, in: Constantin Zopounidis, Panos M. Pardalos (Eds.), Handbook of Multicriteria Analysis, Springer Berlin Heidelberg, Berlin, Heidelberg, 2010, pp. 189–214.

[25] Ana Carolina Scanavachi Moreira Campos, Bertrand Mareschal, Adiel Teixeira de Almeida, Fuzzy FlowSort: an integration of the FlowSort method and fuzzy set theory for decision making on the basis of inaccurate quantitative data, Information Sciences 293 (2015) 115–124.

[26] Renata Pelissari, Maria Célia Oliveira, Sarah Ben Amor, Alvaro José Abackerli, A new FlowSort-based method to deal with information imperfections in sorting decision-making problems, European Journal of Operational Research 276 (1) (2019) 235–246.

[27] Javier Pereira, Elaine C.B. de Oliveira Luiz, F.A.M. Gomes, Renato M. Araújo, Sorting retail locations in a large urban city by using Electre Tri-C and trapezoidal fuzzy numbers, Soft Computing 23 (2019) 4193–4206.

[28] Maisa Mendonça Silva, Ana Paula Cabral, Seixas Costa, Ana Paula Henriques de Gusmão, Continuous cooperation: a proposal using a fuzzy multicriteria sorting method, International Journal of Production Economics 151 (2014) 67–75.

[29] Alessio Ishizaka, Menelaos Tasiou, Luis Martínez, Analytic hierarchy process-fuzzy sorting: an analytic hierarchy process-based method for fuzzy classification in sorting problems, Journal of the Operational Research Society 71 (6) (2020) 928–947.

[30] Feng Shen, Jiuping Xu, Zeshui Xu, An outranking sorting method for multi-criteria group decision making using intuitionistic fuzzy sets, Information Sciences 334–335 (2016) 338–353.

Index

Printed in the United States
by Baker & Taylor Publisher Services